T0276304

BACKVALLEY ⊢ _ . . . . . _ . _

BACKVALLEY
FERRETS

A Rewilding of the Colorado Plateau

LAWRENCE LENHART

The University of Georgia Press · Athens

Published by the University of Georgia Press
Athens, Georgia 30602
www.ugapress.org
© 2023 by Lawrence Lenhart
All rights reserved
Designed by Erin Kirk
Set in Warnock Pro

Most University of Georgia Press titles are
available from popular e-book vendors.

Printed digitally

Library of Congress Cataloging-in-Publication Data

Names: Lenhart, Lawrence, author.
Title: Backvalley ferrets : a rewilding of the
Colorado Plateau / Lawrence Lenhart.
Other titles: Crux (Athens, Ga.)
Description: Athens : The University of Georgia Press, [2023] |
Series: Crux: the Georgia series in literary nonfiction
Identifiers: LCCN 2022062241 | ISBN 9780820364124 (paperback) |
ISBN 9780820364131 (epub) | ISBN 9780820364148 (pdf)
Subjects: LCSH: Black-footed ferret—Ecology. | Black-footed
ferret—Colorado Plateau. | Wildlife conservation. | Rare mammals—
Colorado Plateau. | Aubrey Valley (Ariz.)
Classification: LCC QL737.C25 L458 2023 |
DDC 599.76/629—dc23/eng/20230206
LC record available at https://lccn.loc.gov/2022062241

for Andie,
before Milo

Not just the pine weasel. Life as we know it.

—BENJAMIN HORNE, *Twin Peaks*

CONTENTS

Come Out, Lazarus Taxon • 1

Candle-Powered • 5

Rural Purge • 30

If the Ferret Crosses the Road • 39

This Is Not an Entrance to the Phoenix Zoo • 57

Where's My Little Ferret? • 100

Mourning a Ferret • 119

A Ferret by Any Other Name • 121

Ventriloquism for the Eremocene • 143

Proving Up in the New West • 152

Up Yonder • 164

My Son Was Born to Rob Me of the Glory of Saving
the Black-Footed Ferret from Plague • 169

Extrapolating the Genus • 184

Petri to Prairie • 190

Acknowledgments • 211

COME OUT, LAZARUS TAXON

— . —

On September 26, 1981, a Saturday morning, after having breakfast with his wife, Lucille, maybe a chicken-fried steak like she cooked at Lucille's Café on weekdays on State Street in downtown Meeteetse, ranch owner John Hogg opened the front door of his house in the hopes of finding his ranch dog—a blue heeler named Shep, who was last seen scuffling the evening before with the silhouette of a presumed porcupine—and after looking out at the distant foothills of the Absaroka Range of northwest Wyoming near Yellowstone's perimeter, and looking out at the gap filled by rolling shortgrass prairie, chutes of blue grama covering the Hogg and Pitchfork Ranches, and looking out at the near lawn where Shep usually loped but was hitherto absent, and looking eventually down at the ground immediately at his feet where a mammal—willowy with champagne fur, splotches of sable and soot, its skull blunt, adorned with two triangular ears, teeny legged and long tailed, an offering to the family from Shep—lay supine and stiff, its species unknown to John, so he went to his knees to inspect the carcass closely, and it was down there, in the dirt of it all, where he confirmed he'd never seen such a thing in his whole damned life.

In John Hogg's own words: "I stepped out there and looked . . . There was this ferret . . . I didn't know it was a ferret. It was laying on the ground. I looked at it and pretty soon, well, I picked it up, brought it in, laid it down, showed it to Lucille," who encouraged him to take it to town to be mounted.

The taxidermist, Larry LaFranchi, watched in disbelief as John dumped the small mammal from the gunnysack onto the floor of his shop. The two were stupefied by it. LaFranchi took it to the back and made a phone call, and Hogg never had a say about whether he was going to get his trophy back or not because, it turns out, the heeler hadn't been scuffling with a porcupine but the resurrection of a species twice declared extinct. I imagine Shep and the ferret vanishing in a big ball of violence à la Looney Tunes, the only thing emerging from their smoke cloud terrific growling and yowling, hissing and chattering, maybe a flash of canines or a tip of tail, until death was the ferret's end. But in the case of this story, its death is just the beginning. "Finding that ferret changed my world," Hogg said in an interview. "The ranch wasn't the same after that." And neither was the town of Meeteetse. David Cunningham, director of the Meeteetse Museum, describes what followed as "an onslaught of biologists, wildlife experts, and press." It would also have a considerable impact on how the business of wildlife conservation gets done in North America.

In another interview, Hogg unceremoniously said if he had known how that ferret would disrupt the town, he would have just chucked the body over his fence. It's likely other ranchers had seen signs of the weasel too but kept it to themselves for fear their land would be monitored and sequestered.

And what if Lucille hadn't let Shep out after blue hour? Or what if the porcupine had wobbled to center stage first to instigate Shep's prey drive? What if Shep had buried the ferret in brush instead of depositing it prominently on the front lawn? And what *if* John had chucked that body instead of pursuing his one-of-a-kind trophy? If Larry opted to make a quick buck instead of sharing the secret of this conspicuous carcass with wildlife manager Dennie Hammer?

Had any of them played their parts differently, the prospect of this improbable conservation story would have dissolved. My attention to the black-footed ferret would have been rendered unnecessary, and the course of my life would have been way, way different. Instead, I observe the death anniversary of the Lazarus ferret, September 26, like it's a national holiday—an occasion to meditate on second chances, on a restarting line for a species fated to endure.

———— ◊ ————

Scott Weidensaul, in his book *The Ghost with Trembling Wings* (2002), calls the black-footed ferret (BFF) a "[phantom]: secretive, highly nocturnal, almost entirely subterranean. . . . A prairie dog town is the ferret's universe: shelter, larder, birthing chamber, and tomb, all in one." At night, ferrets slink between colonies, diving through entrance mounds and ambushing tunnels, nests, latrines, and turnaround bays. They'll occasionally breach with emerald eyeshine, their nose, whiskers, and chin slicked with blood, ready to waggle onto the next ingress.

With John Hogg's permission, Dennie Hammer and other conservationists explored his ranch, surveying the prairie dog towns, hoping to find clues that a live business of ferrets was burrowed beneath the ranch.

Hammer and his partner drove the ranch roads for days before spotting the first ferret. It had been thirty-three days since Shep's kill, since Hogg's consternation, since LaFranchi's call to the Wyoming Game and Fish Department. And then, at 6:20 a.m., about as late as a ferret is ever seen above the ground, one scampered alongside the Game and Fish pickup truck. Hammer, on the passenger side, watched it scurry away to a nearby hole. He and his partner followed it to its subterranean destination. The ferret taunted them from the opening, only half-submerged. Hammer recalled that first sustained glimpse: "The picture of his face, the black mask, the Mickey Mouse kind of ears, and the little spots over the eyes. We saw everything we knew we needed to see."

Because prairie dog burrows have multiple points of ingress and egress, the conservationists plugged all holes associated with the system, trapping the ferret known as "620." Hammer sat in a lawn chair with a tarp wrapped around him. It was a frigid twenty degrees, and the ferret was shallow in the trap, not stepping far enough to engage the treadle at first. When 620 was finally captured, he was taken back to camp to undergo surveillance.

From Hammer's original field journals:

0600: Leave camp with b-f-f to release back at the Pitchfork Ranch. . . . The ferret appears to be in good condition, got restless during the night, but always settled back down. Barked at me this morning. 0627: Arrive at Pitchfork Ranch. 0636: Arrive at trap site. 26 exposures on my camera. 0645: Attempted the release but antelope hunters detained us. Temperature about thirty degrees. "620" . . . left the box. Hesitated for two to five minutes and then ran down the road about thirty yards and ran into a single entrance mound. Twenty-seven minutes later, he came up and ran to another, has been repeating this sequence of events ever since. 0830: He's been down below ground for about twenty-six minutes. No one before has ever done what we have just completed in the last day and half: located, trapped, radioed and released a b-f-f. Also at 0705, a golden eagle flew over 620, but didn't attempt to take him. 0930: We lost the signal.

This is how Meeteetse, a Siouan word meaning "meeting place," was the last-ever meeting place for truly wild black-footed ferrets in the United States. Over 128 black-footed ferrets were caught and released thanks to 620's lead. This is about one-third of Meeteetse's human population. The business was monitored for months but was eventually infected by the canine distemper virus. The Wyoming Game and Fish Department developed a recovery plan, including a captive breeding program. In the September 9, 1986, edition of the *Meeteetse Herald*, the bold-faced headline read: "All ferrets captured." The last wild-born black-footed ferret, a single holdout, was discovered in February and joined the others in Laramie.

Of the eighteen captive ferrets, representatives of perhaps the rarest mammal species on earth, only seven would go on to become founders of the extant ferret population, severely limiting genetic diversity. To this day, all living BFFs—from Colorado to South Dakota, Montana to Wyoming, Saskatchewan to Chihuahua, to the reintroduction sites in my own back valley in northern Arizona—are descendants of just seven procreative ferrets.

CANDLE-POWERED

—.—

Forty years after the black-footed ferret (*Mustela nigripes*) was declared extinct, I plug the million-candlepower spotlight adapter into my car's DC port by the gear stick. I reverse the car onto historic Route 66 and drive away from the research trailer. The route is the longest (and longest-lasting) span of America's Mother Road. A series of red-and-white Burma-Shave signs appear along the side of the road, spaced seconds apart.

> YOU CAN DRIVE
> A MILE A MINUTE
> BUT THERE IS NO
> FUTURE IN IT.

There's not much else to look at out here, save for my wife's stoic profile and some water tanks labeled Caterpillar and Camel on the map, so the signs are an entertaining break. Burma-Shave was known best for its roadside signage and not for its brushless shaving cream. It calls to mind the breakup beard I was wearing last time I steered this road.

It was a breakup motivated by the death of a domestic ferret (*Mustela putorius furo*). I'd moved to the desert in a two-car caravan, my ex's Jetta thrumming behind me through West Texas, an extra-large cage shimmied into her passenger seat, in direct line of the AC's stream. Every few miles, she spritzed all three ferrets with water. They swayed in hand-sewn hammocks for thirty-four hours until we reached our final destination, a white-hot gravel alley in Tucson where we could find the rolling gate that opened to our new casita. We pulled through a chalky cloud stirred up by an excavator in the vacant lot across the way.

When I ended up in the hospital a few days before grad school was to begin, medical residents single-filed to poke me, to gawp at my textbook targetoid rash. "Whoa!" they said as my arm blushed and blanched. They said I was lucky I wasn't an octogenarian, lucky I wasn't a toddler, lucky I wasn't a dog, for those infected groups succumbed most readily to valley fever.

"What about a ferret?" I asked. "One of ours has been acting whack."

"I guess it's possible for any mammal to get it," they said. They asked if there were any buildings going up or coming down in my neighborhood.

"There's an excavator and backhoe in the alley," I said. "They seem to run all day."

Chichi, our most beloved ferret, died within a week of my hospitalization. My theory goes like this. We moved to Tucson in the midst of one of the longest droughts the state has ever known—labeled "extreme" to "exceptional" throughout Pima County—or so said the meteorologist with panicky undertones us Appalachians weren't used to. Extended aridity causes cocci spores to proliferate in the Sonoran Desert. Just ask any one of the six author-hydrologists who came to that conclusion in the peer-reviewed journal *GeoHealth*. When the digger came to demolish the alleged coke den in the alley, its bucket cast the fungus into the air. The CDC lists construction as a common spore agitator. That air was then pulled in from the outside via swamp cooler. At least that's, according to a certain website, "How Swamp Coolers Work." Again, it was all new to me. To us.

And then we breathed in that air. Hot, fungal air, which was supposed to be cleaned and cooled by dripping pads and then blown through ducts in the casita. But when we told the landlord I'd been sick, he came to the casita in secret and replaced the cooler's wood-chip filter. (We mysteriously found the old one in the trash.) This is my theory, and I'm sticking to it.

I went to the hospital, Chichi to the vet. My symptoms resolved.

But we couldn't even afford to have his formally diagnosed. We told ourselves that not having the money for him was different than not having the love. Then we broke the news to him.

"You're gonna die," I said.

"We told you not to get sick until after we've won the lottery," my ex said.

I still miss how optimistic it felt to have Chichi around the casita, our winsome diplomat. Our easy and mutual love of him sometimes made loving each other easy too.

By September, we decided maybe we weren't cut out for life in the desert. At least not all of us together.

Within a month, my fiancée was on her way to the Great Basin, where she was to complete a four-month internship in biological conservation: small mammals, mostly mice. And I stayed back, sipping scotch by the pool, letting the surviving ferrets have the run of the house. I'd cosplay as Dar, the brawny hero of *Beastmaster*, who with his ferret sidekicks Podo and Kodo, managed to steal brassieres and avenge his village. But the fun was short-lived. Hadn't my ex and I already suffered three years of long distance? I could only affect ambivalence for so long. Eventually, I grew resentful, grew bitter, grew silent, grew a beard.

BEARDED HIPSTER
PICK UP YOUR PHONE
SAY YOU'RE SORRY
OR BE ALONE.

"What's the difference?" Andie asks. "Between the ones you had with her—the ones in the cage? And the ones out here, in the wild?"

"Do you really want to know?" I ask.

Andie and I are newlyweds. She isn't too sure about this trip—especially considering its precedence in another relationship—but she sets a welcome tone with this question, making it clear she won't begrudge me my past. Won't take the ferrets hostage. She is experienced in relationships, infinitely more capable of neutrality than I am. I want to thank her for not infecting these ferret lands with hostility, for trusting my interest in weasels transcends any residual investment I may still have in my ex.

Before I can answer her question, another Burma-Shave quatrain appears.

Equal parts poetry, punchline, and PSA, the Burma-Shave signs surviving along Route 66 in northwest Arizona portend their own obsolescence. They're cautionary words to a speeding driver, sure, but also predictive of the quietus that would befall the Main Street of America after the passage of the Federal-Aid Highway Act. President Eisenhower, envious of Hitler's autobahn following World War II, insisted U.S. infrastructure keep up with the motorist's need for speed. As a result, Interstate 40, which runs parallel to Route 66 and the Santa Fe Railroad, superseded the Mother Road as Arizona's major east-to-west artery for the second half of the century. Burma-Shave's last manufactured sign read:

> FAREWELL O VERSE
> ALONG THE ROAD
> HOW SAD TO SEE
> YOU'RE OUT OF MODE.

"For starters," I say, "you can't buy a black-footed ferret."

This much she knows.

I tell her that black-footed ferrets, like the Indigenous peoples of the Americas, probably arrived in the New World via a thawed steppe that spanned Beringia, whereas European polecats, like *our* ancestors, have been here for but an eyeblink.

"BFFS were scuttlers. Polecats were sailors," I say.

Aerated crates stocked with limber, musky, dooking polecats were sold to wharfs, where the polecats hunted the cargo-feeding rats that boarded the ships by mooring ropes.

"So the pet ones went back and forth across the Atlantic, just killing rats?"

"I guess some of them did that," I say. "But eventually, they were bred here as working animals. Bred and gradually domesticated."

By the early twentieth century, ferret breeding was a lucrative business in the Midwest. In *Ferret Facts and Fancies* (1915), trapper and fur buyer Arthur Harding discusses how a single breeder, Henry Farnsworth, jumpstarted the new industry, whose annual weasel sales exceeded the human population of Ferretville, Ohio (also called New London), thirteenfold. Single orders were filled for several hundred ferrets at a time.

Ladies coveted their fur. Have you ever seen da Vinci's *Lady with an Ermine*? Now imagine that weasel as a scarf.

Men hankered after them as hunting companions. You know the phrase *to ferret out*? Imagine farmers siccing these little suckers on a crop-chomping rabbit.

I can tell I'm giving Andie more answer than she bargained for, but she nods earnestly as we cruise down 66. She even does her best to look at me admiringly. Down and down the rabbit hole we go.

"Other domestic ferrets were sold into municipal labor," I say.

I tell her how, in the early 1900s, America had the highest teledensity (number of telephone connections per hundred households) of any country due to, in no small part, ferrets. Mr. Cline, superintendent of the Central Union Telephone Company of Indianapolis, deployed ferrets throughout communities of central Indiana. A ferret was "harnessed and muzzled," then sent into ducts, through which it chased a live rat. The ferrets dragged lacing twine by which workmen pulled through a telephone wire. Those first magical telephone calls of the early 1900s were made possible by industrious ferrets that rodded ducts connecting buildings' phone lines. Ferrets continued to work well into the century; if you happened to turn on the TV on July 29, 1981, for example, those glamorous images of Princess Diana's ivory silk taffeta wedding dress were brought to you by the fleet of ferrets who ran cables beneath the grounds of Buckingham Palace.

However (and it's a big *however*), when in dark tunnels—whether interior walls, municipal manholes, or wild prairie dog burrows—ferrets are likely to take unannounced siestas. Their nocturnal nature and frequent sleep patterns make them inefficient candidates for twenty-first-century broadband distribution, though they *are* still occupied by Virgin Media in more rural areas in Great Britain.

I wonder if, by now, Andie is starting to suspect the epistemic origins of this ferret trivia—how I sponged it all during whimsical conversations with my ex. My ex. How now her Jetta begins to creep into the side-view mirror, or so goes the double take, my doleful hallucination. Objects in the mirror grow closer over the years.

On cell phone coverage maps, Nevada is among the least speckled states. Out there, where my fiancée became ex, the dead zones stretch on for miles. The cell phone searches and searches for a signal. Due to its remoteness, the Great Basin was the last explored region in the contiguous United States. Unsurprisingly, Nye County is home to the largest zero-population tract of the 2000 census. I think it would be the ideal place to resume the practice of feeding wire, improving teledensity via ferret.

My only trip to Nye County, Nevada, was to the Nevada National Security Site, formerly the Nevada Test Site or Nevada Proving Grounds, the DOD operation home to Yucca Flat. According to author Gerard Clarfield, it is "the most irradiated, nuclear-blasted spot on Earth." In the nuclear era, this desert stretch of Nye County was famous for its kiloton crater pocks and miles-high mushroom-tipped pillars of smoke. When my ex's voice crackled due to bad reception, I imagined it was the waves of radiation decaying our conversation. My ears strained and pained to hear her voice.

"I think we're breaking up again," I told her before the call always dropped. Though who knows how much she heard of my message.

I think we're breaking up—
I think we're breaking—
I think we're—
   dropped
   dead
   done

During one rare crystal-clear phone call, she implored me to put her on speakerphone, to put her voice next to the ferrets' cage. I roused them from their recently shampooed hammocks, and they sniffed at the sound of her voice with their coffee-bean noses. The call was dropped before I could return the receiver to my ears.

"You've been gone too long," I probably said. "They're starting to hardly know you now."

And just when I'm about to slip into ill-advised melancholy—woe is me o'er the valley to the ferrets—we arrive at mile marker 132, a reflective green sign that triggers the mustelid memory in my braking foot.

Andie points at the iron gate, at Pica Camp Road. It's one of dozens of entry points to the Navajo-owned Big Boquillas's Diamond A Ranch, the largest cattle ranch in Arizona. The scrubby valley is ringed by thousand-foot-steep escarpments. At sunset, the cliffs are pink and ridged like the roof of a mouth. By nightfall, though, especially on slim-moon nights like this one, the Aubrey Cliffs smudge into a broad silhouette carving toward the Grand Canyon. Andie stands in the headlights, a familiar-looking chalk cloud drifting over her. She lifts the chain from the latch and swings the gate open. I roll forward a few revolutions, enough so she can close the gate without crushing my back bumper. She slips back into the car again, and we proceed over dirt ruts, back axles absorbing the shock.

I joke that we should have strung tin cans to the back bumper, let them clatter over the steppe. "Just married," I say like some demented pull-string husband.

She nods. "That we are."

"This *is* kind of like our honeymoon," I say, knowing I'm going a step too far.

She doesn't make eye contact. The semester began just two days after we were married in Sedona. As teachers, we had to postpone our honeymoon until next summer. I know she's narrowed it down to the Maui Channel or French Riviera, Aegean Sea or Coral Sea, Melanesia or Micronesia. Clearly Seligman,

Arizona, didn't even make the long list. Still, quality time like this is rare. And what is a honeymoon but quality time, pink sunsets, a few palm trees? I make-believe the agave shin daggers that pass in and out of view are a stand of stunted palm saplings, a glimpse of a landscape she better deserves.

We've been told by officials that cows have the right-of-way on the ranch. It doesn't take long to encounter the first mob crossing to their companions, who are prone beside the water troughs. I stop for a minute, click on the car's aerial lights, and recheck the map on my knees. It looks like a lava lamp with its multicolored globules indicating the density of the ranch's prairie dog colonies. The area we'll be driving through has as many as three hundred active burrows per hectare. That's three hundred serviceable tunnels trenched through a rugby-sized field. (If you've never seen a rugby field, it's approximately as big as you think it would be.) When the cows have crossed, I gas forward, awaiting the junction where our spotlighting transect begins. Andie slings her arm out the window and clicks on the spotlight's trigger. She develops her technique, using two hands to support the weight. A cone of light illuminates the sagebrush steppe to the east.

One million candlepower is enough to discern our favorite desert plants from the clumps of sage: shin daggers, prickly pear, teddy-bear cholla, barrels and cups of cacti emerging from the otherwise lackluster terrain. There are eyes too, blinking brightly, reflecting the spotlight like a miniature stoplight: red, orange, and green. Most tapeta are pinkish-red and belong to desert cottontail. They jackknife across the rocky earth, nestling behind saltbush shadows. Elsewhere, we see the distant eyeshine of pronghorn, badger, skunk, mice, owl, and cattle. This segment of the ranch, part of a state land trust, is a nocturnal drive-through wilderness. To maximize visibility, Andie oscillates the spotlight, scanning 180 degrees from front bumper to back.

"Well, ferrets," she says, "are you out there?"

The Metropolis Gas Act of 1860 strictly defined candlepower as the amount of light given off by a 2.7-ounce candlestick made from pure spermaceti. Burning at a rate of 7.8 grams per hour, these candles were made of the waxy ester found in an organ in the heads of sperm whales. Spermaceti, from the Latin for *semen* and *whale*, looks milky and smells milky, so it's no surprise that early whalers erroneously believed the substance to be seminal fluid. This means that in the decades prior to the electrification of our cities, candlestick makers thought they were dipping their wicks into melted whale spunk. To create one million candlepower worth of candles, equivalent to the spotlight Andie triggers across the steppe, a candlestick maker would need eighty-four tons of spermaceti, or the equivalent mass of two adult sperm whales—a silo full of white, translucent whale wax.

We pass through the ranchland at just ten miles per hour, occasionally turning onto byroads that run parallel with adjacent transects. This is when other volunteers' spotlights point in our direction. We shield our eyes from the intense light using sun visors, suddenly feeling sympathetic to cows that must endure the roving beams for hours on end. Our nightlong vigil produces billions in collective candlepower across thousands of acres of the Aubrey Valley. Compare this to the approximate four hundred acres a single person can cover in a day. Andie holds the trigger as we scan across the field, hoping for a set of shining emeralds peeking in and out of a prairie dog burrow. Since its presumed extinction in the 1980s, the BFF has steadily reemerged: from a dog-fetched carcass to the live mustelid known as 620 to the eighteen ferrets whose genetic material would be used as a biobank for decades of captive breeding to nearly a thousand wild individuals, a number that ebbs and flows (but mostly ebbs) from one plague season to the next. Currently, the global number is closer to three hundred. Through it all, Aubrey Valley has been one of the flagship sites for rewilding the ferret.

The first flecks of green tapetum lucidum belong to a stocky badger. A nocturnal mustelid like the black-footed ferret, the badger spends its evening hunting for snakes and burrowing owls. Rather than pop up from burrow openings, the badger stands its ground, its broad-clawed forepaws planted in the sand and sage.

"Please keep holding that trigger, would you," I say.

Andie nods.

I run across the steppe, forty yards or more, just to make sure it's not a ferret. When the creature's eyes start running toward me (rather than away), I know we've id'd the correct mustelid. Closer now, I can see the badger's spade-shaped face, the nubby ears, and stripes on its cheeks. I see the buffy fur coating its chest and recall my barber lathering my face with a badger-hair brush just last week. I nod at the animal before spinning away. "As you were."

We finish the transect circuit with no black-footed ferrets to report. The vacant traps clatter in the back as we pull up to the gate. The cars parked at the research trailer mean at least one of the groups has trapped a ferret in this first hour. Andie gazes through the moon roof at the sky's constellations.

"We should really figure out what all these stars are called before we have a kid," I say.

She nods slightly, smiles slightly. Her chin is still upraised. We are thinking, really thinking, about having a baby. Some days she thinks she might be pregnant. We get giddy like there might be three of us in the car. This is not one of those days.

"I'll let you be in charge of the stars," she says.

"What will be your expertise?" I ask.

She thinks about it for a second. "Idioms," she decides. "I'll explain all the idioms to her."

"Her?" I ask.

"Mm-hmm."

"Like what? Which idioms?"

"Not my cup of tea. Scot-free. Spilled milk. Happy-go-lucky. The whole nine yards."

"That will be nice," I say.

We sit, parked, calling out one another's aptitudes, deciding who will take the lead on imparting certain skills to our would-be child inquisitor. She'll take hygiene, Top 40 radio, technology, and shoe tying. I've got sports rules, futurist thinking, basic anatomy, and geographical trivia.

"And ferrets," she says. "You're definitely the ferret guy."

I nod in agreement. "Ready for another go-round?" I ask.

We are at that finite spot where the transect's finish line becomes starting line again.

It's like the most boring level of Mario Kart you've never had to play. I know this ferret stuff is not for her, per se—that she's being a good sport: staying up all night, holding a heavy spotlight out of a window, occasionally searing herself with the intense bulb, otherwise shivering in the constant air flowing through the window, enduring the trippy synth pads and steel drums that boink from my "Spotlighting" playlist on Spotify. And all for a cause that I once shared with my ex.

She shrugs. "Let's do it."

I don't care what she says: this is definitely our honeymoon. "Alrighty," I say. And "I love you."

I shift to drive and blush as I toe-tap the gas. She breathes some hot air into an opening in her gloves before lighting up the steppe again.

The "indefinite moratorium" on sperm whale oil and other cachalot products like candles and scrimshaw went into immediate effect with the passage of Nixon's 1973 Endangered Species Act (ESA). It's the kind of act that would have really pissed off Ahab, the obsessive sea captain who vowed, from hell's heart, to stab at the sperm whale Moby Dick and spit at it to his last breath. The ESA was an expansion of the original 1966 Endangered Species Preservation Act, where one can find the first-ever list of endangered species. Of the seventy-eight species on the original list (also known as the class of '67), three have since dropped out:

Blue pike (*Stizostedion vitreum glaucum*)—delisted; extinct
Dusky seaside sparrow (*Ammodramus maritimus nigrescens*)—delisted; extinct
Longjaw cisco (*Coregonus alpenae*)—delisted; extinct

According to Dale Goble's *The Endangered Species Act at Thirty* (2005), 88 percent of the original species remain on the list, and eight species are "almost certainly extinct, too: Bachman's warbler, Caribbean monk seal, Eskimo curlew, Kauai 'o'o, Kauai akialoa, Kauai nukupu'u, Maryland darter, and 'o'u."

I've spent a lot of hours these past months glossing through academic articles in family studies and reading between the lines of parenting glossies. One listicle, "Ten Reasons Why People Want Kids (and Ten Reasons They Don't)," is just a lazy pros and cons table. I stare at Pollyannaish reason number six: "To Give Your Child the Chance to Enjoy Existence," knowing ecological models indicate we're mostly heading for nonexistence. The Intergovernmental Panel on Climate Change (IPCC) predicts a global temperature increase of 3.5 degrees Celsius will annihilate 40 to 70 percent of known species. I imagine fatherhood will be an endurance act of PR spin on behalf of our liquidated biome—a regimen of smoke and mirrors for the planet's dying years—until, one day, I make the elegiac admission: "I'm sorry I brought you into this world just as everything else was going out of it." According to wehavekids.com, reason number one to *not* have kids, simply put: "environmental impact."

In the introduction to her bestiary *Zoologies* (2014), Alison Deming writes: "Who wants to hear again the sad summary of loss?" There are some who would surely raise their hands. Thoreau, for example, disappointed with ecological deterioration in the wake of species cleansing, lamented that he "wished to know an entire heaven and an entire earth." It's a fantasy we've surrendered ever since Georges Cuvier, founding father of paleontology, established that there were *espèces perdues* (lost species), a concept he debuted after "scrupulous examination" of the mastodon. Before Cuvier, *extinction*, whose Latinate etymology (*extinctionem*) meant something like "annihilation" and applied only to the wiping out of a material thing. Now, *extinction* almost always refers to the biotic world.

Instead of lost species, consider the found. The black-footed ferret, an original from the class of '67, is the single animal species to have twice been declared extinct, only to be downlisted back to "endangered." The BFF's story is an anecdote of unequivocal resurrection. "Lazarus, come out!" and "Lazarus, come out again!" The ferret may habitually recede into its burrow for uneasy bouts of hide-and-seek, but for the forty years since its rediscovery in Meeteetse, Wyoming, it keeps coming back up for more.

It's after midnight. A car zips past us on Route 66, destined for Peach Springs or Truxton or Valentine, Arizona. Maybe even Needles, California. I put my car in drive again and idle toward the cliffs and deep ranch.

Driving a car this slow for so long, I feel my attention drift to the dashboard display. I scroll from the odometer reading (48,211 miles) to trip meter A (116.4 miles) to trip meter B (238.1 miles) to outside temperature (43 degrees) to oil life (56 percent) and back again. These numbers compete with the wilderness that hurtles by the crud-splattered windshield. When I do focus on the road ahead, it resembles the music video for Radiohead's "Karma Police," only dustier. It's scenes like this that remind me why NASA chose this country to test drive its lunar dune buggies in the buildup to the moon landing. It is estimated the soil of the Colorado Plateau is comparable to the surface of the moon.

In this territory, void of cable and cell reception, I must fabricate distraction. Andie rummages through the glove compartment like it's a library. She hands me the paperwork I've asked for, and I pore over the fine print on recent transactions. At five miles per hour, there are only ruts and cattle to run into.

There is an itemized service receipt in my glove compartment recording the date of my last oil change in March. A technician—after checking the dipstick and unthreading the drain plug to let the old transmission fluid ooze onto the pan— poured three liters of new beet-red stuff into a funnel. Once it gulps through the reservoir, the fluid courses through the vehicle's circulatory system, lubricating and cooling it.

A half-century ago, when automobiles single-filed along Route 66, before transmission fluid was an amalgam of toxic chemical additives, motorists used whale oil to get the job done. The oil was sourced from the same spermaceti organ as turn-of-the-century candles. We found half-empty jars of whale oil in my Pap's garage in Wilmerding, Pennsylvania, as we tidied the space after his death, poured the last of the canisters into his Chevy Caprice, the tin glugging until there was just a thin strand of oil threading out. I imagine my grandfather, who suffered from painful plaque psoriasis in his last years, rubbing the buttery whale oil onto the skin of his forearms for relief.

It's not exactly known what spermaceti does for a whale. Most likely, it aids in echolocation; the wax-filled sac becomes a medium through which sonar clicks pulsate to create a subaquatic Doppler effect. At least this is how many aquatic species detect the distance of their prey.

Crickets stridulate like metronomes across the prairie, their music churning in polyrhythmic waves. Some sound meek, others miffed.

"There," my wife says, surely. "Right. There." She clicks the spotlight twice as the emeralds manifest.

This time, I take a trap with me. The burrow complex is not that far from the road, maybe the length of a grocery store parking lot. The animal springs in and out of the mouth of the burrow like a veritable pop-going weasel. A ferret is a weasel, like the one Annie Dillard encounters in her essay, "Living Like Weasels." She and the weasel stand mutually startled, exchanging that long glance inside which she recognizes she "could very calmly go wild." I do not go wild as I stuff the trap into the entrance mound. I watch the BFF recede into its network of tunnels, nests, and turnaround bays, only its nose and whiskers still breaching.

I set the trap, pinning the treadle down with just a centimeter of rusted metal rod, and cover it all up with a burlap sack to simulate darkness, as if this trap is just a dead end of the limitless burrow network gouged out beneath me.

The thing about a burrow network is that prairie dogs, likely aware that a single entrance mound is the architecture of suicide, often puncture as many as two dozen backdoors for escape. They convert the prairie into Swiss cheese, which is perhaps why ranchers took to murdering them en masse (a malicious strain of "species cleansing") for much of the twentieth century. I gently plug all available entrances and exits to the system with a stack of empty Big Gulp cups—eleven in total—and canter back to the car. Andie records the GPS coordinates, takes a few field notes— "REAL. LIVE. FERRET." is her way of saying we've positively ID'd the species—and we drive away with plans to return in less than an hour.

⎯⎯⎯ ⁂ ⎯⎯⎯

Whether in Seligman, Arizona, where historic Route 66 commences, or Peach Springs, the tribal center of the Hualapai Indian Reservation, there is a constant insinuation of activity, with antique cars parked, some even double-parked in kitschy road stop gravel lots that sell little more than candy bars and postcards. The decrepit towns appearing along the Mother Road in northwest Arizona are the basis for Pixar's Radiator Springs (from the film *Cars*). Totter around the antique cars, and you'll see all of them are underused, just parking lot props for cutesy photo ops. It's obvious that their ignitions haven't been keyed in years. Some of them are so dormant, it's likely they still contain a few ounces of whale oil. It's all an elaborate dramatization, a way to make business seem booming.

Stick around long enough, and you'll hear an East Coast family trying to get their ever-loving-cent's worth on their 66-themed vacation. Three squealing kids encircle the salvaged cars. The boy's father quotes a line of flattery from *Cars* in his best Richard Petty voice: "You've got more talent in one lug nut than a lot of cars has got on their whole body." When the eldest son asks what a lug nut is, the father fails to explain. Keep eavesdropping as the children ask naive questions about Seligman, about the disuse of Route 66. Based on their answers, it's unclear if the parents find Seligman romantic or revolting, or just as likely, an indifferent spot to stop for some cheap gas before the Grand Canyon exit.

When someone hears me mention the town—and I speak of it often—my admiration is unambiguous. Ignoring its current motto (Birthplace of Historic Route 66), I replace it with: Re-Birthplace of the Black-Footed Ferret.

<hr />

At some point during the third circuit, my wife stops spotlighting. I'm speeding to thirty now, almost forty on straightaways— way too fast on these farm roads, whose mud-packed tire tracks were formed by a wider chassis, the super-sized pickups whose drivers are invited to Diamond A Ranch on other nights to hunt pronghorn antelope and trap coyote. We bump through ruts and brake for cows proximal to the road. We are racing back to the burrow, to the trap, to (we hope) a newly caught black-footed ferret.

I park and walk toward it: the burrow: the cage: the hoped-for ferret. The grass clumps are frosted beneath my boots. They crunch like I'm walking over a field of celery. I click on my headlamp as I lift the burlap. Even though this trapping process is for the ferret's own good—in the trailer, it will receive inoculation and a PIT tag—it feels momentarily diabolical to capture something that figures itself wild. But the treadle has not yet been stomped. I check the Big Gulp plugs, each still lodged in place. I pace every part of the burrow network; one of these steps—I can't know which—positions me directly above that black-footed ferret, this most endangered mammal. My body's gravity is a literal force acting on its fragile habitat. I wonder if I've inadvertently imprisoned it inside an excellent prairie dog buffet, if its jowls are coated in dark red blood, its carnassial teeth gnawing clean through the bone. Don Katz has noted ferrets have the

"spinal flexibility of a snake and the jaw musculature of a pit bull."
Beneath me, does the prairie dog bleed out as it twitches by the
sated ferret's side?

There is an invisible roadway beneath me, as much as fifteen
feet deep and sixty feet long. I try to visualize its throughways
and byways, stop offs and intersections. Sometimes, a prairie
dog colony connects to another, like a country road linking two
sparse towns. Indeed, like Route 66, the single tunnel grants
tourists like the BFF more lodging and dining options. In my
mind, I'm fake-snaking a fiber optic cable through the burrow as
if preparing for laparoscopic surgery. *Where are you now, ferret?
And now?*

I turn around, sorry that I'll have to report to Andie there's
nothing there. Not yet.

⸻ ❦ ⸻

I have taken to calling our future child Superpredator, a name
Andie reasonably loathes. I say the word like it's "Junior" or
"Buckaroo."

"I bet Superpredator will be so smart she'll be the one to teach
us the names of the constellations," I might say.

And my wife responds, "Please don't call our baby that."

In ecology, superpredator refers to an apex predator (for example, the human species) that exterminates its prey so widely
the consequences are potentially irreparable for global ecologies.
Lack of empathy, an impaired conscience, and disregard for the
future are characteristics of *Homo sapiens* in the Anthropocene.
Conservation scientist Chris Darimont writes in *Science* magazine: "The species that we target are thus far in considerable decline; however, predators in the wild generally achieve a balance
with their prey populations such that both persist. . . . Humans
function as an unsustainable 'super predator,' which . . . will continue to alter ecological and evolutionary processes globally."

By calling my future child Superpredator, the inane art of baby
naming is postponed through eco-self-criticism. Some bioeth-
icists crusading for a small-family (even no-family) ethic are

taking it a step further. Take philosopher Travis Rieder's prov-
ocation recently on *All Things Considered*: "Maybe we should
protect our kids by not having them." It's an inversion of the
logical fallacy repeated in the glossies: "To Give Your Child the
Chance to Enjoy Existence." Notice how obviously the problem
(*Why have a kid?*) is resolved when it's already worked out in the
hypothetical answer (*You already have one.*).

———— ● ————

The Center for Biological Diversity has come up with a novel
approach to advocate for wildlife ecology: distributing over five
hundred thousand condoms. The condom wrappers feature
an illustration of an endangered species along with a catchy
contraception-as-conservation couplet. The center calls attention to the link between human population growth and the
current (sixth) mass extinction. Rather than educate would-be
fornicators about the same old ("proper use of this condom may
help prevent the spread of sexually transmitted diseases and
pregnancy"), the memo transforms the prophylactic into an ecological tool for protecting rare and endangered species.

DON'T GO BARE . . . PANTHERS ARE RARE.

WHEN YOU'RE FEELING TENDER . . . THINK ABOUT THE
    HELLBENDER.

BE A SAVVY LOVER . . . PROTECT THE SNOWY PLOVER.

IN THE SACK? SAVE THE LEATHERBACK.

WRAP WITH CARE . . . SAVE THE POLAR BEAR.

SAFE INTERCOURSE SAVES THE DWARF SEAHORSE.

COVER YOUR TWEEDLE . . . SAVE THE BURYING BEETLE.

USE A STOPPER . . . SAVE THE HOPPER.

WEAR A JIMMY HAT . . . SAVE THE BIG CAT.

HUMP SMARTER . . . SAVE THE SNAIL DARTER.

SAVE THE SPOTTED OWL . . . WEAR A CONDOM NOW.

FUMBLING IN THE DARK? THINK OF THE MONARCH.

BEFORE IT GETS ANY HOTTER . . . REMEMBER THE SEA OTTER.

CAN'T REFRAIN? REMEMBER THE WHOOPING CRANE.

And my favorite (for its slight condescension):

FOR THE SAKE OF THE HORNED LIZARD . . . SLOW DOWN,
LOVE WIZARD.

Author Jonathan Franzen was once asked in an interview in the *Guardian* whether one's fondness for the natural world necessarily leads to social isolation. Franzen's response: "If you take a devotion to other species to its logical conclusion, you reach a point of pretty radical misanthropy." Some mornings, I feel more radical than others. By midday, though, *every* day, I've got ferrets on the brain. Sometimes, it's more reckless than that: I dedicate all my thoughts to them. I've decorated my office in such a way that I'm reminded of the black-footed ferret no matter which direction I swivel my chair: a newspaper article to the north, two framed prints south and east, and the laminated Audubon/ Bachman quotation to the west: "It is with great pleasure that we introduce this handsome new species."

When I first saw the catalog of endangered species condoms, I was a little peeved that there was no BFF condom. I imagine the Center for Biological Diversity's resident condom poet, stumped and slouching at a desk to this day, an index finger rubbing through a rhyming dictionary, unable to conjure a perfect couplet for the ferret.

Being underground is perhaps as animal as it gets. I think of my cousins' husbands, how their first order of home-owning business in suburban Appalachia was to construct man caves for themselves, to trick out their basements with pool tables, liquor cabinets, surround sound, and deer antlers. When I am invited into their vestigial dwelling places, I'm mostly biding time till I can return to the main floor. If I stay too long, I fear the plaster will mineralize into limestone, the pillars will extend into stalagmites, the fireplace will glow Promethean, and the stairwell will be barricaded with scree.

On my first hike through the Lava River Cave in Flagstaff, my friend and I spontaneously slipped into caveman caricature. He made a grouchy guttural sound like a depressed Tim "the Tool Man" Taylor, and I returned the sentiment. With headlights affixed to our foreheads, we could see just ahead of us in the lava tubes: three adult chaperones guiding their sixth-grade class through a fork in the cave. "Go left if you want to walk straight through. But if you choose the right, you'll have to crawl on your knees." Those who went to the left maintained their bipedal posture, while the others, embracing their inner animal, scrambled through on all fours across sharp basalt rubble.

How animal am I? How animal could I be?

The eccentric environmentalist Charles Foster has earnestly lived liked a badger in the Mayfield Valley of the United Kingdom—blindfolded on all fours, very low to the ground, his nose muzzling the dirt, gorging on worms, and sleeping by day in a hollow. The *Guardian* has called it a form of extreme camping, but for Foster it's more than that. "In order to be properly human," he says, "we've got to be properly animal." Evolutionary biology professor Marc Bekoff concurs. He believes modern Americans "are really craving to be 're-wilded.' They're craving to be reconnected to nature."

It's after 3:00 a.m. now. Even with the one trap set, we continue scouring for more green tapeta. We can set as many as four traps at a time. Since we began, my wife has twice burned her flesh with the heated glass of the spotlight. Her wrist is sore. No matter how much hot coffee steams in the thermos, fatigue sets in. I pull over, and we switch roles. Now, she drives while I squeeze the spotlight's trigger.

Sit alongside someone for long enough and the tolerance for casual humor and small talk eventually disintegrates.

"How sure are you that you want to have a child?" she asks at some point.

It's been a while since she's asked me this one. I worry I'm the one being trapped now. I try to compute the percentage, worry that anything less than 100 percent will register as "not so sure."

"I'm sure," I say, and leave it at that.

I know she worries that my sarcastic mentioning of Superpredator suggests a lack of seriousness. It's true that stock photos of paternity make me queasy. But when I look at old albums with empirical photos of *my* dad—cuddling me during a couch nap, howling through chain-link at Little League, massaging burrs off of my treehouse with sandpaper—that's when my intuition, call it future FOMO, whispers that I will not be happy until I've had a chance to be "dad" too. As someone whose depression often fetters him to the bed, though, and drives him to drink to the bottom of every bottle in sight, I'm worried I won't be happy regardless. And that my kid will come to know it—in unfair ways. That's my secret reason *not* to. Add that one to the list, wehavekids.com. That's why, I should admit, I'm really not so sure.

Researchers have been storing black-footed ferret semen in liquid nitrogen for nearly three decades. Sourced from seven Meeteetse males, especially the prolific ferret known as Scarface, the semen is "transabdominally inseminated into the uterine horns of female conspecifics," to borrow the not-so-sensual language in *Animal Conservation*. This method helps preserve genetic diversity among future captive-bred BFF populations. It's kind of like if Queen Elizabeth II (born 1926) was artificially inseminated with spermatozoa from her very-great grandfather William the Conqueror (born 1028). With their genetic forefather twenty generations removed, these BFF kits are genetic history obliquely repeated. Despite the reliance on inbreeding, time gradually restores the species' genetic diversity. Sure, these captive-born ferrets may inherit some of the physical traits of their forebears, but their main inheritance is the remarkable chance to be rewilded to the prairie.

As a genre, BFF literature is a diminutive one. Dig into the classics for a couple weeks, and you'll soon find all that's left is a lot of research on ferret semen. I've read every article I can get my hands on, most recently on low-voltage electroejaculation, and how genome resource banks ensure genetic integrity, and the ideal temperature threshold for slow-cooling ferret semen. Rachel Santymire and her team blew the case wide open in 2007: it's twenty-five degrees Celsius, not thirty-seven!

Because "getting pregnant is a game for two" (so says one of the more irritating books on our coffee table), I've been reading a lot about my own semen too—about morphology, motility, liquefaction, and pH. I sometimes worry about my "swimmers" to the point of daydreaming of sperm heads that resemble Michael Phelps. I've found when I try to recall the facts from my reading, though, I'll occasionally transpose facts about ferret semen with ones about human semen. I imagine a nurse in scrubs, running from a bathroom to a lab, mistakenly swapping containers.

I once had ounces upon ounces of BFF (best friend forever) semen in my refrigerator. My college roommate collected his semen in glass vials with baby blue plastic lids. He stashed those vials in the condiments drawer of our shared Frigidaire, where they looked oddly palatable amid the mayonnaise, tartar sauce, and ranch dressing. Hoping to become the highest-volume donor at the university's forensics lab, he spent much of that month panting behind closed doors, searching for the kinkiest porn du jour. Now he's the father of four superpredators himself. From my distant vantage (social media), it kind of looks like a blast.

I wonder if my semen is potent enough to burrow through the gelatinous coat of Andie's eggs. I've twice lingered in the reproductive aisle at Walgreens, reading the backs of at-home sperm count tests, wondering what I would even do with such a number.

It's more morning than night now, and we're running out of chances to trap the ferret. We chase the coordinates back to the burrow, where we park on the crepuscular roadside before killing the engine. She sets the timer for a fifteen-minute nap while I activate the hand warmers. I power recline my seat. With the comic slowness of a dental chair, I fall parallel with the prairie. I stare through the moon roof, blinking the stars black, feeling subterranean.

There is actually a way to dive deep beneath this prairie. For $20.95 plus tax, an elevator will lower you twenty-one stories down under the surface. Once an ancient seabed, the Grand Canyon Caverns is now a massive complex of dry rock formations whose limestone bedrock is made up of a slurry of shell and bone from long-gone oceanic species. Weeks ago, as we went below, I imagined a burrow-level button on the elevator wall. (*Floor Negative One, please,* I wanted to say.) Instead, we proceeded to Early Carboniferous depths.

The tour guide pointed out a mannequin of a giant ground sloth named Gertie, whose dimensions were extrapolated from a sloth's skeletal remains found in the cave. While the Pleistocene was known for its megafauna—from wooly mammoth to saber-toothed cats to cave bears—it was also the epoch in which the BFF emigrated from Eurasia to North America, member of the mammalian march across the Bering land bridge, evader of the crack-soled footstep of its larger-than-life cohabitants.

Examining Gertie's taxidermy, I dream up her de-extinction. Considered a loss for eleven thousand years—compare with the BFF, "extinct" for just two years before its re-emergence—how would she find the planet now? Would this very late Holocene appeal to her? Would Arizona Game and Fish Department coordinate with Big Boquillas to help reintroduce the twenty-foot giant ground sloth alongside the twenty-inch ferret, allow it to graze for yuccas and grasses alongside the cattle? The parking lot to the caverns is a literal stone's throw away from the ranch. I chucked a pebble across Route 66, watched it arc and crash with a spray of dust before one of Diamond A's gates.

Elsewhere in the caverns is the "largest, deepest, darkest, oldest, quietest motel room in the world." As soon as I heard about the cave room with its seventy-foot, sixty-five-million-year-old ceilings, I shared a link with Andie.

"Honeymoon?"

"No way," she said.

For eight hundred dollars a night, you can rent the way-dark Grand Canyon Caverns cave room, and according to testimonials, incorporate it into your all-American vacation, meditation practice, or honeymoon lovemaking. Imagine conceiving a child just around the corner from Gertie, fits of pleasure echoing for miles across the undiscovered skeletons of the last mass extinction. There, in the dumb black of the cave room, one can conceive a superpredator of their own.

———— ✦ ————

Just like that, there it is: the black-footed ferret hunchbacked in the trap. It chuckles, unable to retreat past the treadle to its burrow. I shimmy the trap free, take the juvenile with me. It swings along my denim thigh as I cross the steppe to the suv. I knock on the window and hoist the weasel toward Andie's eyes. They blink at each other. When I set down the trap in the compact hatchback, the interior light reveals its buffy fur peppered with black. I see its belly slung low against the cage. Its face twitches in abiding rage. Its entire body quivers, actually. I crouch to be near it, inhaling the musk as I say, "Ride or die, buddy."

———— ✦ ————

It only takes a couple minutes for me to come up with a couplet of my own, just as good, I think, as the ones on the existing condom wrappers:

———— ⸭ ————

It's like we've got a kid in the backseat. So tiny, the ferret is probably just five months old. Every time it chitters, I look in the rearview mirror where I can't even see it. Instead, my eyes fixate on
the space where a car seat would go. Suddenly, we're in a car
commercial. It's a perennial heart warmer: a nuclear family is off-
road again, giving the vehicle's suspension a run for its money.
With each jolt to the tires' shock absorbers, our eyes close with
fearful laughter. We're all smiling omnidirectionally, and the sun
is just coming up. All we're missing is an Americana melody. A
reedy harmonica hyperventilating over stuttering guitar, a faint
brush of drums binding it all together. It's all so feel-good I feel
I could just take off my shirt, whirl it round and round my head
like a helicopter, launch it heavenward.

When the ferret chitters again, Andie and I glance at each other.
It feels good, this being three, regardless of the musky scent slowly
filling the car. I put the windows down. Andie is calling out names
for the BFF in case this is its first capture. Sunrise is minutes away. All
the other ferrets will drift to sleep just as the horses are let out from
stable. This one, though—our big find—will be out past curfew. We
see the horses race astride, nearly a dozen, as if on an invisible track.
The dust they kick up lasts only for a minute, and when it's gone, the
steep Aubrey Cliffs manifest again on the horizon. Pronghorns stand
still as if posing for a painting. Some nibble forbs, others grasses. And
prairie dogs, the ones who survived the murderous night, stand up
on hind legs at their burrows' dusty mounds, victorious.

By the time we reach the Mother Road, we've agreed on the perfect name. We start calling back to it by its name, letting it know it's
in good hands. It responds with a loud clucking sound, validating
our tired efforts to be fun captors. We're buoyed. For a long moment,
we're so giddy with good feelings that it's like we'll just skip the trailer,
drive on, take this beast of a baby home, and love it to death.

RURAL PURGE

—•—

In the way back of an Olive Garden on Valentine's Eve, stirring sugar into an espresso under a speaker playing Sinatra—would somebody fly him to the fucking moon already—I refuse to believe the biscotti I just ordered, smelling sweetly of anise and fennel, can't be dunked into the demitasse cup. I rub the cup's rim with lemon zest and nibble the cookie to fit the circumference. I would have preferred to meet Jennifer Cordova at a local joint downtown, something a little less freezer-to-table, but seeing as it's Valentine's and we both have partners waiting at home, it seems more appropriate to meet over the sexless optics of unlimited breadsticks and endless pastabilities. Not to mention, it's the closest restaurant to my house, unless you count the Circle K roller grill with its sweaty hot dogs and taquitos. That, and my parents have mailed me enough Darden gift cards to play Go Fish. I dunk again, and half the espresso shot is absorbed by the cookie.

The gray Game and Fish truck pulls into a spot in the parking lot, a little over the stall line. Jennifer hops down to the asphalt. It's rare for a BFF volunteer to see her in daylight. Usually, our interactions are during the punch-drunk hours of middle-night. She'll wait for our call from a roadside inoculation trailer. "We got one," I'll say between swigs of thermos coffee. The ferret chitters in my hatchback as the cage rattles. "Awesome," she'll say, a bit drowsy. "Bring it in then."

But today she's in my neck of the woods, meeting colleagues in Flagstaff to plan preconditioning pens, which are for a month-long purgatory for captive-born kits scheduled for rewilding.

The outdoor enclosures are essential in instilling and assessing skills kits will need in the wild. They're also discussing the conservation implications of the government shutdown in nearby national parks.

There are college sweethearts seated throughout the dining room, taking selfies with augmented-reality filters: heart eyes, cat ears, flower crowns, and puking rainbows, whatever floats their marinara boats. As much as I want to get straight to BFF business—peruse the minutes of her latest meeting, swap gossip—I feel like I should first give small talk a try. It's been five years, and I know next to nothing about Jennifer.

"How'd you meet your husband again?" I ask as if she had shared the story once before.

"Oh, he hunted prairie dogs in Seligman," she says, referring to the polarizing keystone species.

"He sounds like a ferret," I say. I can't help but imagine her betrothed to a ferret. It somehow makes more sense than her dating a man who kills the ferret's prey.

"I met him at the Black Cat," she says, referring to Seligman's dive bar, the only real meeting place in town.

Prairie dogs are known agricultural pests, feeding on the same vegetation as livestock. I imagine Jennifer's husband as the star of that YouTube video where a man sprays a field with a semiautomatic rifle, laying to waste dozens of peeping prairie dogs. Last century, one could actually make a living that way. On a game forum, one nostalgic shooter writes: "I remember when the ranchers would pay you to shoot the sage rats." Now, most hunters beg around at cafés and feed mills for the privilege or pay outfitters upward of six hundred dollars per day for a bunkhouse, grub, and a brick of .22s.

"I don't have anything against hunting or guns," she says. "You can't when you live in a place like Seligman."

I bite my tongue. Jennifer had once shared she grew up in Newtown, Connecticut, which is in the richest county in the richest state in the United States. She even went to Sandy Hook Elementary in the 1970s. It is arguably the epicenter of gun control now, where the state's supreme court has recently paved the way for victims' families to "subpoena internal documents on how the gun companies have marketed the AR-15, which has become the weapon of choice for mass shooters," according to the *Hartford Courant.* The decision could mean unprecedented liability for Remington.

I try a more tactful challenge. "You mean there's not a single gun control advocate in Seligman?"

She shrugs. "I haven't heard of one. Anyway, I convinced my beau to donate some of his prairie dogs to the ferret freezer. He's the one who keeps our meat pops stocked."

It's around this time that the waitress takes our orders—plain-ass spaghetti for me, pasta carbonara for Jennifer.

"And your wife?" Jennifer asks. "She's a biologist?"

"No," I say. "That was my ex. She's the one I spotlighted with years ago."

"Oh," Jennifer says. "I thought you all were engaged."

"We were," I say. "But a lot got in the way."

Jennifer turns silent.

"Do you go to the Black Cat often?" I ask.

"I wouldn't say often, but when I do go out, yeah, yeah, that's the place."

Jennifer moved to Seligman in 1999 to construct nest boxes for the BFF project. Before that, she made display cabinets for retail stores in Tucson, a skill that came in handy when applying for the full-time position with Game and Fish, which at the time required just as much carpentry as it did conservation know-how.

"Seligman back then was . . . there were no stoplights, no sirens, and just these real pretty sunsets," she said.

"In other words, Seligman was as it is now," I say.

"But it was solitary," she says. Early on, she picked up the *Seligman Bulletin* to familiarize herself with the rhythms of the town, if there were any. On page one, they listed the birthdays. "Happy birthday, Bob Johnson!" it read. On page two, though, this story: "Robert Johnson Murdered His Wife Sunday."

"It made me wonder what else was going on in the town," Jennifer says. In other words, what do people do when no one's watching?

It calls to mind the Western gothic tale by Annie Proulx "Fifty-Five Miles to the Gas Pump." In the story, Rancher Croom, "that walleyed cattleman" with "stray hairs like curling fiddle string ends" dashes off the top of a cliff while Mrs. Croom busts through attic padlocks and discovers the corpses of his paramours. The story ends with these ominous lines, which could serve as an unofficial slogan for any far-out town, Seligman included: "When you live a long way out you make your own fun."

At first it makes sense. I think of the forms of fun I've had in rural Arizona: seated in the grandstands of the Tohono O'odham rodeo, trawling the fancy chicken coops at the Coconino County Fair, tapping my boot soles at a fiddle contest in Payson, whistling at antique cars on 66 in Williams, stoking bonfires outside hogans in Tsaile, and of course spotlighting for ferrets in the Aubrey Valley.

For some, rural fun can sound like an oxymoron—quaint at best, ironic at worst. Like Rancher Croom's "own strange beer, yeasty, cloudy, bursting out in garlands of foam," brewing is a perfect example of making—indeed, manufacturing—one's own fun. With no library, playground, movie theater, concert venue, skating rink, ski resort, shopping mall, candy shop, observatory, arboretum, escape room—nothing of the sort, not at all—one must look within for inspiration. One must be a maker of fun.

I think of the adventure course about a mile from Olive Garden with its kinetic rope swings, zip lines, scrambling walls, hanging nets, and wobbly bridges. Riotous from birthday parties and corporate retreats, it is, according to Tripadvisor, "Guaranteed fun!" But drive an hour to the west, and fun isn't a sure thing. I read the reports on missing kids, imagine them wandering off in search of the possibility of fun. There are a lot of young boys about the size of a burlap sack. One's in a Batman shirt, jacket tied around the waist, last seen in black snow boots. Another's wearing that iconic red plaid lumberjacket with pajama bottoms. Look for his tan boots. The one boy who has made it so far as "fun" was punished for it. He was caught shooting rabbits, leaving their corpses to decompose on the side of the road. It's an awfully hypocritical citation considering Seligman's most famous café is the Roadkill. I imagine the boy rolling his eyes at the restaurant's sign as his grandparents drive him to the county's juvenile court.

There's something about Proulx's story that rubs me the wrong way, though. Structurally, it's two paragraphs and a sentence. The first is from Rancher Croom's limited point of view and the second is from the missus's. And then the point of view slips just for that last sentence. It's a spooky declarative from an omniscient source, detaching from the intimacy, ringing like some sadistic chamber of commerce slogan. This slippage calls into question the narrator's position within the story. In or out?

There's this quote from the midwesterner Thomas McGuane about how people who live in flyover country, himself included, "figure out what is going on elsewhere by subscribing to magazines." Writing from the inside, it's clear in its self-deprecation. If spoken from the outside, though, his words would wound. I begin to wonder if Proulx's last line has anything to do with fun at all—if perhaps it's incidentally "making fun" of rural life.

———— ◊ ————

Jennifer still remembers the first time she went to the Black Cat. She made plans to go with a coworker, and her supervisor belly laughed at the idea. "You girls have all your teeth," he said. "You're going to be popular."

"We thought he was kidding," Jennifer said, "but when we got to the bar, it was like an episode of *Hee Haw*."

It takes a minute for her to explain *Hee Haw* to me—something about a variety show with country music interludes. She pauses as the waitress hovers over her entrée with a rotary grater.

"Yes please," Jennifer says, and the waitress cranks away. Parmesan falls like movie-set snow.

She says she used to look the other way when she passed houses with junky yards as if one could just not see the scrap heaps—the mounds of tires and hubcaps and mismatched wood; stacks of aluminum siding and louver shutters and three-tab shingles; fallen fence posts, discarded plastic toys, and clusters of baling wire. As if she could just look beyond the clutter to the cliffs, let the sunsets blind her to the offending bric-a-brac.

Jennifer could have never expected that a couple years in, her house would be indistinguishable from her neighbors'. One day after work, she nearly drove past her subdivided ranch because she didn't recognize the yard. The drum had stopped spinning in her dryer, so she dragged it to the front yard to repair it. "It was around Halloween," she says, "and because the dryer was kind of like a high-top table, I was carving some pumpkins up there. And there was this one jack-o'-lantern—its teeth were falling out of its head, and I tried to stick 'em back in using toothpicks. There was a dryer hose hanging midair, a toolkit surrounded by wrenches and clamps. It was like a bomb had gone off. Quite the sight."

She says this with a hint of embarrassment, as if to say, this is about when I started blending in—how her lot became part of the motley backdrop of the rural West.

We drift to ferret talk as usual. Jennifer invites me to the groundbreaking of the conditioning pens her new intern is building. She says I should accompany her husband on a prairie dog hunt too. We both know it's time to go when she starts comparing the firmness of ferret testicles to the peas in her carbonara.

I order more biscotti to go—and a black-tie mousse cake, a Valentine's sweet to take home to Andie.

——— ⚬ ———

I watch *Hee Haw* when I get home from the Olive Garden, smirking occasionally at the corny jokes of the residents of the show's fictional town, Kornfield Kounty. Originally used as voice commands for plow horses, *gee* for left and *haw* for right, the *hee haws* in this show are mostly launched heavenward. It is pun balanced with observational humor—and the set is decked out in cornstalks, haystacks, hay bales, tractors, wagons, and barns. The characters wear straw hats with plaid and overalls, bandanas drooping over their chest pockets. They unconvincingly clutch at props like pitchforks and scythes, fiddles and rhubarb, jugs and their coonhounds' ears. And there, in the background, are the Hee Haw Honeys, an asinine ensemble of young women who are meant to catch your eye with their risqué farmer's daughter costumes, but really, the most conspicuous thing about them is the way they lounge in the background with no apparent connection to the humorists in the fore. It's like trying to watch a political debate at a Hooters.

There's animation amid all this live action too, including the titular donkey braying, a pig that tidies up the screen between scenes with a broom, and other bipedal farm animals. There are banjo duels between Grandpa Jones and Stringbean and satirical ditties from Opry legend Minnie Pearl. If you can look beyond the bushy sideburns of *Hee Haw* cohost Roy Clark, just try to answer the question he poses in one of his songs: "Do you believe this town?" No, I mostly don't.

If I get caught in the filter bubble of Google's search engine, deceived by the trappings of instant access ("Seligman" yields 7.1 million results in 0.72 seconds), I might forget how biased, how polluted my algorithm has become—influenced by click and search history, encrusted with decisions I've made when no one was watching, a positive feedback loop of "intellectual isolation," to borrow a phrase from internet activist Eli Pariser. In other words, it can be malicious to "visit" rural America from the bubble of a suburban home office. My prejudice is likely to override even the most precise search syntax, resuscitating stereotypes of farmworkers and the working poor. Like in Lorrie Moore's analysis of *Making a Murderer*, an entire town stands "socially accused . . . [the townspeople are cast as] outsiders, troublemakers, feisty, and a little dim."

By coaxing the black-footed ferret into the literal spotlight, who have the ecotourists of Seligman dismissed to the metaphorical shadows of this town? I scold myself for my impudence. My oversights. I've snubbed these, my extended neighbors, and mistaken them for just part of the scenery.

———— ● ————

Born in 1970, Jennifer wasn't even a year old when depictions of the countryside began to flicker from her television, canceled as part of the "rural purge." CBS, which had earned a disparaging reputation as the "Country Broadcast Station," decided to spontaneously nix *Hee Haw, The Beverly Hillbillies, Green Acres*, and *The Andy Griffith Show* spinoff, *Mayberry R.F.D.*, an acronym for rural free delivery. Overnight, rural programming transitioned from ubiquity to obscurity. Shortly after, *Mister Ed, Petticoat Junction, Lassie, The Red Skelton Show*, and *The Jim Nabors Hour* were purged as well.

With Jennifer as Gen Xer and me as millennial, we could only visit Mayberry, Hooterville, Kornfield Kounty, and the Ozark transplants of Beverly Hills via the jalopy of syndication. Reruns are inherently historical, made even more so when in black and white and depicting premodern dramaturgy and situational comedy. Appearing during program blocks on TV Land or CMT or Nick at Nite (and now, YouTube), it's like the wholesome characters have been exiled to some kind of off-network retirement home. Come to think of it, the only live depiction of rural life I've ever known was via radio. Situated on the prairie's edge, Lake Wobegon from Garrison Keillor's *A Prairie Home Companion* lifts a flattering mirror to the sons and daughters of America's first generation of homesteaders.

Granted, Jennifer encountered these shows during a period when "naive but noble 'rubes' from deep in the American heartland" (a phrase from the Museum of Broadcast Communications) still had lingering relevance in the cultural imagination. As programming moved to the metropolises and suburbs, one couldn't help but wonder if the rural purge was, as television writer Chris Morgan deems, "one of the bigger overcorrections the medium has ever experienced."

Not so coincidentally, developers were simultaneously bulldozing rural America, making way for the suburbs. The new sitcoms modeled a lifestyle for families new to the burbs who had no template for how to go about their days in their cookie-cutter homes.

I think of the Appalachia I almost knew in western Pennsylvania, a wilderness forfeited to strip malls and subdivisions—all hyperconnected by arterial pikes and foggy hollers, and all those lanes whose namesakes came from my friends' great-grannies. I resented my hometown for having paved over the kinds of wilderness that were still extant in the surrounding townships. The suburbs are, by definition, the opposite of "a long way out."

The consequences of the rural purge were not just cultural but also ecological. Just as America turned its attention away from "flyover country," the era of Big Agriculture began. Deep grasses were uprooted, imploding the continent's greatest carbon sink. Critters scrambled toward unspoiled acreage. And corn, soybeans, and alfalfa were wallpapered across the landscape. By the time the first crops grew tall, everybody was channel surfing. We had long tuned out.

IF THE FERRET CROSSES THE ROAD

—•—

The line for free lunch is dozens of uniformed employees from state and federal agencies, who are apparently starving. They shuffle through in their straw hats, broad vests, faded jeans, and cruddy boots, and fling gobs of various casseroles onto their Styrofoam plates. One woman, either a member of the media or an invited volunteer like me, asks no one in particular, "Isn't there any elk?"

As a vegetarian, I'm accustomed to picnic disappointments, to peeking over rims of bowls only to find meat and more meat, ham in the potatoes, bacon crumbled on the salad. By the time I've reached the end of the buffet, I realize the only things I can eat are the sugar cookies. I set my naked plate down, a little self-conscious, and take a cookie for each palm.

There are two styles of cookies, actually. In my left palm, I am holding the black-footed ferret. Dark icing accentuates its bandit mask. I nibble its paws. The other cookie is meant to look like the ferret's prey: a prairie dog. These two species are, after all, the occasion for our afternoon gathering on Double O Ranch in Seligman, Arizona, just northwest of Prescott, capital of the former Arizona Territory. Almost two-thirds of Double O's high desert landholdings are leased to the Arizona State Trust, and in a matter of minutes, through the auspices of a Safe Harbor Agreement, it will become the twenty-sixth, and newest, BFF reintroduction site in the country.

I gnaw on the limbs of one cookie or another while ogling a makeshift wall of memorabilia leaning against the outside of a trailer. These poster-board collages depicting twenty years of

BFF conservation here in the Aubrey Valley will likely be forgotten until needed for subsequent anniversaries—twenty-five, thirty, fifty, however many until the population is viable or extinct. Everybody's favorite part of the exhibit is the taxidermy duo—a ferret's limber body midambush, arched over a prairie dog nearly its own size. Transferring the cookies to my left hand, I step toward the taxidermy and stroke the pelages with my right. The fur is coarse. The static enactment of the food chain before me—just a gasp before the ferret's fossorial teeth puncture the prairie dog's neckline—feels ironic considering I'm the one doing all the chewing. By now, I've eaten all but the cookie heads, not sure whose dignity I'm trying to preserve— mine as a vegetarian, or theirs. It's yet another reminder that even if animals don't make their way onto my dinner plate, I'm still the apex predator in this triad. The mashed cookie on my tongue suddenly tastes gamey.

I always drive to Seligman with a full tank and an empty stomach. It's a little more than an hour from my home in Flagstaff, and I make the trip every three months or so when I need an altitude adjustment. At almost exactly one mile above sea level, it's still 1,700 feet beneath the alpine heights of Flagstaff. In the early evenings, the sun gilds the asphalt horizon all the way to Seligman. I cross my finish line on the sidewalk at Roadkill Café.

Years ago, Roadkill promised to grill any creature that had succumbed to the Mother Road. I was skeptical at first. I figured hunters were encouraged to bring in deer or elk steaks, presliced and wrapped in newspaper, something simple like that. But when I asked the waitresses, they doubled down on the mythos: "Anything they wanted." The wood-paneled restaurant crowded with taxidermy might as well be the Colorado Plateau Museum of Natural History, give or take a few jackalopes. There are coyotes, wolves, quail, antelope, deer, elk, buffalo, rabbits, snakes, prairie dogs, javelinas, and others. The creatures are elaborately collaged into a diorama that could double as a menu. Just point at the snout, and it's yours. I always order a double house salad, extra hard-boiled eggs.

I once met a woman named Chris who told me her daddy would take the family to Roadkill for special dinners. To get there, he'd gas up the car and drive a section of Williamson Valley Road that he knew from hunting—dirt-packed with divots, a wave of rabbits hopping across. In Aurelie Sheehan's story "Rabbits," a woman drives her station wagon over a road sidelined by fields with warrens and streams on either side, "all kinds of rabbit habitat." She drives slow as her headlights illuminate "little gray streaks," the bunnies "zigzagging, frantic, stupid," and inevitably "there would be bumps." I imagine Chris's daddy a little more reckless, a little more hungry. I imagine his wagon hatchback or truck bed stacked with limp cottontails. As she tells it, I can see him presenting them proudly to the waitress at the café, a noose strung around their unlucky feet.

While people linger at the picnic benches—eating seconds, swapping jokes in the midday glow of this commandeered parcel of ranchland—an Arizona Game and Fish intern drags a podium onto the pasture, shimmying it strategically behind an intact cholla cactus. She tries several angles so as to place the podium optimally, to frame nature as spectacle. Until finally, the sixty-two-degree angle, the field of view of a normal camera lens, is void of water tanks. The few houses perched on the southern canyon are out of sight as well. It's just cholla, podium, and an orange butte at the would-be speaker's back. It's ready-made for all the illustrators, photographers, videographers, and journalists in attendance. It's ready-made for me, too. Maybe I'm just being paranoid, but this angled illusion that we're standing on virginal wilderness is too far from the truth for my taste.

The December 2016 issue of *Sierra* features a manifesto by sociobiologist Edward O. Wilson. Calling for the dedication of half of the planet's surface to nature, he writes, "the surviving wildlands of the world are not art museums. They are not gardens to be arranged and tended for our delectation. . . . The wildlands and the bulk of Earth's biodiversity protected within them are another world from the one humanity is throwing together pell-mell." I've been trying for years to give up my selective vision of wildness. Rather than sneak my lens through the chain-link like so many others do, fake-photographing the bison at Mormon Lake Lodge as if they're on an actual roam, I capture their captivity, their jumbo fenced-in faces. I snapshot the sign too:

NAME OUR NEWEST BUFFALO. BEST BABY NAME GETS FREE
STEAK DINNER AT MORMON LAKE LODGE & STEAK HOUSE.

Even the ferrets that will be released in a few moments are only wildish. Bred in captivity in Colorado and flown in by a pilot (who won't be in attendance; he's fixing the plane), the ferrets are now resting in a private trailer, like actors between takes. Their paws have not yet touched the dust that will become their habitat. Just a few acres away, prairie dogs are scooping away the earth, forming occasional mounds that look like oversized anthills. Occasionally, they stand upright, their forepaws limp at pectoral level. I wonder if they understand the suicidal nature of their toiling, that by reconditioning the entrance chutes they are making it easier for their new starving guests to find a way in.

Earlier today, just after taking Exit 123 to Seligman, I saw a shiny speed bump extending across the center of both lanes. After ten years in Arizona, I have never seen a substantially large snake (just a few checkered garters in juniper brush), so I braked for the bend and approached the bump as if it were a gas station bell hose—as if the snake would ding when I rolled over it. After I pulled over and parked on the roadside, I could tell it was the constrictor *Arizona elegans*, also known as the glossy snake. The corpse was over three feet in length. I stood over it, studying the middle third where a tire had flattened it. Its pink intestines popped out of the olive casing. The jaw was unhinged, the teeth pointing at the air around it. Looking into the wide-open eyes, black beads still aimed at their destination fully across the road, I wondered if this would be a fit feast for the café down the road. If I had a shovel, I would have scraped, hoisted, and dumped the snake into the brush, let it blend again with the hundreds of square acres of semiarid grassland around it.

In a chapter in *Roads and Ecological Infrastructure* (2015), David M. Marsh and Jochen A. G. Jaeger claim that because exploratory and migratory behaviors are heritable, animal populations "could, over time, adapt in ways that reduce their risk of road mortality." That is, through successive generations' mistakes, a species can learn efficient ways to cross a road or avoid it via culverts. But it's hard to imagine how a snake, whose slow, rectilinear motion—requiring the coordination of dozens of muscles connecting rib and skin, lifting the belly, scale by scale, from the ground, replacing itself a smidgeon farther each time—could ever move "efficiently" across a road.

It may be that these thirty deadly feet of Arizona highway will, over time, signify an obstacle that snakes will refuse to cross. For example, Swiss conservation biologists Anette and Bruno Baur determined that a twenty-six-foot road acted as a complete barrier for 168 of 169 snails. I imagine the solo snail who managed her pilgrimage across the road inspiring a chorus of bravos from the research group. While mollusks, which move via wavelike pedal locomotion similar to a snake's rectilinear motion, are rarely the subject of road-planning conversations, there is something ecologically reassuring that studies like this exist, that researchers would fuss over a mollusk's path across a road. As I stood over the snake on my way to Double O, I couldn't help but imagine a ferret caroming to the other side, making dooking sounds through the clumsy choreography of its "weasel-war dance," all in pursuit of new habitat, only to be whomped by a semi.

In a few minutes, the seven ferrets will come out of their trailers, emerging to flashbulb fanfare, before being escorted to their new home on the range. As one of the most endangered mammal species in North America, they deserve it. Their celebrity is thanks to their collective endurance. And yet, after decades of conservation technique and gadgetry, thousands of acres of habitat on loan from ranches and Indigenous tribes, and tens of thousands of hours of labor by zoologists and volunteers, their wild population is a meager three hundred globally—less than a quarter than that of the widely elegized Bengal tiger. Theirs is survival by proxy. It seems likely the black-footed ferret will always be endangered.

Due to a recent plague die-off, there are only nine confirmed BFFs in the Aubrey Valley today. This is way down from 123 five years ago. While researchers investigate the usual suspects— plague, drought, wildfire, and agricultural activities—there's a new culprit this time around. Local mycologists suspect the vector-borne fungus coccidioides is to blame. They make the case that as the climate changes throughout the state, heretofore undiscovered strains of the fungus have begun to emerge in the Colorado Plateau. The theory goes that when these spores are stirred by wind, farming, or construction, BFFs—ever low to the ground—inhale the spores into their lungs and contract acute cocci (valley fever), the same infectious disease that hospitalized me my first weeks in Arizona. If it is cocci that's extinguishing Aubrey's ferrets, there may be no cure. Even if it resolved itself in my case, through bedrest and gooey antifungal medications, it's unlikely small-mammal respiratory systems will be able to fight off the disease. In this case, it could spread to the skin or bones or even cross the blood-brain barrier. If this *is* the reason for the swift die-off, then veterinarians are going to need more than plague vaccines to save the ferrets. The lead conservationist, Jennifer, is doubtful, though—of this and any anomaly.

While everyone else speculates, Jennifer takes action. She made a call to colleagues in Colorado, making a case for a shipment of ferrets to Arizona. According to Bruce Finley's article in the *Denver Post*, the National BFF Conservation Center outside of Fort Collins is a "40-year, $55 million national project [meant] to restore [BFFs] across Great Plains grasslands from Canada to Mexico." The biologists agreed to Jennifer's request, meaning they had to spend a long night scoping and wrangling seven ferrets to be airlifted by private jet to Seligman. Once a military arsenal where the U.S. military and Shell made chemical weapons and DDT, the center is located on an unlikely patch of prairie. The $2.1 billion cleanup of this military-industrial disaster area saw the arsenal converted to a wildlife refuge and the home to the largest captive population of BFFs in the world. The experiment may be reaching its limits, though. Finley writes: "The refuge, sandwiched between Denver International Airport and an expanding metropolis, may have exceeded its carrying capacity for ferrets, mortality data suggest. At least six wandered away from prairie-dog colonies and were killed by vehicle traffic on Peña Boulevard." If not by plague, then by Peña Boulevard.

"How fast are we driving species to extinction?" Wilson asks in his manifesto. "As a consequence of human activity, it is believed that the current rate of extinction overall is between 100 and 1,000 times higher than it was [200,000 years ago]." Which raises the question: "How well is conservation working?"

———— ♦ ————

The celebrants are milling about the staging area now, tossing away plates, sipping Gatorade, occasionally peeking into the windows of the trailer to see if they can glimpse a ferret. I overhear someone say it's Jennifer's mother who baked the cookies.

"Not just a pretty face. She can cook, too," a man says.

It's the kind of thing I would chide my dad for saying but seeing as I'm not this man's son and everyone else is yukking at the misogyny, Jennifer's mom included, I end up staring at my boots.

As supervisor of Arizona Game and Fish Department's BFF Program, Jennifer is the reluctant hero of the reintroduction. In twenty years, Jennifer's mother has never laid eyes on the weasel herself despite her daughter's dogged work to reintroduce the ferret to the Colorado Plateau—to Diamond A, Espee, and now Double O. It's kind of like how my own mother scrolls through all of my online publications, seeing the text but not reading it, only to tell me how she likes the author photo I've chosen.

As I watch Jennifer's small actions—consolidating casseroles, leafing through sign-in sheets, dutifully laughing at that man's streak of unfunny jokes—I realize I've never seen her so gregarious. I squint and think I detect trace levels of pride—what with federal agencies, the media, and even her mother all there to see *her* show, *her* ferrets. Still, she is characteristically deferential—hiding her face when the camera comes near, standing on the edges of conversations she's obviously central to, and mostly letting others fill in the conversational blanks. She'd just as soon let somebody start a sentence with "I think" even if she could start the same sentence "I know."

For example, the group is discussing translocation, trying to cobble together the particulars of research by Samantha Wisely. Published in *Conservation Genetics*, the article recommends the "translocation of 30–40 captive [BFFs] per annum" to certain reintroduction sites. By moving the ferrets from one place to another, researchers can mix up the genes and improve the overall population, "[alleviating] the effects of bottlenecks and drifts" associated with a kindred gene pool. In populations as small as these—there are just a dozen or so ferrets capable of breeding on any transect of ranch—genetic diversity is hard to come by. For the BFF, the severe die-off that occurred in the late 1970s—caused by prairie dog poisoning, sylvatic plague, and general loss of prairie habitat—reduced the population to fewer than twenty, countable on my fingers and yours.

———— ⚬ ————

I'm talking with a local named George, along with a couple of ranch hands. We're standing off to the side as if to suggest we are only observers.

George jokes that he's "only here for the free food." He points out his house over the canyon, a short ATV ride away.

"How about you?" I ask the cowboys. "What do you think about the ferret?"

"They got us out of work this afternoon," one says, "so we're off to a great start."

As we wait for the speakers to queue at the podium, the intern who had first arranged the podium steps up to it again and reluctantly waves at us.

"I've got a part here," she says, lifting a sheet of plastic. "It came from the bottom of a Nissan." Even here, definitively off-road, we've managed to bring the effects of the highway with us. A man wearing a "Save the Black-Footed Ferret" T-shirt claims it and walks toward the parking area.

George talks to the cowboys about trapping.

"What kind of trapping?" I ask. "Coyotes?" I only have a microsecond to premeditate the pronunciation. Having read Dan Flores's *Coyote America* (2016), I'm well studied in the political implications:

> Simple pronunciation . . . can serve as a clue in coyote politics, if not a hard-and-fast rule. Defenders and supporters of coyotes, usually (but not always) from educated, urban backgrounds, tend to pronounce the animal's name *ki-YOH-tee*, with the accent on the second syllable and a *t* so soft it's almost a *d*. Americans from rural backgrounds—who commonly fill the ranks of those who manage coyotes, shoot and trap them, or fear them and want them killed—struggle with a three-syllable name, a rendering that apparently sounds pretentious. Or maybe as a word out of the Southwest, *ki-yoh-tee* just sounds too fancy, perhaps too Spanish. In any case, to rural people the comfortable name is *ki-yote*, accent on the first of the two syllables.

The pronunciation, Flores claims, is like asking people what they think of John Wayne: "It's immediately diagnostic of a whole range of belief systems and values."

I opt for the latter pronunciation, but because that's not how I typically pronounce it, it feels put on. When they don't wince, I mention the first BFF was a "poor specimen" first found by a trapper near the headwaters of the Platte River in Wyoming.

"He stuffed its carcass with crushed sagebrush and sent it along to the Audubons."

"Yeah?" George asks. As in, *So what.*

John James Audubon was nearly blind by the time that package arrived, so he just kind of ran his fingers through the pelage. And his son John Woodhouse Audubon made a plate depicting the weasel thieving eggs from a nest by the river, which was an unlucky guess. That plate appears in a three-volume mammal project known as *The Viviparous Quadrupeds of North America* (1846). In it, Audubon's naturalist buddy the Reverend John Bachman writes: "It is with great pleasure that we introduce this handsome new species." Despite the hearty introduction, though, it took a quarter century for a *living* specimen to manifest, leaving skeptics to assume the black-footed ferret was mythological. I don't tell George any of this, though.

What I do say is this: "It's strange. Some company in Saint Louis shipped eighty-six ferret pelts to the American Fur Company in the late 1830s, but between 1920 and 1950, there's only mention of twelve ferrets in trapper records. Nobody's been able to explain that."

"Not a lot of fur on them," one of the cowboys says. This comment echoes the experts who suggest burrow trapping was just too much work for such a small pelt in the shivery middle of night.

"Yeah, but clearly it was enough for the trappers in previous generations," I say.

"Hm," says the other cowboy.

If I were feeling more combative, here I'd mention the fact that 98 percent of prairie dogs were slaughtered in a government-sponsored "control program." That prairie dogs provide essential ecosystem services like "groundwater recharge, regulation of soil erosion, regulation of soil productive potential, soil carbon storage and forage availability"—this according to conservation biologist Lourdes Martínez-Estévez and others. That the holes prairie dogs dig are not some villainous plot to mangle livestock but are the mechanism by which those services are provided. That the genocide of a keystone species, in tandem with the conversion of 95 percent of its native range to croplands, was bound to have severe consequences. That, in architecture, a keystone is what allows an arch to bear weight; without it, everything collapses. That the earth's eolian collapse in the Great Plains was due, in part, to the prairie having lost its keystone. That a regional sandstorm—no, Dust Bowl—is what you get when amateurs (homesteaders) replace the experts (prairie dogs). That when the collective archive of trapper logs averages just 0.3 ferrets a year, one might be inclined to ask *Where are all the fucking ferrets?* and not *How much fur is on its back?*

For the next half hour, a slew of ferret lovers speak. Jennifer is obliged to go first, despite her general distaste for public speaking. I'm convinced she's holding up her hand not as a shield from the sun but to cleverly hide from the camera—to force the photographer to use another visage for the news story. Even though this is primarily a publicity event for the Arizona Game and Fish Department, Jennifer can't overcome her aversion to the public. It's an authentic aversion—childlike, something I feel like she's still scheduled to grow out of, but not today. She swiftly vacates the podium, introducing a wildlife specialist, a grassland coordinator, a conservation-and-science director, a fish-and-wildlife manager, and a game-and-fish retiree.

They praise the voters and volunteers of Arizona. They cry out: "Embrace the weasel!" One person dubs the Aubrey Valley the "premier site for ferret reintroduction," while another suggests "the recovery belongs to the north." Someone skeptically mentions the Navajo's claim that the ferret has made its way to their reservation. Everyone is doing their best to avoid politics on this day of celebration. For twenty years now, Seligman residents have been in a halfhearted staring contest with the BFF. When was the last time somebody invested this kind of money and time in the people of Seligman? Sure, by virtue of a positive feedback loop brought to you by ecotourism, the ferrets, whose monitoring requires volunteers to travel from afar—to lodge and dine in the town—represent a slight boost to the local economy.

Mostly, though, the residents recognize the way their lives are valuated alongside a ferret's. They feel that difference.

"Sure are a lot of people came to see these critters," one of the ranch hands says under his breath, scanning the crowd of fifty-plus.

"What, they gonna come to see you instead, huh?" his friend ribs in reply.

"But no. This really is a lot of people for our area, for one day," he says over his friend, to me.

Earlier, he had mentioned how he was kicked out of two high schools, for antisocial behavior in both cases, how he'd spent most of his life in incidental solitude whether in GED online classes or the surrounding acreage.

"Usually, we just get people wanting to shoot at animals out here, not stand around and look at them."

We agree it kind of feels like Groundhog Day. I tell them about how I grew up near Punxsutawney, how after the shadow play is over, the whole town turns its attention away from the weather lore and toward day drinking.

"Maybe that's what we should do once this shindig is over with," one of the ranch hands says.

The other agrees with a goofy smile. "See you at Black Cat," he says.

"I would," I say, not even sure I was included in the invitation. "But I've got to get back to Flag. I teach this evening."

At some point during the proceedings, the Endangered Species Act of 1973 (ESA) is invoked, and the presentation gets a little muddled. With the ranch hands listening in, the speakers seem to lose track of their audience. The ESA is praised for its inherent flexibility. Then it is rebuked because it impinges on landowners. People in the audience glance at the ranch hands to see if they flinch. Later, a retired conservationist points out one of the biggest misconceptions about the ESA. "We're not trying to save every last rat in the country, people!" he says. By referring to the ferret as a rat, he is not only family switching (from Mustelidae to Muridae) but also code-switching: appealing to some least common denominator. If it scurries near your ankles, it's a rat, he seems to be saying. In so doing, he disabuses everyone from the notion that he would ever be the type to put a ferret's needs above a human's.

No matter what the ranch hands think about the ESA—and there's no telling with their prolonged poker faces and steady slurps from soda cans—it's clear that the BFF is still extant because of the legislation. According to legal scholar J. B. Ruhl, the ESA determines which species to protect and which threats to regulate and can serve as "a viable way to respond to [the] ecological reshuffling of species." As we approach what ecologists refer to as a no-analog future, one in which our usual ecological models will lose their predictive power because of our accelerated transition into the zoologically morbid, the ESA can be tapped as a tool that guides adaptation measures while ramping up ecopragmatism. Ruhl even goes so far as to say the ESA should be adapted for climate change—that land managers should be coerced by the statute to aid in the safe passage of climate-threatened species through the tenuous corridors of the Anthropocene.

"Stewardship over ownership" is a tenet shared by many ranchers in Arizona. The famous Babbitt ranching outfit, among the first to open its gates to the ferret, invokes famed naturalist Aldo Leopold in its constitution, saying it intends to "[change] the role of *Homo sapiens* from conqueror of the land community to plain member and citizen of it."

In the midst of the sixth mass extinction, we can no longer frame species loss and ecosystem collapse as an "either/or choice between mitigation and adaptation," Ruhl argues. In coordination with the Black-Footed Ferret Recovery Program in Colorado, zoos throughout the country are developing vaccines and *ex situ* reproductive techniques to allow ferrets to endure bouts of plague while maintaining their genetic diversity. Most famously, eight BFFs were born, sons and daughters of frozen sperm from the original Meeteetse line. In the case of a small breeding population, says JoGayle Howard and a team of conservationists, artificially mating with a distant progenitor would significantly increase genetics while decreasing inbreeding.

When the ferrets are brought from their trailers, people howl. Their cages are set into three truck beds. I climb into the first. On my knees, I peek through the lattice, wondering if this one is a veritable chip off the old liquid-nitrogen block. How far, I think, this species has come since it was first described in Audubon's *The Viviparous Quadrupeds of North America.* And yet it's mostly the same. My eyes scan upward from the black nib of the cylindrical tail to the interspersion of fine and coarse hairs on the ferret's underside. I remember the one time I touched a living BFF. It was anesthetized, limp in a trailer, as it was inoculated. I closed my eyes, thinking of Audubon, blind and desirous as he ran his fingers through the fur of the first ferret corpse known to the Euro-American world. With its Mickey Mouse face, it looks like the kind of creature you might ask to sign your Disney autograph book. One loud chitter, though, and I know to back away and leap to a seat above the wheel well.

In the entryway hall of our house, Andie has hung a large black-and-white print of a *Life* photograph by Andreas Feininger. It's twenty-four inches of cumulus sky above six inches of asphalt. There's a Texaco station, two cars, and even, it seems, a hitch-hiker. When she first hung it, I told her it was uncanny the way the scene reminded me of Seligman. There's something about the way a photograph and small-town America both have a habit of getting frozen in time. Over the months, the resemblance grew so strong, I had to look it up. Turns out, it *was* Seligman.

From our driveway, you can hear the Santa Fe Railroad chuffing east to Winslow or west to Williams, especially on Sundays. On windy days, you can even hear the traffic on Route 66, which runs parallel with the tracks. If you time it right, pull out of the driveway just as you hear the first in a series of low-pitched whistles a third of a mile away, you can catch all the train-tripped green lights on 66 and travel at the same pace as the train.

Three miles down, on the right, there's a series of motels chock-full of 66 kitsch, none more so than the 66 Motel. There's even a brewery called Mother Road. All but one of its beers is named for the highway—the only exception being the Conserve and Protect Kölsch Style Ale, whose proceeds go to the Arizona Game and Fish Department to promote wildlife conservation (#cheerstoAZwildlife). It's my go-to. I crack open the can, tilt back my head, glug with eyes closed, and imagine I'm standing on the main street of Seligman. There, you can see the small white house where Angel Delgadillo grew up. Son of a machinist from Jalisco, Angel used to stand in front of his house with his many brothers and sisters, waiting for the sun to dim just so. And when the long line of cars came rolling into the city for one last piping hot meal before California, their headlights like a continuous projector bulb, the young Delgadillos would dance to live piano or banjo, trombone or drums, even their daddy's "gee-tar" (they were a family of instrumentalists), and their silhouettes would project onto the white house. It was as if they were on television, Angel remembered, recounting the anecdote as part of the Route 66 Oral History Project. "We would make shadows on the walls. We would dance and play, and we would stomp on each other's shadows to erase each other," he said.

Sitting in his barber's chair, Angel recalled what happened on September 22, 1978. At 2:30 p.m., Interstate 40 officially opened, bypassing that stretch of Route 66, taking passengers away from the Seligman business district. "The state wouldn't forget to put signs up for us," Angel told his older brother, Juan. But it did. "And the world forgot about us."

The fictional setting of Radiator Springs in Pixar's *Cars* is based on Seligman. In one scene, the race-car protagonist Lightning McQueen is parked at a scenic vista. McQueen, who is based on Muhammad Ali, Kid Rock, and at least for this scene, Angel Delgadillo—personified, mechanized—watches the stream of cars on the interstate, and says, "They're driving right by. They don't even know what they're missing."

By the time the *Cars* creators interviewed Delgadillo, he had been promoted to Mayor of the Mother Road, having established Seligman as the Birthplace of Historic Route 66—a deceptive epithet meant to reclaim traffic lost to the interstate. Sixty-six was actually "born" in Springfield, Missouri; Seligman was just the first town to dub its bit of the road "historic." Still, Seligman lays claim to the longest uninterrupted stretch of original pavement from the Main Street of America, its 159 miles aiming west for Kingman and its nostalgic Arizona Route 66 Museum.

Now, thanks to Delgadillo's efforts, thousands of drivers have returned to Seligman to pay their respects. With all these nostalgists drifting through, road mortality for small animals is certain to increase; it may be only a matter of time until the Roadkill Café is coerced to resume its "you kill it, we grill it" policy. In the past year, I've already seen a handful of prairie dogs splayed on the asphalt, and Jennifer's team has released multiple ferrets on one side of 66, only to capture them on the other side. They've even crossed the interstate. "They must have found the culvert and went beneath the road," Jennifer said. "Or who knows, maybe they just went over the median."

Ferrets may wise up before long. Ecological models have shown it takes an average of fifteen vehicles per minute for a road to become "an absolute barrier" to otters, a *Mustelid* cousin to the ferret. Regardless of the ferret's ability to adapt, it will be increasingly important to remember that, as one study concluded, "the fragmentation of habitats . . . [is] associated with reduced species richness." And in Aubrey Valley, the primary fragmenter of habitats is Route 66.

From the Historic Route 66 General Store in downtown Seligman, you can follow a series of country roads that require some serious zooming in on your map app of choice: Fort Rock Road to Sol Lane to Powerline Road to the staging area at Double

O. See how this wilderness is barely so? If we set aside more land, "populations of species that were dangerously small will have space to grow," Wilson says. "Rare . . . species doomed by development will escape their fate."

We wait for the cage door to whip open, for the first ferret to scuttle onto Double O's land. Its coffee-bean nose and white whiskers breach. They name her Lucy in case they need to refer to her later. After a few moments, all of us silent, only the road noise whooshing behind us, the ferret falls into an entrance mound for a nap until night.

I recede from all the high fives and chitchat. It's getting late and I have a class to teach. I jog back to my car, race to the I-40, and speed all the way to Flag.

There's no time to change my clothes, so I figure I'll just hide myself with the podium. My students wonder if I'm auditioning a Western costume for Halloween, which is still a couple weeks away. It's hard for them to believe that this might be what I look like when I'm not on campus: boots, jeans, flannel, and a cowboy hat. The students take turns telling me how I might go about embellishing the costume to look more like a scarecrow or an urban cowboy, like Jeremiah Johnson or the Sundance Kid, like Louie the Lumberjack (our university's mascot) or a pioneer hipster from Bushwick. *I'm not trying to look the part*, I want to say.

At the top of the hour, I clear my throat. I should start talking about writing now, but I find myself wanting to talk ferrets instead. Maybe it's the podium; I can't help but imagine it's the same one from the ranch, that it's my turn to speak on behalf of the species. I give my students a writing prompt based on the 1,500-square-foot fictional map that artist Jerry Gretzinger has been working on over the past fifty years.

"Think about the fictional world you've been writing about," I say. "Draw a map of the city, town, village. Try to capture it all: cities, suburbs, farmlands. Everything you can think of." They work their pencils for ten minutes, drawing grids for city streets and curvilinear forms for country roads, squares for homes and rectangles for high-rises, circles for fountains and ovals for pools, each page a clutter of development. Then I instruct everyone to pass their paper to the right. "I want you to introduce a void onto your peer's map. Draw a big blob somewhere on it. It should take over about half of the map. Fill it in. Make it totally opaque so that there's no trace of what was there before." Students are strategic about where they place the void. Some try to avoid major monuments. Others aim for the busiest parts of the maps. Roads are bisected, buildings demolished, housing developments undeveloped. "Okay," I say. "Give the map back to its creator."

"What the hell, man?" one student says to the classmate to his left.

"See what's happened to your map. Study the void. It's now a genuine wilderness. What will your characters do with it? Will they pave it over or encourage it to grow?" I mention E. O. Wilson's ideas about the subject, about the ideal of a Half-Earth. "For now, let's write a scene about the wilderness. Let's all take good care of it."

THIS IS NOT AN ENTRANCE
TO THE PHOENIX ZOO

—·—

"Okay, it looks like I'm approaching a golf course?" I say. "There's a putting green on my left." These bourgeois oases are regular fixtures on the periphery of Sonoran Desert roads.

"Is this you in the white?" Bradley asks.

The golfers' putts are all inside the leather. I look away from them to glimpse the man I'm talking with on the phone. I come to a complete stop at a chain-link roll gate and stare through the windshield at the curator of conservation and science. He's leaning against the wheel of his own golf cart. It's that awkward part of a short-distance phone call when the device itself becomes unnecessary.

"Yeah, that's me," I say as our eyes meet.

I hold the phone to my ear for a few seconds more, watching the man on the other side of the gate—the thumbnail portrait I've known from my inbox now animate and life-size. Bradley has grown from a few pixels tall to six foot six, his limbs spilling from the cart, where he's uncomfortably hunched. His bangs are glazed to his forehead. A walkie-talkie rests on his lap. We share a breath or two before hanging up.

I raise my hand in clumsy salute. A redundant way of saying: *Is that you?* He raises his too: *Yup.* This charade doubles as an ad hoc security checkpoint. Bradley squints until he's certain that I'm the guy who's been bugging him.

My email requests to see the black-footed ferret breeding center at the Phoenix Zoo had spanned several years and employed a series of stratagems including the pleading professor, the demanding artist, the noble citizen scientist, and the harried journalist. Everything but the sitcom farce of a man casting a preteen as a terminally ill Make-A-Wish kid who just wants to see the ferrets breed before she dies.

In order to get to this exact location, this back entrance to the zoo, I had to plug in a discrete address Bradley had sent via text. Just for today, just for me, the zoo is on Marigold Lane and not on Galvin Parkway. When the GPS prematurely announced my arrival, I had to geolocate the rest of the way down the road, disobeying a half-dozen signs discouraging my advancement. THIS IS NOT AN ENTRANCE TO THE PHOENIX ZOO, the signs read consecutively. Noncompliance meant I was getting ever closer to a bona fide Jurassic Park. This off-exhibit part of the zoo is, after all, home to a once "extinct" species whose reintroduction to the natural landscape is a conservation spectacle. The captive breeding happening on the other side of this gate is the subject of a bioethical debate not unlike those inspired by Mary Shelley or Michael Crichton.

Bradley pokes at a keypad, and the gate slides right. My foot lifts from the brake pedal, and I idle forward, staring at his back, at a print shirt with what appears to be clip art watermelons.

My father-in-law once told me golf carts are legally allowed to drive 19.9 miles per hour. Bradley's must be souped-up—going 25, maybe more. I try to keep up, but he can swerve around the speedbumps that force *me* to slow. At each hump, I peek around.

To my left, I see a patchy fairway through the hundred-foot-tall nets erected to keep golf balls from hooking into the conservation center's solar roofs. I imagine ninety-nine balls caroming off the netting and an occasional one soaring over it, landing in the nearby hyena or leopard enclosures. To my right are zoo facilities. It feels like I'm driving around the backside of a grocery store, or parallel with an industrial park. There are multicolored dumpsters, heavy-duty garbage cans, pickup trucks and delivery trucks, cherry pickers and scissor lifts, and dozens of golf carts—probably more than they have at the Rolling Hills Golf

Course next door. There are pieces of corrugated cardboard and wood pallets and crate boxes, sawhorses and scrap wood, the ubiquitous detritus of shipping and receiving, strewn across the asphalt. Some service doors are rolled open, revealing the silhouette of some enigmatic project—perhaps a habitat reno for one of the 1,200 animals in residence at the zoo. I wave at a facilities worker who takes her 7:00 a.m. cigarette break in the shade of a broken-down Dippin' Dots stand.

As Bradley turns right into his spot, he points with his left hand at a dirt patch where my car is meant to go. Even though I had watched the temperature double on the digital dash over the past two hours—during the six thousand–foot descent from nippy Flagstaff to balmy Phoenix—I'm still surprised by the feel of hot air when I step out of my car.

"Good morning, Lawrence," Bradley says.

"Hello," I say. "Hi."

Before making eye contact, I notice it's not watermelons after all but a familiar graphic: a skeletal profile of a T. rex over a blood-red backdrop: the *Jurassic Park* logo stamped all over his torso.

"You can just follow me in," he says, his hand outstretched, grazing the cinder wall.

I gauge my ecodepth several times a day as Andie and I—okay, it's mostly me—deliberate over this decision to reproduce. I am trying to declutter my decision-making, which is to say: desocialize it.

I share my reasoning with friends at a bar. One friend returns from the bathroom and asks for a recap.

"What did I miss?" she asks.

Another friend offers: "Just some more breeder bullshit."

I nod politely.

On another occasion, an older African student who wears a jumbo crucifix around his neck listens as his female colleagues assure him, again and again, that they have no intention to reproduce. He is gobsmacked by their disregard for what he perceives to be a biological imperative. He is the last one left in the room, and he is looking at me like he's cosmically offended. "What do we do about these girls?" he wants to know.

Elsewhere, we have friends who admit they aren't having kids because they're "too selfish" about the potential for career advancement and creative opportunity. And we have friends who have had kids but rarely speak of them—just the varying strategies for disengaging with the responsibility: edibles, in-laws, an office halfway across town. We have friends who "can't afford it." And those who can but are too frugal. Worst of all, we have friends who are utterly self-righteous, who offer sarcastic warnings via email like this one from my good friend Will: "According to the U.S. Department of Agriculture, raising a child from birth to age eighteen will cost, depending on your income and spending habits, between $174,000 and $345,000. We won't factor in college since by the time little So-and-so is eighteen, most institutions of higher learning will probably have already MOOCed themselves to death. Besides, there will be few sustainable job opportunities left in the post-Uber economy except transporting waste outside the 1 percent's oxygen-rich floating bubble communities."

While Will won't be our child's godfather, he offers (unhelpfully) to be the "godless antifather." He sends me a poem by Weldon Kees that begins with a baiting image ("Looking into my daughter's eyes . . . ") and ends with a switch ("I have no daughter. I desire none.").

It takes time to purge all these ideas, I want to explain to Andie. Instead, I dumbly say, "I'm still thinking." Thinking isn't the problem. She just wishes I'd think for myself. For a whole season, I ask the existential question, tritely plagiarized: To be or not to bring somebody into being. Eventually, I find the schematic from the Voluntary Human Extinction Movement (VHEMT).

"How deep is your ecology?" it asks. "Take a sounding." A cartoon figure wearing a hardhat leans over the edge of an open pit. The possible depths are labeled as psychostratigraphic layers: superficial,[1] shallow, knee deep, hip deep, deeper, profoundly deep, radically deep, and abysmally deep.[2] This makes ecological thought sound like a competition, which in some academic circles, it absolutely is. VHEMT self-identifies as profoundly deep: "Humans are too great a threat to life on Earth. The species should be phased out." Or as their motto goes: "May we live long and die out."

I follow the instructions at the top of the diagram to discover my own ecodepth: "Go down until you disagree, then go back up one level." Depending on the day, I'm a proponent of deep or deeper ecology, gradations on the relationship humans are meant to have with nonhumans and wilderness. As if by some kind of misanthropic osmosis, when I'm near Will, I feel "profoundly deep" enough to tell my wife I think we'd better not.

At some point, though, the semester gets busy and I stop inviting devils to perch on my shoulder. By fall, the deliberation is over. My wife and I are trying, in spite of all we've been told, to have a child. To desire it too.

———— ❦ ————

I left for the breeding center at 5:00 a.m. It took two hours: zooming past Mountainaire, where my therapist lives in a gabled house with gingerbread eaves; past the roadside silhouette of an elk so large it had to be a statue but was real, a buck leading his gang to the fatal edge of the road; past the mangled guardrail where a sleepy trucker left his overturned haul; past the "fire activity" sign and the film of smoke that resembled fog; past and through that reeking smoke that circulated through my car's vents like a coffee roastery; past the juniper woodland, which was somewhere burning; down and past the 5 percent grade that runs east of Sedona; past the rest stop where my ears always pop

1 We should take good care of our planet, as we would any valuable tool.
2 A quick annihilation is too good for humans. A horrible, fatal illness from outer space is only fair.

from elevation drop; past the hillside glitter of Jerome, whose converted bordellos and overfull junkyards and active mining pits look like a lousy solar farm from the distance of the highway; past the exit signs for the Cliff Castle Casino and the public service billboards forewarning gambling addiction that can ruin families; past all the roadside crosses, RIP; past the RV grounds rife with skunks and Doritos dust; past cows tromping over prickly pear daggers to graze at the kelpy-looking patches of grass; past ephemeral streams in rocky gulches, born of snow-melt and gravity; past the mature juniper tree in the median that someone decorates for Christmas with oversized bulbs and wisps of tinsel; past the super-bloomed Sonoran periphery, brightly carpeted with poppies and lupines and owl clover and penstemons and brittlebush and fairy dusters; past signs for a fiddle contest and signs for donkey crossings (next ten miles) and a well-placed billboard for the university where I teach; past Bloody Basin and Horsethief Basin and Black Canyon City and other grisly place-names; past a dead cottontail by the sign for Bumble Bee (which some call Bumblefuck); past the first grove of saguaros, their arms raised like football officials' as a field goal is booted through the posts; past the cars in the slow lane whose bumper stickers signal Wildcat or Sun Devil or Lumberjack or other mascotly pride; past hot-air balloons floating magically above the Superstitions; past the planes that are passing me, low from the drag of their takeoff from Sky Harbor Airport.

Within two hours of backing out of my driveway—that half-moon departure from under a pine branch where an early bird cooed shy vocal exercises—I became a limp arm hanging from a window in the twelve-lane berserk of the Phoenix freeway, watching the pulse of the brake lights before me, a strip mall security car issuing a gentle SOS.

With so much attention paid to the wild populations in the Colorado Plateau, it's easy to forget there are ferrets in the south as well—captive-born and living, albeit indoors, in a desert that could never approximate their natural habitat. I took the freeway exit like I was banking on a racetrack, a madman who hadn't seen a wild ferret for months—save for the one who was "re-introduced" in the Aubrey Valley, who had literally walked out of a cage and into her own wildness, diving exponentially into freedom, into a burrow that must have felt like home. I was damned excited for this next-best thing: an *ex situ* population of frankenferrets living under the panoptical surveillance of zoo conservation.

The breeding center is a biosecure environment, meaning the doors close behind me like they mean it. We pass through an administrative hallway and end up in a tight space with lockers and shoe racks. Every cranny is labeled with a staffer's name. Bradley instructs me to put booties on over my shoes and a surgical mask over my face. I offer to wash my hands too.

"You don't have to do that since you won't be touching the ferrets," Bradley says, emphasis on the YOU WON'T BE TOUCHING FERRETS part. He has a way of sneaking ground rules into conversation without making me feel infantilized. He has me pegged, correctly, as the type who might take liberties. That, and the operations manual says that as supervisor of this facility, it is his responsibility to make sure "no one other than immediate staff will be permitted in the main BFF rooms" during pairings. And yet, here he lets me be.

Over the sound of suds, I hear Bradley's radio. In the zoo proper, somebody's asking for a favor. "I'll be there in a minute," comes the reply. "I just need to get the tiger in." Which leads to the question: *The tiger is out?* It's a reminder that there are other endangered species nearby, ones with more celebrity than the black-footed ferret. Any zoo seeking accreditation from the Association of Zoos and Aquariums (AZA) is mandated to "participate in conservation work that benefits wild populations." In an article in the *Journal of Environmental Education*, researchers analyzed language from 160 mission statements from nationally accredited zoos to determine how conservation figured into zoos' missions. These terms regularly appeared: conserve/

protect the species, rehabilitation, reintroduction, species survival plan, husbandry, captive breeding, conservation advocacy,
promote conservation, advocate stewardship, promote awareness, facilitate conservation, and conservation for generations.
Categorically speaking, all of these activities apply to the Phoenix
Zoo. This is why there are more black-footed ferrets caged in this
Sonoran Desert compound than there are in their native sage-
steppe habitat up north.

"Are you ready?" Bradley asks, standing before the door.

"I am."

"You're in luck," he says, "We've just started pairing the ferrets.
You might get to see something special today."

———— ✦ ————

In *When Species Meet* (2007), philosopher Donna Haraway
writes that a Species Survival Plan (SSP) requires coordination
among organic, organizational, and technological bodies. It is:

> a trademarked complex, cooperative management program of the
> American Zoo and Aquarium Association (AZA) . . . [including]
> World Conservation Union's specialist groups who make assess-
> ments of endangerment; member zoos, with their scientists, keep-
> ers, and boards of governors; a small management group under
> the AZA; a database maintained as a regional studbook, using
> specialized software like SPARKS (single population and records
> keeping system) and its companion programs for demographic
> and genetic analysis, produced by the International Species
> Information System; funders; national governments; international
> bodies; stratified local human populations; and, hardly least, the
> flesh-and-blood animals whose kind is categorically "endangered."

Add to BFF conservation a fleet of drones to administer plague
vaccines to sustain their prey, and one begins to appreciate
the scale and complexity of the commitment. Humans have
so thoroughly involved themselves in the SSP that, to a distant
Martian spectator, it may seem like the ferret-ferret-human
ménage à trois is the only way to ensure the species is reproductive. Haraway has gone so far as to characterize the dissolved

boundary between human and animal in U.S. scientific culture as the mythological birthplace of the cyborg, the two species so imbricated as to simulate bestiality.

Meanwhile, zoo patrons hoping to engage intimately with endangered species can typically do so from the awkward distance of snail-mail charity. For a small donation, one can make the dubious claim that they've adopted a tiger, giraffe, elephant, orangutan, or snail. (However, few people will adopt a mollusk.) If these adoptees are to be the donor's zoological progeny—per the parlance of adoptive parents—then let them be cute, as endearing as the visage of a niece or grandson on a well-angled phone screen, something to make you *aww*. Studies published in *Biological Conservation* have shown that a species' affect-related characteristics—namely charisma, including phylogenetic similarity to humans and the feasibility of it sharing human habitation—positively correlate with its selection for this symbolic adoption.

But that's not the only factor. Another trend shows a species is more likely to be adopted if its species epithet appears early on in the alphabet. Study authors write, "Animals were listed by name in alphabetical order on the adoption program's website . . . [and] people are not willing to spend much time on choosing the species they wish to support, but go for the first animal displayed once they have decided to support a conservation program." Sucks to be a walrus, warthog, wolverine, wombat, woodpecker, and so forth. As the International Union for the Conservation of Nature (IUCN) Red List grows, with the extinction surging to one thousand times the background rate, natural selection is likely to be rife with lazy speculation, gradually subsumed by free-market capitalism.

———— ◆ ————

It's an overlarge room, a little bigger than a college basketball court, with cathedral ceilings and puffs of insulation dangling from the rafters. There are windows overlooking desert landscape, letting some natural light eke in, but the room is mostly saturated by the fluorescence of light racks. There are cabinets on the perimeter labeled glassware, cameras, water bowls, corner beds, masks/gloves, and breeding supplies. I am standing in the center of a corridor with a roll cart loaded with gloves and chemicals, a wash basin with bleach and disinfectant, and other instruments suggestive of just how clean, safe, and protocol-following this place is meant to be.

Most of the facility is occupied by rows of cages. The spacing of the rows is reminiscent of the scene in which two velociraptors slink through a dark stainless-steel lab in Spielberg's *Jurassic Park*, tapping their dewclaws on the linoleum and inhaling the scent of hidden children. There are three rows of ten cages, all elevated like the ones in pet stores, but a little more expensive and industrial looking. Whereas three or more domestic ferrets can be crammed into a single cage, these ferrets are solitary. And for now, invisible.

Each wire-mesh cage looks empty—like the ferrets have yet to arrive or like they've just flown the coop. Rather, there's an egress at the center of each cage; it looks something like a toilet's hole, and the ferrets have flushed themselves down into black tubing that helixes toward the floor, connecting to a heavy metal nest box where they sleep. Because it's early morning, the time when most ferrets tucker out, they are all—all thirty of them—in a dimension that is invisible, *away*. Each ferret seems to have been replaced by a clipboard where all of their biostatic secrets are stored.

Kevin emerges from the prep room adjacent to the main corridor. He is masked and gloved, in booties and scrubs that reveal the tops of tattoos and tan lines. I try not to look at his topknot, a hipster hairstyle BuzzFeed once described as balancing a rubber band on one's head. Instead, I stare at his pretty eyes.

"Hey," Bradley says. "This is that—" and then he trails off while nodding in my direction.

"The guy you—?" Kevin asks. It's his turn to acknowledge me with a half-sentence.

This time, I nod. "Lawrence," I say, reaching out for his gloved hand.

After a vigorous shake, Kevin looks down at his glove, and realizing I've defiled it, yanks it off, finger by finger.

Bradley asks how long I'll be here—an obvious, if gentle, reminder that I shouldn't loiter for any longer than I had requested. I had initially said it would only take an hour in the email, but now that I see the facility's size, I'm prepared to ask for more.

"When's lunch?" I ask.

"Eleven."

"Maybe eleven then," I say. "If that's alright with Kevin," diffusing the authority.

Kevin shrugs.

Bradley shrugs too before leaving.

I crack my knuckles and begin by asking Kevin about his tattoos, a safe icebreaker.

"Are those ravens?" I ask. It can be difficult, trying to tell the difference between ravens and crows, kraas and caws.

"Yeah, it's Huginn and Muninn," he says. Because he's wearing the surgical mask and I'm unable to read his lips, I don't exactly catch what he has to say about the birds. I decide it's probably a primer on their role in Norse mythology, how they fly over Midgard and deliver messages to Odin. Every tattoo is a hyperlink.

"Cool," I say. "What about that one?" I point at the double-digit graphic.

He hesitates. I can tell he'd rather not.

"It was my best friend's college basketball number," he said. "He committed suicide."

"Ah, shit," I say. "I'm sorry."

I look far away from his collar bone to the ferret cage in the farthest corner.

After a couple hours scrolling on Airbnb, a deep search for the perfect stranger's home for our baby-making needs, Andie and I agreed on Casita Bellissima, a historic adobe within walking distance to the plaza in Santa Fe, New Mexico. We started with the reviews, where one hyperbolic individual claimed there were "angel sprinkles everywhere." Unconvinced, we clicked through photos. The first set focused on the private patio—for "dining al fresco." It was surrounded by pear trees, wisteria, local sunflowers, a waterfall, and a custom mural of sticky, heliotropic flowers. Inside, the walls were made of a bioshield clay and slathered in a raw clay paint. There was clay in the Saltillo tiles in the kitchen and bathroom too. The ceilings were beamed with wooden vigas, and piñon was stacked in the kiva fireplace. There were antique prayer chairs and a 1920s artist bureau, plus an Italian velvet sofa filled with down. Every modifier in the listing's description, right down to the citrus zest and rosemary sprigs in the soaps perched on the clawfoot tub, was meant to amplify the organic nature of this space. This casita was *made* of organisms, of varying life-forms, and therefore seemed conducive to forming new life. By the time we saw the chili wreath hanging from the French doors leading to the bedroom, I shifted the pointer to the "BOOK NOW" button. The unilateral nudge was meant as a small joke, but when Andie didn't flinch, I went through the motions of typing my credit card digits and messaging the Superhost. I nearly told her about our intentions with the place, thinking it might flatter her. "This looks like the number one place in Santa Fe to make a baby," I typed, but Andie shook her head and I replaced it with something more generic.

When I first entered Casita Bellissima, I was transported back to "Verona," an Old World refuge I had constructed in the Pennsylvania wilderness of my early teens. There, I had hollowed out a wooded pocket within a massive brush pile and supported it with beams fashioned from uprooted saplings. Under the oak canopy, I hung curtains from hacksawed vines, staked citronella torches into the earth, and cobbled the contours of room shapes using hunks of shale and claystone rock. The goal, of course, was to build a shelter, where my high school girlfriend and I could have sex without the paranoia of parental surveillance. At the center of it all, in that pocket of brush, was a product-defected Tony's Got It! mattress. I found it dumped unused in an Irwin alleyway and dragged it for over a mile along a stretch of Route 30, through several discreet streets, and finally over the curb into the terra nullius of Verona.

Out there, we feared pregnancy and STDs like any teen who aced sex ed, but most of all Lyme disease and hunters. It was in Verona that a fellow trespasser heard our clumsy humping and lifted his rifle, aiming for deer, peering through the 18x zoom night-vision scope, ready to count antlers, only to discover our teenage fuck instead of his would-be eight-point buck.

His voyeur eye squinted into the optics for too long, rendering us wilderness pornography. There's no naked like crosshairs naked. I wished for a blanket that resembled his fleece: one hundred square feet of mossy oak mimicry.

"Lare!" my girlfriend whispered under the weight of me. As in, *What do we do?*

I stared at her head, imagining an exit wound. It's a well-known fact in Pennsylvania that the tastiest deer are the ones who are shot directly in the head. If the animal has too long to panic or run, its muscles become filled with lactic acid. "Ever had a glass of good-tasting acid?" asks outdoor outfitter Realtree.

I remember thinking that if he didn't look away soon, we should just run.

It took a moment to realize the hunter wasn't supposed to be there either. Hunting season was nearly a month away. And now our underage bodies presented him with a second reason to vacate. I shifted to my knees and made a demonstrative "Y" with my arms—as if M-C-A would be next. The poacher lowered his rifle and trekked back in the direction of his car.

Until then, we were in the habit of spending a lot of our money on pregnancy tests. My girlfriend had amenorrhea, perhaps from an eating disorder, and for many of the forty-three months we were together, she had no menses. Most months ended with the ritual of a pregnancy scare. In other words: a dramatic trip to CVS, and not Rite Aid, where her grandmother was a cashier. We spent what little money we had on condoms, pregnancy strips, and a package of Swedish Fish or some other red herring.

After the episode with the hunter, though, we decided to stop wasting our money on the pregnancy tests. Sex was a reckless thing no matter what, we wagered.

"What if I get pregnant?" she asked.

"If you get pregnant, then *we'll* be pregnant," I assured her with unearned confidence, as if I were rehearsing lines for a teen drama starring Julia Stiles. She liked the sentiment. Come to think of it, it sounded vaguely like the first stutterings of family planning, which was farther than my parents ever got.[3]

If someone had told me that by my ten-year high school reunion, I'd be staying in a stranger's pueblo-style house in the American Southwest, using a peer-to-peer hospitality network with the hopes of conceiving a child with a woman from California who ingests prenatal vitamins twice daily—that we'd be outsourcing the particulars of our family planning to an app on a computer phone that color-codes our reproductive itinerary down to the hour, I'd probably have responded, "No thanks. The future sounds too fancy for me."

And yet, here I am. Here we all seem to be—at "organic" Casita Bellissima—going through the motions.

While this facility has produced an average of twenty ferrets per year for twenty years, their four hundred ferrets pale in comparison to the kits produced in the other five locations throughout

---

3 During a class presentation on "family lines" à la Toni Morrison's *Song of Solomon*, I shared my family's immigration paperwork—from County Kerry to the port of entry at Ellis Island. I followed the lines of descent for four generations until my birth a century later, 1989. But our class valedictorian—calculus whiz, high school quarterback, future Notre Dame premed, future Harvard Medical, future orthopedic surgeon, future dater of my high school girlfriend—did the simple arithmetic that I had failed to notice. "You said your parents got married and then had you," he said. "Yeah?" "Well, it's the other way around—if they're celebrating their seventeenth anniversary this year like you said." I said I must have gotten the dates wrong, but that night at dinner, my parents gave the valedictorian an A on his math. They used the word "mistake" in an ambiguous way. Was the pregnancy a mistake? Or me, the baby?

North America. The BFF Conservation Center, for example, has had upward of two hundred in a single season. The National Zoo had a baby boom in 2010 that resulted in the birth of forty-nine kits. Reproductive physiologist JoGayle Howard attributes the success to excellent husbandry and management practices. "After many years of research, our knowledge about the reproductive biology of the black-footed ferret is extensive. This species comes into estrus [heat] only once a year, and determining the optimal time for breeding is critical to reproductive success."

A lot can go wrong in a breeding center too. Maybe the pairings, as prescribed by the studbook keeper at the Smithsonian, do not result in genetically viable embryos. Male ferrets are notorious for their reproductive inefficiency; just see K. N. Wolf's paper in *Zoo Biology*, which says that, until he can overcome the most common snags—tiny testes, uninspired sexual positions, aggression toward females in heat, no ejaculate, poor aim, or shooting blanks—a male ferret will be known as a "nonproven breeder." Even when a male *is* "proven," the pregnancy may end in spontaneous abortion. Or shortly after her whelping, the mother might cannibalize her litter. Worst of all, though, a season may pass in which the female ferrets aren't even in heat. This was the case at the Phoenix Zoo last year, meaning breeding season came and went, and the thirty ferrets—each of which are valued upward of $1.3 million in state, federal, and zoo resources—remained *just* thirty ferrets. And I used to think the ferrets at the pet store were pricy. I could buy ten thousand domestic ferrets for the price of just one captive *Mustela nigripes*.

Unlike humans, who ovulate upward of five hundred times in their reproductive lifetime and could in theory get pregnant any month between puberty and menopause, ferrets have only a handful of chances to reproduce. Because they live only three years in the wild and max out at six in captivity, most ferrets only have three chances to get pregnant. These once-per-year ovulations are so light sensitive that once, when a zoo staffer left a door cracked, the ambient light from a desk lamp in a room adjacent to the breeding center terminated all chances of estrus.

Just like that, a couple dozen ferrets weren't born. My dad used to scold me when I left the light on in unoccupied rooms, tabulating the cents like a CPA. Imagine the catastrophe of leaving a small light on and squandering millions of dollars' worth of ovulation.

"That didn't happen here, though," Kevin clarifies when he sees me writing that down. He wants me to know he would never make such an amateur mistake. "It was somewhere else."

I'm surprised Kevin has the sole responsibility to oversee this delicate production. Because he's the only person *to* shadow, it feels literal: I walk just behind him, but not so close as to trip him up if he suddenly changes direction. It feels funny, the two of us so close in such a large space—kind of like two sweepers on a curling sheet. I am exactly the shadow that I asked permission to be.

This is the BFF paradox: in celebrating all the ways it's hanging on, we fail to see the ways in which it's already extinct. If we entertain, for the moment, the idea that dead is something you *can* halfway be, then the BFF is it: the human hand so heavy in its breeding, conditioning, feeding, and inoculating that they're not just a relict organism but a cyborg one to boot.

Even humans who have created the biosecure environments meant to inspire BFF's longevity know better. While humans seek sex in organic spaces, returning to the garden for sex and honeymoons, they sequester once-wild species to the sterile facilities of their imagining—a panoptic brothel that relies on technological seduction. As Haraway asserts in her manifesto, we have moved away from the organics of domination and toward the informatics of domination: representation to simulation, organisms to biotic components, reproduction to replication, organic sex role specialization to optimal genetic strategies, biological determinism to evolutionary inertia and all of its constraints. Informatics are the life support required for ferrets to survive. To return to organics (or "nature") is to begin the countdown to extinction. The Panopticon is Foucault's promise of a noncorporal penality designed to "take away life, but prevent the [ferrets] from feeling it."

When I described the breeding facility to Andie, she put it just like it is: "Sit here in this cage and get fucked." Her critique is mostly about choice, access. Without that, she argues, they cease to be a real species. It sounds reasonable enough until I remember my cousin who spent almost two decades and hundreds of thousands of dollars trying to engineer her own pregnancy. They had reached Will's upper estimate for the cost of raising a child before the baby was even an embryo. According to the Pew Research Center, one-third of American adults say that they or someone they know have undergone fertility treatment, which often involves third-party reproductive technologies in which their only option is to pair with egg donors, sperm donors, or surrogates. These conditions, in which informatics succeed where organics falter, are necessitated by the same reproductive and genetic limitations ferrets face. There is nothing romantic about a cryobank, where men ogle dirty mags and ejaculate into Tupperware, nor the room where women are given pelvic exams, follicle-stimulating hormones, their eggs extracted under anesthesia. And yet, this is where sex begins for so many couples cut off from the kind of access others enjoy.

I remind Andie of my cousin's story, of her son who's now eight years old. "Remember him? He was at our wedding? Are you saying he's not real?"

She points out that he's a single organism, not a species.

We have a semantic war while I neglect to remind her of how my cousin framed the conception. After all the in vitro fertilization attempts failed, she gave up. And then it happened, unassisted, by happy accident at age forty-five. "A miracle," she had said. "*Au naturel.*" True enough.

———— ⚬ ————

Kevin begins with a vaginal wash of a ferret named Indigo. Wearing extra-thick work gloves—"They can get you," he says, "a lot of pressure without the puncture"—he pats and scrapes the cage until a ferret pops through the platform's hole. She's vexed and stretching, her whiskers twitching. By the time he scoops her into a transport trap, a second ferret scurries up the tube, emerging from the same hole.

"I thought they were kept individually."

"Yes, except for the ones with clipboards on the *tops* of the cages," he says. "We've got pairs in there."

"So, who's that?" I ask, pointing to Indigo's mate.

"We call him Jager."

I scan the other rows to find two more paired cages. "If the clipboard's a-rockin', don't come a-knockin'," I say.

I prefer to think Kevin can't hear me through my surgical mask rather than face the fact that I'm not that funny. He closes the enclosure, and I follow him to the front corridor, Indigo swinging at his side.

He sets the trap on the cart, where she trembles.

"The red is a good sign," Kevin says. "It's the color of his saliva on her fur."

I had heard this before—that the hobs restrain the jills by their necks before intromission, that all breeding is "essentially rape." Indigo's shivers intensify as Kevin lifts the trap to eye level so that he can see her vulva. He draws saline into a medicine dropper, shallowly inserts the pipet, and squeezes the dropper's nipple, thus flushing out the saline. By releasing the nipple, he withdraws any new material from Indigo's vagina.

"We're checking to see if there is sperm, and to get whatever fluids are in there out so that we can test them," Kevin says as he lowers the dropper and squeezes once more, transferring her superficial, cornified squamous epithelial cells to a blank slide.

He returns Indigo to her cage. In the wild, a ferret would dive immediately into the nearest hole. Indigo, though, remains on the upper deck of her enclosure. I imagine it's because she wants to know who I am. The operations manual would refer to me as a new stressor, someone who makes "unnecessary noises"; by virtue of my thousand questions, I haven't kept up my end of the bargain to keep "talking to a minimum." Or maybe it's because she doesn't want to return to the sexed-up Jager, who waits for her in the nest box. Or maybe she's eager to know the results of the procedure? She's looking at us like, *What the fuck was that all about?* At three years old, she's endured this twice before. I look at her chart, a log of her weight and diet July through January, followed by a series of reproductive checks February through mid-April. She was "Paired w/ Jager" yesterday, and today is the sperm check.

"So how about these names?" I ask.

"What do you mean?"

"Who names the ferrets?"

"Well, because none of the ferrets ovulated last year, we didn't get to name any. Before that, though, the old director wanted names to do with the habitat. He doesn't work here anymore, so I think we'll be able to do fun names again."

Kevin says he's holding out hope for a *Lord of the Rings*–themed round of naming.

After a quick disinfecting of the equipment, we end up in the prep room, where Kevin dyes the slide purple and adds a fixative. "Sometimes there's just one sperm head on there," Kevin says as he squints at the slide. "They're extremely small."

I am standing over his shoulder when a volunteer biology student from Arizona State University (ASU) joins us in the prep room. She checks in—with the computer first, then Kevin.

"You're the only one today," he says.

She looks disappointed. Her arms are folded, her fingers fanned and covering the eyes of her wolf tattoo.

"If I get done early, I can help you clean the cages," Kevin says.

"Okay."

"Have you ever cleaned paired ferrets before?"

She shakes her head, a little disgusted.

Just before she leaves with her bucket and gloves, Kevin thinks to introduce me.

"Oh, Chandler, this is a writer. So if he's creepily watching and writing down everything you do . . ." He trails off. It reveals how he's been processing my presence. I remind myself to give Kevin some space.

"Okay," she says to him. "Good to know." She smiles at me before trudging away, off to row one, cage one—to a yearling named Nitrogen.

———— ◦ ————

The app signals Andie's fertility with a leaf symbol. It looks conspicuously like one of those fig leaves used to conceal female genitalia in ancient art. With six fertile days per calendar month lit up green like a speedometer reaching its ecopotential, we have to be strategic about intercourse. A fertility magazine recommends every other day, so we plan for sex on either side of the app's estimate, assuming some margin of error: the first, third, fifth, seventh, and ninth of the month. We approach the act with incidental reverence—like we're not ourselves but procreative archetypes lifted from "some unconscious 'folk' memory" from Igor Stravinsky's *The Rite of Spring*. It is a form of roleplay in which we levitate from the textbooks of our sexual education. Then the app's calendar goes blank with infertility and sexlessness for a week and some days. Just when we think it's time to claim our lottery ticket, to raise a glass of nonalcoholic champagne, my wife shows me she's added a note to the calendar: a transparent red droplet (spotting). A couple days later, an opaque one (menses). Not this time. We're back to waiting for the leaves.

———— ◦ ————

While Kevin repeats the procedure for the other two paired females, I stay behind in the prep room to study the pairings markered on the "breeding board," a whiteboard that looks like a tabloid mapping and branching its gossip columns. I imagine the intimate breeding information before me after it's gone through an ASU Greek-life rumor mill:

INDIGO'S FLING WITH JAGER

JAGER CAUGHT CHEATING

CREOLE IN TEARS: BEST FRIEND TELLS ALL

COOKIE ADMITS AFFAIR WITH YIPPEE

TORN BETWEEN TWO LOVERS: CRUSH MUST CHOOSE
  BETWEEN THRIPS & SIOUX
ROCHELLE & SHOOTER: DID HE CHEAT? LIES, TEARS &
  BETRAYAL
SHOOTER & KORRA CAUGHT! ALL THE DETAILS INSIDE . . .
THE OTHER WOMAN SPEAKS: MY AFFAIR WITH SHOOTER
WOODFORD A VIRGIN NO MORE! A NIGHT TO REMEMBER
  WITH PABST
WOODFORD TELLS ALL

In reality, there is nothing frivolous about these pairings. First, the technician checks the males' testes. "They should be firm but have some give," Kevin says. "Like a grape, but smaller." I immediately think of the circumference of a boba straw and those balls of tapioca that settle at the bottom of the tea. Four weeks later, hydroejaculation shows if the sperm is adequately concentrated. For females, once the vulva begins swelling, technicians perform lavages, flushing out cells that line their vaginas. Those cells are then tested for cornification, which essentially means the cells have lost their nucleus and become large, irregular, and flaky. The cells stay this way for a full month, at which point yearling females should be paired with proven males.

"Why not pair the younger ferrets together?"

"The yearling males don't know what they're doing," Kevin says with a little condescension.

A male and female yearling would spend their entire mating period in a squabble. According to the U.S. Fish and Wildlife Service BFF Managed Care Operations manual, "some males will chronically attack females and cannot be bred."

The breeding readiness of any pair is then balanced with their potential to sire offspring that are genetically diverse. The studbook keeper and curator at the Smithsonian Conservation Biology Institute, Paul Marinari, plays genomic matchmaker, reviewing the pedigree of possible pairs at all sites. Marinari knows the historical details of all captive-born ferrets' births, deaths, locations, pairings, and parentage. These studbooks don't exist for just any species. One study shows that half the animals extinct in the wild have active studbooks. And over 40 percent of all studbooks are for threatened species. For the black-footed ferret, a species descended from so few founders, this chain of recordkeeping represents one of the most complete studbooks of any species on earth. Marinari's primary goal is to avoid—or in the case of the severely bottlenecked BFF, minimize—inbreeding. The closer the cousins are—in genetic genealogy, they call it IBD for "identical by descent"—the more likely their alleles will be replicas from a common ancestor. In Marinari's world, only opposites attract.

One column on the breeding board, reserved for future whelping dates, is blank. My eyes scan from its aspirational heading (*DUE*) down to the ledge for markers. The blankness feels like a prayer.

Some ferrets begin screeching. It sounds like the spasmodic sparring of two overwound mechanical toys, the grinding of their gears amplified by the acoustics of the extra-tall ceilings.

Kevin runs back into the prep room. "Hear that?" he asks. "That's ferret sex." You can tell he thinks I'll like that.

"Oh really?" I say, trying to match his enthusiasm. "Good looking out," I add. I wouldn't have known the difference between that and, say, a ferret having a loud and horrific nightmare.

"Yeah. They get after it," he says.

I peek out the door in the direction of the enclosure. It isn't far from where Chandler is on her knees, scrubbing the walls and floor clean to a rhythm probably dictated by the song in her headphones but also subconsciously matching the rough ferret sex happening at her side.

I nudge the mouse, and the computer lights. I see the nest boxes, one per square, full of paired ferrets cuddling like () or)(. But then one square looks like a sexy wrestling match. I can see their mouths open, the origin of the harsh and constant sound. The pixels can't keep up with Luzius, who's uncompromising in his mounting of Applejack. He uses his canines as he would to chow down on a prairie dog; except rather than kill her (her throat is only an inch or so away), he only gnashes them down enough to have a paralyzing effect on her.

It occurs to me that this is why there are Ethernet cables trapezing from the ceiling of the facility. Used year-round for the live ferret stream on the Phoenix Zoo's website, the same one I watched compulsively after my ex had left with our three pet ferrets, it's offline for just a few weeks while the ferrets are paired. I used to think the reason it went offline is because something dire had happened—like the ferrets had been placed in quarantine after being exposed to a deadly disease or something. I can't imagine what a young web surfer might think if she were to stumble upon the image of Luzius nonconsensually attached to Applejack, gripping her scruff like he's about to pull off her weasel mask. As the operations manual puts it, "experience suggests that even if a female's cytology indicates she is ready to breed, the BFF may not agree." At two-thirds the size of her male counterpart, a jill "can hold off" all thirty-two ounces of male mounting.

If you've never seen the Wally Van Sickle drawing of proper ferret sex—and shockingly, not many people have—here's how the managed care operations manual describes it: "A promising breeding attempt is one in which the male mounts the female's back, and secures himself by grabbing the female around the flank with his front legs while holding the female's scruff on the back of her neck in his mouth. The female's tail is held to one side to allow breeding. Males and females usually remain in this coupled position for one–two hours. They must remain coupled for 15 to 30 minutes for the male to ejaculate."

When Kevin notices me watching them for a little longer than I had planned, he moves away from the glass slides and chemicals he's been fussing with. He stands behind me like a dad who has just discovered his son watching an obscure porn clip.

"These all get recorded. We have to watch them later for good positioning."

It amazes me, the idea that among all the other things in the Phoenix Zoo's cloud, there are hours and hours of ferret sex footage. I'm reminded again of the architecture of surveillance, the Association of Zoos and Aquarium's agenda of panopticism all in the name of engaging patrons in conservation. In reality, they are simply using the affective cuteness of the ferret as an "ambassador species" to help reestablish prairie dogs, a keystone species, in the Great Plains.

"What happens if it's bad positioning? Do you have to teach them?" Even as I ask the question, I know the answer is obviously not.

"No, no. They either have it or they don't," Kevin says.

While waiting for the slides to set, he moves on to other ferrets to see if they're ready for pairing. He lifts them, their vaginas at eye level. Sometimes he has to blow on the fur to part the hair to see if the vulva is swollen. He takes a few notes and decides there's a few prime for pairing.

I wouldn't have realized how near it was to lunchtime if it weren't for the sudden chatter on the radio. Someone announces there are leftovers from a catered breakfast in the front of the zoo. Another person asks for the message to be repeated. I look restlessly at the slides, wondering if they'll be ready before lunch.

As Kevin prepares medicine for a couple of sick ferrets, I snoop around a bit more. I stare at a hand-drawn comic magnetized to the fridge: an upright cartoon ferret, its paw clutching the handle of an ajar refrigerator, tail on the tile floor and head peeking inside: "No prairie dogs!! We never have anything good to eat anymore!"

"They don't eat prairie dogs?" I ask, wondering what the ferrets will be having for their lunch hour.

"Nope."

Now I open the refrigerator and lean in like the cartoon. The freeze-dried bags on the shelves are stacked with dark coils of meat labeled *TORONTO*. In the baskets below, there are jumbo bags filled with whole frozen rats.

"Toronto?" I ask.

"That's horse meat. Some guy drives it down from Toronto every week since we aren't allowed to slaughter horses for meat in the United States." The ferrets get a special diet, he explains. Virtually all of the other animals receive food prepped in-house by his fiancée and nutritionists like her. "She does nutrition for all of Monkey Village," he says with a hint of pride.

I think about the Torontonian driver, can't help but imagine him waking up on a Monday morning and taking off for Arizona. I figured even if he drives an above-average amount in a given day—say 550 miles—it would take him ten full days to make the round-trip delivery. I decide there must be at least two drivers on this route, two horse-meat shippers passing in the night. Do they rendezvous for a late dinner in Missouri, maybe Oklahoma? I imagine them shearing the meat off dry-rub ribs while the horse meat stays cool in the trailers.

"Welp, I have to get going," the southbound driver might say. "The ferrets are expecting me." And the northbound driver nods, "Yep, and my family's expecting me."

"That's a weird twist in the food chain," I say. The prairie dog genocide of the mid-twentieth century was due in part to the fear that the "cockroaches of the prairie" and other denizens of their colonies would stud the ground with ankle-breaking burrow mounds and ruin the equine and bovine residents of the range. Now ferrets were actually eating ground horse meat? It's probably the biggest indicator of how far from wild these ferrets are.

"We give them the rats on the weekend," Kevin says. "The ones with abscesses and broken teeth get horse meat exclusively, though. We think the rat bones are too hard on them as they get older."

I stare at ferret photos on the wall. "That's Wink and Chimo," Kevin says. He's getting good at answering my questions before I even ask them. "We take photos of some of the really special ones. Before they die."

"These?" I ask. There are framed paw prints labeled with ferret names: Barry, Dell, Mae, Roni.

"When they die, the vets have ink they can save them in." You can tell Kevin thinks it's a touch sentimental. But then I remember he's done the same thing with the tattoo on his collar-bone. I glance at it again, then away before he notices.

He turns his attention to the cells fixed to the slides. "I think they're ready."

When I'd run out of ways of being social—having exhausted topics like Kevin's mom's real estate business, upshots of the various wedding venues he and his fiancée are considering, and his personal list of Phoenix's top breweries (Wilderness being number one)—I turned to social media. Kevin doesn't know it, but while he fiddled with the chemicals, I found his Twitter feed, which is mostly retweeted memes starring Marshawn Lynch (NFL) and Michael Scott (*The Office*). The two are infamous for their reluctance and eagerness to speak to the camera, respectively. There's some aggro-male stuff on there too—repeat images of Stone Cold Steve Austin (WWE) and professional gambler Dan Bilzerian calling PETA "cunts" for their criticism of Steve Irwin's legacy. As is usually the case with Twitter, it's unclear if Kevin endorses these messages or just finds them amusing. Utterly un-self-conscious, his is a very different Twitter presence than I'm accustomed to. My feed is mostly full of mind-numbing self-promotion, doomsdayism, purity tests, and virtue signaling. His only original thoughts seem to be in his unofficial position as armchair quarterback for ASU's mediocre football team.

The retweet that most catches my attention, though, is Jeff Goldblum quoting a famous line from a role he once played in the *Jurassic Park* franchise: "Yeah, yeah, but your scientists were so preoccupied with whether or not they could, they didn't stop to think if they should." It's an interesting case of life imitating art imitating life. In other words, Michael Crichton courted renowned paleontologist Jack Horner as a consultant for his novels and even adapted his likeness into protagonist Alan Grant. From there, Goldblum was cast as mathematician and chaos theorist Ian Malcolm, who issues this Promethean warning to Grant. Now, though, decades later, Goldblum (and not his character) reissues the warning via tweet to the actual paleontologist—or rather, an article celebrating Horner's latest invention. The article discusses an ongoing collaboration with geneticists to create a "chickenosaurus," reversing the bird's evolution through strategic manipulation of alleles so as to express a tail, arms, hands, and mouth. Having already transformed the chicken's beak into a snout, Horner claims "the tail is the biggest project" remaining.

As Kevin leans into the microscope, his top knot flops forward. I watch him pin the first slide beneath the stage clips, correcting the condenser and light intensity, turning at the focus knobs. This is probably the biggest difference between the work Kevin and Jennifer Cordova do: he looks into microscopes while she looks through binoculars. Databases versus maps. Cells versus litters. Cages versus fences. Vulvas versus tapetum lucidum.

I wonder if Kevin can even appreciate the gravity of his work. On several occasions today, he's said something along the lines of "I don't even know how they come up with some of this stuff" with respect to conservation cytology. It's not an indictment on his competency—not at all—just a sign of how rapidly, how ingeniously techniques are developed in this discipline. In *The Re-Origin of Species* (2018), Torill Kornfeldt writes, "gene technology and biotechnology are developing at the same rate today as information technology did in the 1990s, possibly even faster." The field is so accelerated that media can barely keep up with broad trends, let alone their ethical undergirding.

Ian Malcolm breaks this issue down as he addresses John Hammond, whom Crichton describes as the "dark side of Walt Disney": "If I may . . . Um, I'll tell you the problem with the scientific power that you're using here: it didn't require any discipline to attain it. You read what others had done and you took the next step. You didn't earn the knowledge for yourselves, so you don't take any responsibility for it. You stood on the shoulders of geniuses to accomplish something as fast as you could, and before you even knew what you had, you patented it, and packaged it, and slapped it on a plastic lunchbox."

I think of E. O. Wilson's call to "set aside about half the earth's surface as a natural reserve." In an interview with the *New York Times*, he says, "I'm not suggesting we have one hemisphere for humans and the other for the rest of life. I'm talking about allocating up to one half of the surface of the land and the sea as a preserve for remaining flora and fauna." What if this kind of ethical retreat extended to zoos as well? What if member zoos of the AZA were required to maintain half of their properties for off-exhibit conservation? In the case of Phoenix Zoo, the largest privately owned, nonprofit zoo in the United States, that would amount to 62.5 acres for conservation activity and 62.5 for its other purposes. Nominally, these are gift shops, stroller rentals, food kiosks, corporate retreats, proms for bourgeois high schools, a welcoming committee of flamingos and enclosures for the who's who of zoological children's books. At the very least, they could probably convert half of their fifteen wedding venues to conservation facilities, thus accommodating a few more embattled species. It would be a good look for a zoo whose namesake city has gobbled up more wildlife habitat than any other in the western United States. The half zoo is probably all people want to see anyway. I can't remember the last time I set aside enough time or energy to visit all the crannies of a zoo in a single day.

I'm imagining a zoo with half. Half the desert groves (their shaded ramadas halved too), half the farmland and half the hide to handle in the petting part of the zoo, half the amphitheater and half the aviary, half the caverns and half the lagoons, half the savanna and half the fake-ass safaris. I imagine a zoo with half the invertebrate hollows, half the snake-induced squeals and otter-induced *aww*s, half the glass-to-glass human-on-monkey paws. Half the forests and half the jungles. I imagine a carousel with half the radius, half the hand-painted, skewered menagerie. Half the dizziness, half the busyness. I imagine *this* would be a sustainable zoo.

Now that I think of it, Kevin probably *was* endorsing the disparaging tweet against PETA. If the organization had its way, all zoos would be shuttered, resembling the Old Los Angeles Zoo, which was abandoned in 1965. Its grottos, walls, and enclosures are vibrant with layers of bubbled graffiti, and in an ironic twist, the grounds, built by humans, are now inhabited by humans alone. Friends picnic on ham sandwiches in the same spaces where lions once gnawed on beef bones. PETA claims that even the "best artificial environments can't come close to matching the space, diversity, and freedom that animals want and need." As a result, animals "lose their minds." They develop zoochosis, causing the animals to "rock, sway, or pace endlessly," and veterinarians have no choice but to feed them antidepressants and antipsychotics.

Kornfeldt attributes our interest in de-extinction with nostalgia, a chronic desire for a lost world more biodiverse than our own. Unfortunately, biodiversity is a concept that will be increasingly associated with the past. It's one of the hardest lessons we aren't ready to learn, that mea culpa needn't always be accompanied by human remedy, that there is an ethical difference between *could have* and *should have*, and sometimes we need to suffer our own consequences, languish in this species loneliness we've imposed on ourselves. If we heed Ian Malcolm's call for "humility before nature," we'll realize that, in many cases, there is no going back. To paraphrase his take on unnatural history: "God creates ferrets. God destroys ferrets. God creates man. Man destroys God. Man creates ferrets." It seems that, for him, these last two are simultaneous processes.

Kevin's eyes are fixed to the eyepieces of his microscope, invisibly playing the laboratory click-counter at his side like it's a telegraph. His fingers tap at two knobs, tallying the first hundred cells in some kind of cellular Morse. He lets me take a look.

Living in a dark sky city known as the birthplace of Pluto, I've become accustomed to looking through telescopes. For a few seconds, I'm convinced I'm looking at the surface of the moon, that its many craters are filled with lunar water.

"Notice how many of the cells stained blue," Kevin says.

It's true, the golf-ball orb is speckled with cells that resemble turquoise Fruity Pebbles. There are a few sallow pebbles too, and in the top right, a dark wine stain with a single fleck of fuchsia.

"I counted just one cornified cell in one hundred," he says.

Whereas a ferret in heat has mostly cornified (that is, no-nucleus) cells—indeed, it's the indicator she's ready for pairing—a bred ferret has no such cells. This is because ferrets are induced ovulators, and once copulation has taken place, the epithelial cells inside the vaginal wall transform. After having it explained to me repeatedly, I understand the mechanisms but still can't see the forest for the trees.

"What's that mean, though? One cornified cell?" I peek from the eyepieces to the click-counter, witnessing his tally.

"That means this one is probably pregnant," he says. You can tell he's giddy. "You're good luck," he adds unnecessarily.

"Wow. Which one is this? Thrips?"

"Thrips," he echoes.

"So that's like the first of the season?" I ask.

"First in several seasons," he clarifies. "It's not a done deal. Now we have to check the calendar for forty-two to forty-five days to determine the due date.

I do the math and add the whelping date to a calendar in my phone. "THRIPS IS DUE TODAY" I type. I'm parroting the exact language Andie had used for her childhood friend Heather, whose due date is also that week. "It isn't sarcastic," I'll later have to explain to Andie, even though seeing them side by side in the week view does make me smirk.

"So we'll increase Thrips's diet, and if she stays about the same weight, that means the extra calories are going to her kit. If she gains weight, though—well, then she's probably not pregnant."

He starts clicking the knobs for Creole's slide, and it's a very different story. The numbers are practically inverted, with the majority of her cells cornified, meaning she's still in heat. The image—like pale pink Himalayan salt—is much less impressive, aesthetically speaking. It's more like a close-up of a kitchen countertop than an undiscovered planet.

"She isn't ovulating," Kevin says. "We'll have to put her with a new male while she's still ready." This is known as "recycling" her estrus. Meanwhile, the male she was just with will have three days to recuperate.

The process is repeated for Rochelle. "Hmm, this one is tough. It's one of those that's hard to say because some cells are both colors. We might have to do another check tomorrow."

"So it's a yes, a no, and a maybe?" I confirm.

Kevin nods. While he checks cells for ferrets who haven't yet been paired, determining if they're ready—Thistle, Mandolin, and Ludmilla—I go to congratulate Thrips. Her mate, Crush, is sleeping in the nest box below. She's up top, drinking water, still recovering from the confusion of the wash. I share the news with Chandler, who's elbow-deep in the last cage of a row.

"Really?" she says. "That's great."

We both stand before the cage, staring at Thrips, whose pregnancy—when considering the scale of the facilitation, namely the facility, third-party data analysis, human touch, the implicit machinery of conservation, all of it infused with big money—seems pretty inevitable. Haraway reminds us that cyborgs are "creatures simultaneously animal and machine, who populate worlds ambiguously natural and crafted." The embryo in Thrips's belly seems one sprocket or bearing away from being cyborg itself.

Though it feels cheesy to say it aloud, I do it anyway: "Congratulations."

Chandler doesn't seem to notice, so I lean in closer to Thrips.

"Congratulations," I say again.

By the time I return to the prep room, Kevin has added Thrips's whelping date to the whiteboard, the only date listed under that aspirational column. He radios Bradley to let him know.

"Is Lawrence just about done in there?" Bradley asks.

He's not asking but telling me that I'm done.

I thank Kevin for our time together and start to walk away, but then pivot back. There's something I forgot to ask. "Kevin, just one more question."

"Yeah?"

"Do you think about the ferrets after the day's done? Do they ever keep you up at night?"

"Not really."

"I mean, do you find yourself thinking of ferrets in your daily life?"

He explains that, really, he's a herp guy, that all the technicians rotate through all the endangered species at the zoo. But then he concedes: "I do have positive feelings when we can send the ferrets to the wild."

Positive feelings? I want to interrogate the euphemism, his way of maintaining rhetorical distance, keeping things professional and scientific with these, his furry clients.

Before I leave, he asks me to bring him his phone while he refills the chemical trays. I can't help but notice he's received lots of hearts from someone on the screen display—his fiancée, I presume. I imagine a text exchange with this same euphemism. *I love you,* she might say. His response: *I have positive feelings about you too.*

<hr />

I stayed after school some nights, designing the high school yearbook from a small annex of a classroom where a favorite teacher of mine, Ms. Renny Thompson, taught night GED classes to all the pregnant teens who had recently and mysteriously disappeared from our halls. I sometimes peeked in to ask Ms. Thompson a question, hoping she would take the bait and let me join them for a few minutes at the top of each hour. Because of the circumferences of their waists, the ones in their third trimester had to sit sidesaddle in the old tablet-arm desks.

Ms. Thompson sometimes went off script, trading cloze usage lessons for life lessons. "You don't know who's going to have your back just yet," she challenged one of her students, Erica. "He may say he's going to be there for you, but what if he changes his mind? What if his parents change his mind for him? What if it's another woman?"

Erica shook her head.

"Just look at *me*," Ms. Thompson said. She had already regaled the students with her anecdote about her husband leaving her and her son one Christmas morning. Ms. Thompson didn't want sympathy. She wanted to inspire vigilance.

"Of course, if you get someone as reliable as Larry," Ms. Thompson said, "everything will be just dandy."

I shook my head, equal parts false modesty and genuine refutation. I ran them small errands under the guise of chivalry, taking Ms. Thompson's singles to the vending machine, where I got one of each candy bar, filling their water bottles and filing their sensitive paperwork in the front office, even driving them home if their boyfriends or mothers didn't show.

"Are you seeing anyone?" Erica asked me as I pulled up to the curb of a house filled with battered toys. Her mom had kids just a couple years older than hers would be.

"Yeah," I said.

"Oh," she said. After a thoughtful pause, she asked, "Can I give you a kiss on the cheek anyway?"

Weeks later, when I mentioned it to my friend Geoff, he said something to the effect of "if you're dumb enough to be a pregnant teen, you don't deserve to—" and then went on to revoke several basic human rights. It took me a moment to place the derision as he voiced "pregnant teen." Our rival school was Penn-Trafford, whose acronym (PT) was weaponized as "Pregnant Teen," an insult apparently.

"Seriously," Geoff said. "We don't need them flopping any more steamers in the gene pool."

"You're not serious," I said. "Erica's sweet."

But then I realized he was quoting our favorite band, NOFX. The song "The Idiots Are Taking Over" goes on to call the "breeders" god-fearing nationalists who feel it's their "duty to populate the homeland." It's not unlike Harvey Danger's paranoid one-hit wonder, "Flagpole Sitta," which whines about "the cretins cloning and feeding."

Even though Geoff was joking, I resolved to sneak these girls into the yearbook at any cost. I started rifling through the stacks of photos submitted to the yearbook room. It wasn't fair that they were missing from all the ho-hum photos taken throughout the school year: hammy talent shows, nonsensical spirit days, archaic school assemblies, overhyped dances, gawky club photos. But then I realized they were all present for the powderpuff football game, all of them prepregnant for just that one evening. I placed their faces into the extra-large frames, my secret homage to them, my weak-ass way of having their back, of being Ms. Thompson's prophecy, self-fulfilled.

Sometimes, I think I want to be the husband of a pregnant woman more than I want to be the father to a child. In solidarity, I am reading articles about getting pregnant and being pregnant. I am researching body pillows and seasickness bracelets. I am pretending to be a spendthrift when it comes to Andie's request to hire a doula to be on her "birthing team." I am reading reviews of local ob-gyns and watching YouTube videos with Lamaze breathing exercises, trying to get a leg up. I am trying to figure out where I can go to try on one of those silicon Moonbump pregnancy suits made by prop makers to help men strengthen bonds with their pregnant wives. I am dipping my toes in the waters of rituals so unfamiliar I might be becoming someone else. It's fun to pretend I can be perfect even when I know I'm mostly prone to emotional inertia.

My wife knows best that I'm way more excited about the pregnant ferret than I am her pregnant friend. She might even wonder where my loyalties lie when it comes to her own pregnancy prospects. Sure, I've memorized which days have leaves on her fertility app, but isn't that just because I'm anticipating our next sex? If Ms. Thompson were here, she would say it like it is: "You don't know who's going to have your back just yet. He may say he's going to be there for you, but what if he changes his mind? What if a ferret changes his mind?"

I want to say goodbye to Bradley, so I end up sitting in the only chair available to me. It's under a showerhead in a stall that feels like a top-notch hide-and-seek spot. I listen in on Bradley's conference call with, as best I can tell, other zoologists, veterinarians, and game and fish officials. His door is open, and it's not like I can turn my hearing off. They are discussing an apparent squirrel orgy happening just outside of one of the zoo enclosures.

"We removed nineteen squirrels last week," a voice says. "And it's already fifty this week. We've got to break up that breeding party."

They then begin talking about a less prolific (i.e., endangered) squirrel, one whose breeding is so limited—females are in estrus for less than a third of a day per year—that zookeepers are constantly fine-tuning the ritual, stopping short of organizing a Bacchanalia Rodentia that could inspire in them some mating compulsion. The Mount Graham red squirrel is the other endangered Arizonan mammal species in the zoo's custody. After lightning struck their only habitat in the ten thousand–foot elevation Pinaleño Mountains, their populations shrunk from 250 to just 32. Other endangered species mentioned on the conference call agenda include the Chiricahua leopard frogs, Gila topminnows, narrow-headed garter snakes, California floaters, desert pupfish, and springsnails.

I remember reading about the snail species in an article in the *Arizona Daily Sun*: "Can a miniature monsoon-storm machine save a super-small endangered snail? Bradley Poynter sure thinks so." Is it just me, or does that "sure" sound sarcastic? At only a few millimeters wide, these snails are essential to Arizona's riparian ecosystems. In the article, Bradley describes the rudimentary engineering that goes into making a micro monsoon. "If we want to get really fancy," he says, "we can get a speaker system and a strobe light" to emulate thunder and lightning, "but I think the rain will probably be enough."

Each of the endangered species faces its own hazards, mostly instigated by humans—habitat loss, disease, and competition with nonnative predators, among the most common.

Because of a poor audio connection, I lose track of which species they're discussing. But Bradley's speaking of them like he's a vocational nurse. "Bob is on heart meds," he says. "Al may have heart issues too. We're at a very frustrating point here." His team has been watching for behavioral cues, but "none of it is getting us any reproduction."

"Well, the whole intent was to figure this stuff out," a voice responds. "Have you considered artificial?"

"It's never been done before," Bradley says. "We'd have to bring in experts, develop the technique. There's also equipment, feasibility . . ."

The other voice presses. "It seems like the obvious next step."

Bradley pauses. "We can't even figure out when they're ovulating for us. It's hard to do in vitro without that. If you have a secret or something up your sleeve . . ." He's throwing up his hands more than he's soliciting genuine feedback. With that, they all decide the next step for this mystery species is a longer-phase introduction. Bradley ends the call with an update on one specimen's uterine scars. He then hangs up in a hurry as he does a reference check for a new employee.

That's when I pop my head in. He waves me in, and I sit next to an aquarium with the largest plecostomus I've ever seen. It sucks the algae off the glass like a dog licking gravy off a plate, somehow avoiding the snails, which are about the size of the O on a keyboard.

Bradley leans back in his springy office chair, wincing slightly from an invisible pain. I ask if he's okay, and he explains that he was an offensive tackle at Western Illinois. That, and his decades-long obsession with third-wave ska, means his spine is tender. Between all the gridiron blocking and punk-club skanking, his back is shot.

"I can't even do fieldwork now." He recounts the time he propped open the jaws of the largest crocodile in the United States with a crowbar. "Those days are in the past."

"You have a raven tattoo too," I say, taking in his ink. "Huginn? Or Muninn?"

"This one's a crow," Bradley clarifies. "Eastern European mythology. But, yeah, Kevin and me are crow bros."

I raise my eyebrows. "Did you hear the good news?" I ask.

Bradley's face goes blank.

"That Thrips is pregnant?"

He nods. "Oh. Yep. You're good luck."

Hearing it a second time makes me realize it's a platitude around here.

"How many whelping dates do you need on that board to get the ferret downlisted?" I ask.

It's a hyperbolic question. There's no way that fifteen BFFs in a single facility could birth litters big enough to singlehandedly downlist the species from endangered to "just" threatened. But Bradley tries to answer anyway. We discuss the downlisting criteria from the AZA's Black-Footed Ferret SAFE Program Action Plan:

- Conserve and manage an *ex situ* breeding population of black-footed ferrets with a minimum of 280 adults (105 males, 175 females) distributed among at least three facilities.
- Establish free-ranging black-footed ferrets totaling at least 1,500 breeding adults, in 10 or more populations, in at least 6 of 12 states within the historical range of the species, with no fewer than 30 breeding adults in any population, and at least 3 populations within colonies of Gunnison's and white-tailed prairie dogs.
- Maintain these population objectives for at least three years prior to downlisting.
- Maintain approximately 247,000 acres of prairie-dog occupied habitat at reintroduction sites by planning and implementing actions to manage plague and conserve prairie dog populations.

"What would it take to delist them entirely?" I ask this knowing full well the ferret has been in an ecological limbo since humans thought to establish a list a half-century ago.

"Well, that's the whole reason we're here," he says. The conservationist's paradox is that they exist in the hopes that they won't have to.

The metrics for delisting are, naturally, more robust than those for downlisting. Free-range adults must be double that of a threatened population, with a higher percentage of them breeding. Discrete populations must be tripled. Their range should encompass an additional three states. And there must be a half-million acres of prairie-dog-occupied habitat. This is the equivalent of the entirety of Phoenix and Tucson's metropolitan areas converted into one mega prairie.

"You're going to need a bigger dry-erase board if that's ever going to happen," I say.

"Yeah," he agrees. "At this point, the breeding we do is just enough to keep the wild populations going, to replace the ones who succumb to plague." In this regard, captive-born ferrets are kind of like understudies.

This somehow prompts a non sequitur about a turtle, which reminds me that while Kevin is a "frog guy," Bradley is a "turtle guy." Neither of them are "ferret guys." I guess that's me. He asks, "Hey, did you hear about the Yangtze giant softshell turtle?" At first, I thought he said, *Did you hear the one about the . . .* , so when I said that I hadn't, I was expecting he'd tell me a joke.

Instead, he tells me that the last known female died in a zoo last week. "There's a pair in Vietnam, but they're so old nobody knows how to sex them."

I am looking nonplussed, still waiting for the punchline, when Kevin enters the room.

"Lunch?" he asks Bradley. Kevin crouches for a closer look at the snails in the aquarium.

"Yeah, sure, let's go," Bradley says, leaping up. Late to remember his manners, he adds, "You're welcome to come watch two biologists eat Chipotle."

I say no, but not because I don't want to. The invitation just doesn't feel all that genuine. It's a long ride back to Flagstaff anyway.

"Okay," Bradley says. "You can follow us out then."

I trail behind his car toward the security gate. The windows go down, and the Crow Bros' arms extend out, cigarette smoke drifting magically up from their fingers. It's like they're sharing a postcoital smoke on behalf of the ferrets in their keep. Even though it's a proud day in the breeding facility, I suspect they're probably talking about something else: offense or defense or special teams, frogs or turtles or springsnails. They turn their way toward Chipotle, and I turn mine toward home. I wave goodbye. Maybe they see it.

A Phoenix essay should sprawl like the city itself. A helicopter chops over the stopped-up freeway. Inside, a traffic reporter narrates the scene I'm inside of. I'm nearing the second hour of this terrific jam, looking around for a bottle to discreetly pee in. That morning, it had taken me the same amount of time to travel from the signage of elk crossing to burro crossing—and now, I've barely progressed a half-mile in that same span. I begin to wonder if a truck has flipped, if this is an emergency procedure for a radioactive spill. The only thing that keeps me hopeful is the realization that it's the same interstate they'll use someday to transport the newest ferrets to the wild.

The highway is Arizona's least segregated space. Arizona cities are particularly efficient about containing their Chicanx enclaves. Sociologist Andrew Ross has demonstrated in *Bird on Fire* (2011) how Phoenix has enacted a form of ecoapartheid as mediated by the trickling Salt River. Some will naively claim the state is defined by its easy multiculturalism, but what they actually mean is that the suburbs have mastered the art of commercial Spanglish. The real vibe is best expressed by this vigilant blogger on City -Data.com: "My advice on Tucson is stay as far North and East as you can afford. . . . Tucson has some really affluent areas and some pretty gritty ones"—the underlying wisdom being money equals security. This is probably why the state is one of the few that spends over a billion dollars in annual prison expenditures.

If you are inclined to subscribe to this brand of "wisdom," then steer clear of south of Phoenix, south of Tucson, and most obviously, south of the border.

In January 1931, the ADOT-published magazine, *Arizona Highways*, then ten years old, featured an article by Mrs. Lamar Cobb, wife of one of the architects of Arizona's highways. Cobb writes: "It has come to be said that roads are the physical symbol by which to measure the progress of any age of people. [Frances] Byrne, in 'Highway Construction' says, 'If the community is stagnant the condition of the roads will indicate the fact; if they have no roads they are savages.'" I'd like to think, instead, that civilization is not measured by the presence of its highways but the comportment of its motorists.

This afternoon, drivers are picking and picking at their collective nose, struggling to flick their boogers free. Kids mosh restlessly in the backseat, or poke at the levers of the games on their electronic pads. Some cars are so dirt caked that they resemble mobile adobes. Meanwhile, incendiary tailgates argue over bygone political campaigns. The most despicable, obviously homespun, among them reading: "GABBY HAD IT COMING" with a rifle's silhouette—this, in reference to the "Blue Dog" Congresswoman Gabrielle Giffords, who narrowly survived her assassination attempt in a Tucson grocery store parking lot and is now a gun control advocate. I glare at the driver, but he looks coy where I expected smug. He knows the reason I've taken offense, and he looks absurdly apologetic. It seems he's trying to telegraph: *The sticker came with car.*

Every driver wears shades or squints against the sun. A bug lands on my knuckles and skitters, choreographically, to a Fugazi bass run. What if the radioactive spill I'm imagining can't be contained? What if all of us on this roadway are equally doomed?

At some point, I notice just about everyone has put their windows down like we're all sharing the same back patio. It's like the communal tunnel scene in *Independence Day* just as the aliens attack. As the air cools to *just* warm, arms make their way out of windows. It seems a slight majority of people have tattoos. There are bands on biceps, crucifixes on wrists, mythological beasts on deltoids, cryptic symbols on triceps, cursive names on trapeziuses, and fairies on skulls, tucked behind ears.

I think I'm overdue for my first tattoo. In high school, my dad recommended I draw my dream tat on my inner forearm each morning every day for a month. If I still had the urge after that, he promised to sign on the guardian line of the consent paperwork. Prone to taking notes on my hand, I wanted to get a sheet of college-rule paper permanently inscribed on me—a place to jot my to-dos. Eventually, I gave up on the idea.

For the first time since fifteen, I think I'll get a tattoo. I know I'm probably feeling impulsive because I want to do something, anything to overcome this traffic lull. As journalist Tom Vanderbilt writes, "Traffic [is] as much an emotional problem as it [is] a mechanical one." I'm recalling Chandler's wolf, Kevin's ravens, Bradley's crow, and think I'll get a black-footed ferret. It will be superimposed over the part of my arm where I used to draw that blank piece of paper. I could have never guessed that my high school to-dos—furtively buying condoms, dragging a mattress to the woods, surprising my girlfriend with an a cappella telegram for Valentine's Day—would one day be replaced by the image of a ferret. That the most urgent to-do as an adult would be to obsess over an obscure prairie weasel.

"The vets have ink they can save them in," Kevin had said of the memorialized ferrets, their paws inked out on framed paper. I think of how when I started writing about the BFF, I'd hoped the same thing, that I could be a *writer* whose ink would save the species. It seems improbable now. More people will see my tattoo than will ever read my book. I think of how many opportunities it will afford me to talk about ferrets. Every time somebody asks, "What's up with that tattoo," I'll lean into the invitation.

At some point, the society of the freeway breaks down. Maybe we're all stricken with some kind of collective unconscious dread, all realizing something is really wrong up ahead. People are creating their own lanes, speeding past the rest of us to the exit ramp, a move apocryphally permitted only for people with passengers who are in active labor. Others reflexively block these rogue drivers, trying to restore order. After becoming familiar, even trusting, of the half-dozen cars surrounding them, drivers resist the occasional newcomer who tries to cut in. It's a form of anthropophobia. People use their horns to angrily punctuate others' driving behaviors. Some flick cigarette butts toward the road. Afraid it will cause another Maricopa County brush fire, I try to align my wheels with the cherry and put it out. One man gets out of his car to flag down a passing motorcycle trooper. He thinks he's owed a personal explanation for the delay. He waves his arms like he's about to fly away.

When I need to merge, I skip a few cars ahead, not many really, until I think I've found an opening in front of a station wagon, but its driver won't have it. She thinks I've just zoomed to the front of the line from miles back. She decides she'll singlehand- edly deny me my diabolical dream of arriving at the radioactive scene a few seconds before her. She wags her finger at me, shakes her head. She wants me to feel shame. I respond by nodding, and we sit there, a picture of pettiness, like two idiotic bobble heads who can't cope with a little traffic stress. *You have me all wrong,* I wish I could tell her. *I know what you think happened, but it's not like that.* Instead, we are sitting side by side, telepathically cursing each other out.

In the white-hot rage of that scene, I feel myself taking another sounding. I think my ecodepth in this one moment is of the "abys- mally deep" camp. Proponents at this depth wish outer space would unleash a horrible fatal illness to painfully wipe out all of humanity. And what an ideal scapegoat the Phoenix metro area would make for a group promoting human extinction. Called the most unsustainable city in the world, Phoenix is boundless by design. There are contracts for more master-planned commu- nities on the horizon, destined to make the city sprawl well over fifty miles. Climate researcher Jonathan Overpeck calls the mas- sive heat island of Phoenix "the urban bullseye for global warm- ing in North America."

What's more likely than a disease unleashed by outer space is a truck overturning—like the one I had seen that morning, wheels parallel with the road, its trailer flattening a guardrail—that its contents could be spent nuclear waste on its way to not-so-distant Yucca Mountain, and that its spillage could result in the flow of tens of thousands of doses of lethal radiation. Later that night, I'll discover it was just a beer truck, but for that long spiteful moment, nodding and nodding at a stranger, I wondered if life for all of us behind the wheel was over—a fanatical VHEMT dream come true.

Part of the rage that seizes us on an interstate is our own complicity in habitat destruction. We can't even see the furthest lane to our left, let alone riparian, parafluvial, or hyporheic ecosystems. We can barely see the tops of the arms of the cacti on the upland ecosystem. I think we are just mad at ourselves, at each other—that we could have made something so violent as a road and became dependent on it.

Instead of facing more traffic, I retreat at the next exit and end up at a brewery—and not one on Kevin's list. I drink while searching for the script to monologist Spalding Gray's *Swimming to Cambodia*. After recounting the breakdown of civility in his apartment complex, he asks the rhetorical question: "But I say, how does a country like America—or rather how does America, because certainly there's no country like it—begin to find the language to negotiate or talk with a country like Russia or Libya if I can't even begin to get it with my people on the corner of Broadway and John Street?" Likewise, how do we come to collaboratively care about or for another species if we can't even yield to our own on I-17?

Just as I'm convinced the last thing we need is more people, my wife calls. Andie wants to know if I've left the zoo yet, and when I'll be home. "It's a leaf day," she reminds me. I imagine her winking as she says it.

WHERE'S MY LITTLE FERRET?

—.—

Standing over the terrestrial orifice of a prairie dog entrance mound is kind of like straddling the hole of a squat toilet. It is a geological vertigo: the earth punched out, agape. A means of escape for something smaller, luckier than I. It's not hard to imagine what's immediately beyond a hole in the ground. In the case of a toilet, it's a trapway, a weir, an outlet and flange. But then? Subterranean, the burrow is an invisible architecture, its habitat impenetrable to all but maybe the human forearm. In *Discipline* (2011), Dawn Lundy Martin writes: "Are holes things with ends to them, or do they go on forever? One must decide." To get eye level with the mound, lie prostrate on the prairie floor or prop on elbows like an end-zone photographer. Intimacy in nature always requires such sacrifice: a forfeiture of one's stature—a meeting of the ecological other halfway, and often more. Even there, with the eye hovering over the opening—indeed, a burrow's door co-extends with its peephole—there's nothing left to see after the first kink in the complex.

"Nobody really knows what it's like down there," says Richard White, director of Tucson's International Wildlife Museum. "There's nothing in the literature about what a burrow looks like." He claims that, when he staged the black-footed ferrets at the museum, he was merely improvising the adorable scene. After eagerly opening the package from the U.S. Fish and Wildlife Service, he cleared his desk and let the kits' freeze-dried carcasses thaw there like chicken dinner. The twee website for Perpetual Pet ("The Perfect Plan for the Perfect Pet") explains freeze-dry taxidermy like this: "The animal is carefully prepared and posed, supported by a custom-made framework. It is placed into a sealed vacuum chamber at extremely low temperature. Over time, frozen moisture is slowly converted into a gaseous state, and then extracted." Only, imagine this explanation typed over a background of pastel paw prints parading diagonally toward the corner of your screen. Once the baby ferrets were thawed, White had only a few minutes to get the positioning right before initiating a permanent freeze and exiling them to the museum's penultimate diorama.

In the competitive world of taxidermy, *taxi-* is the art and *-derma* is the material. Without real hide and pelage, a model is not categorically a taxidermy at all; it is dismissed as a "re-creation." Without *taxi-*, though, the ordering or arranging of the skin (as in *tactics*), there is no lifelikeness. Anthropology Professor Jane Desmond writes, "Taxidermists whom I've spoken with commonly use *taxi* as a verb—they taxi the skin into place over an adhesive-covered body form, adjusting it this way and that for a perfect fit." In the case of a freeze-dry taxidermy, though—the animal with all of its original parts—the taxiing is more like a forceful splaying, a manhandling ballerino plying his petite dance partner into arabesque into échappé into grand jeté, pose after pose as he arrives at some locomotive verisimilitude. "The expert taxidermist will calculate the effect of a curving neck on a leap and will shorten the stride to maintain a believable sense of momentum," Desmond writes. "Each part of the body will be visually and kinesthetically balanced against the others."

The freeze-dried bodies before me are a far cry from the taxidermy of yore. In one historical account of nineteenth-century taxidermy, George Shrosbree reflects on his taxidermic childhood, in which he helped his parents prepare an animal's skin with salt and alum. They'd take turns putting rods in the legs and then bolt the leg irons to a board, which had been slipped into the center of the pelt. Then, "the mammal was suspended feet upwards to a beam, and stuffed full of straw and shavings . . . or almost anything on hand . . . the skin being sewn up when no more could possibly be crowded into it. The specimen was then stood on its feet, and pounded into shape with a club." And if this wasn't crude enough, many of these figures were then dragged to a public proscenium, where the arrogant taxidermist would stage and block their lopsided inventions in scenes of anthropomorphic taxidermy (a "tableaux"), dressed like your great-great-grandparents, waltzing like them too.

Lucky for Richard White, little taxiing was required for these ferrets. The kit carcasses in his care were so young that he just mewed them up in the soporific womb impersonator of a nest burrow—downy and catatonic, so submerged in the group snuggle that their bodies' perimeters swirl into one conjoined blur of fuzz. Even to me, the arrangement looks like child's play.

Save for a small family squealing their way through the murderous McElroy Hall behind me—an auditorium crammed with hundreds of trophy heads representing the fauna of Africa, not Arizona—I'm all alone in the museum. I can't resist depressing the button that makes the nest chamber glow. Under the light, the kits transform: whitish to champagne. An average litter size, these three babies nestle with eyelids fused shut. Blind through their first month of life, they rely solely on their mother, who conveys shreds of prairie dog meat to the nest. The kits, who initially weigh no more than one or two quarters, will be nourished and confined in the chamber until July, when they're ready for their first aboveground foray. Any sooner, and they'll be easy prey for eagles, owls, badgers, foxes, and coyotes. For these specific ferrets, though, the nest is a tomb. I stare at them, realizing they never have and never will venture aboveground.

These kits are the charismatic center of the *Bringing Back Wildlife* exhibit, a diorama depicting some combination of desert scrub, steppe, and chaparral. Above ground, there are four species of quail, plus coati, javelina, and white-rumped pronghorn. But the real drama is below. The entrance mound inverts through the surface of the earth like one of those coin donation funnels. This plunge happens deceptively at eye level, allowing the viewer an uncommon glimpse into subterranean infinity. Not far down, there is a turning bay. Animal behaviorist Con Slobodchikoff says this allows the prairie dog to turn comfortably or let another animal go past—like a cul-de-sac or highway pullout. The turning bay resembles my wife's pearlike womb as depicted in the ultrasound. She is pregnant now, and the fetus—our fetus—often fidgets and flutters in the sonographer's short films. He or she is well on his or her way to a full somersault. I ask Andie if she can feel it, the baby swaying in her womb. "Sometimes," she says. I look at her. She is populated, obviously tired. I caress my gut and imagine the turning bay before me, inside me. In the homestretch of the first trimester, our fetus weighs just a half-ounce more than a newborn ferret. "To find all along there has been room for another," Lia Purpura writes in *Increase* (2000), "to feel *increase* in the crowded space I am becoming."

After the turning bay, there are two vacant air chambers, a nesting chamber with a taxidermy of a prairie dog caching grass, and that other chamber with the three snoozing ferret kits. If it is tableau, it is *tableau vivant* (painting that *seems* living). Rather, it is more of what art historian Karen Wonders has called an ecological theater, an "illusion of wilderness." The final intersection bends at a right angle and acts as an emergency ramp back to the surface. The whole thing looks like the first page of a maze activity book, or maybe a cubist sketch by M. C. Escher. It is more burrow than I've ever seen, and still not nearly enough.

Scanning all the ferret specimens—the kits warmly below ground, a juvenile male on vigilant hindquarters above, and the mother scuttling between worlds—I am reminded of Donna Haraway's observation in "Teddy Bear Patriarchy" that dioramas tend to present animal groups so that "each animal is an organism, *and* the group is an organism." In this way, "taxidermy fulfills the fatal desire to represent, to be whole; it is a politics of reproduction," where nature is hygienic and impossibly still. "They are actors in a morality play on the stage of nature," she writes, "and the eye is the critical organ." Critical because, with the glass forbidding entry, "only the gaze can penetrate." One knows it is unnatural to inflict their gaze on a ferret for more than a few seconds. Any conscious ferret would dash into the earth, and once down there, she should be invisible, following that infinite vector of escape. There's also the issue that it is barely noon, and no ferret would be aboveground during a museum's business hours. I try to ignore all the dioramic dissonance and understand it's simply a privileged glimpse of my favorite species, albeit without pulse or power. There's little difference between this deathly episode and the nights I've greedily hunched over those anesthetized BFFs I shuttled back to the Route 66 RV. It is impossible to be lifelike *and* alive. This central irony of taxidermy has been iterated by scholars again and again. Jane Desmond: Death is "prerequisite to the process of creating lifelikeness." William Lindsay: "The one thing that qualifies a specimen to illustrate life is the one thing that they are singularly lacking."

An hour ago, when I arrived at the museum—a faux castle with a moat, turrets, and battlements—I held the door open for a young mother and her two daughters. They look like they'd arrived by accident, like they'd actually meant to go to Tripadvisor's number one Tucson destination, the Arizona-Sonora Desert Museum, which lies just on the other side of the Tucson Mountains. I looked demonstratively at the sign on the desk, hoping the mother would take my cue: "This is not the Sonoran Desert Museum." But they moved immediately toward the bathroom.

The older girl who was not that old said, "I'm going to use the potty without you" to her mother. It was barely threatening, and yet the mother looked at her nervously. It seemed to register like the first in a series of threats. *One day, I'll empty your nest.* Meanwhile, I paid my admission and wandered solo through the lepidoptera room, tens of thousands of thoraxes gingerly pinned to foam, the insects' wings stretched midflight, my favorite belonging to the scarlet-tipped wasp mimic moth. When the family entered the room moments later, I decided to move on, even though I still had a few hundred iridescent moths and beetles and butterflies to check out. I gave them a casual nod that suggested: *Hey, this room is something else. Enjoy, but without me.*

Over the course of the next few rooms and galleried corridors, I had tried to outpace the family—casually at first, but then more intentionally as I proceeded through the museum's discrete rooms. It felt ironic, evading these anonymous kiddos considering my own child is on the way—descending sluggishly into Andie's birth canal. Whereas a mother is validated from day one for her generous carriage, able to "claim for [herself] the social credit to which [she feels] entitled," according to anthropologist Linda H. Layne, it seems the father must suffer from imposter syndrome until the commencement of the so-called fourth trimester.

I knew that my prolonged immobility at the ferret exhibit would eventually mean having to share a social space with the family again. I wondered what ferrets like these would think of us humans. Due to our mutual blondness, I cast myself as the presumed father-husband of this brood. If it were commonplace to "taxi" the human species, would we not be a prototypical grouping for the entire human organism? When they enter, we become a tableaux vivant of happenstance—staged and study-able, life mirroring the lifelike.

The older girl bolts past me, diving into the child's burrow beneath the diorama like Alice into the fantastical rabbit hole. What begins as a slide tackle ends in a pure disappearing act. Her movement is so spontaneous I decide she's either been to this exact exhibit before or she's unusually knowledgeable about the space syntax of kid-friendly museums. Her little sister notices it too—curious, but not enough to wriggle from their mother's arms. While I had seen the play burrow opening, I can't claim I had discerned its function for all the minutes I had been standing before it. Like one of those meerkat mazes in a children's zoo that allows kids to scurry alongside active mongooses, pop up their heads into a plexiglass dome, and peep parallel across the earth, this tunnel is darling, interactive. The older girl uses her palms and knees to crawl to the center of the burrow, rubber soles chirping off the fiberglass. Her short ecstatic breath echoes as she follows the tunnel to its abrupt end. Unlike the zoo, though, where she can actually commune with small mammals, she is eyeing death up close. I wonder if she thinks of it as death.

Rachel Poliquin has claimed there is pedagogical power in this "intimate experience of encountering a long-dead animal face to face." Once a child is convinced the animal is, in fact, dead—one museum director notes that the ultimate confirmation is when the kid gets to poke the taxidermy in the eyeballs—they can begin to reflect on death itself. Researchers Dawn Sanders and Jill Hohenstein have shown that middle-class parents avoid the topic of death due to its emotional valence. In a taxidermy gallery, however, parents may feel liberated to speak rationally about death.

The girl is sobbing. Her mother stands next to me and calls after her. "Where's my little ferret?" she asks softly. I glance at the kits in the nest chamber. When I envision the girl deep in the tunnel, she is more kit than kid—a miniature of the child I had seen only a minute ago.

"Where's my little ferret?" the mother's question pours again into the burrow. And then, a few seconds later, she's asking: "Elsie?" This follow-up, now in a register of concern, belies the zoomorphic charade. Just like that, the little ferret becomes a little girl again.

"Do you want me to go in?" I ask, trying not to sound too presumptuous. She looks at me like she's got some kind of maternal software in her eyes, scanning me for cruelty or perversion. I stand up straighter, tug at my shirt's side seam to smooth the rumple. Suddenly, I feel like I'm auditioning for a role I don't even want.

"I'm going to be a father soon," I blurt. And just like that, I've told the first person.

Andie had asked me to heed her superstition, to not tell anyone through the first trimester. It's the usual span of secrecy prescribed by ob-gyns. Some withhold for even longer. I recall a professor at Pitt who announced her pregnancy only after the birth of her child, a custom from her Russian Orthodox Jewish family that left many in the department confused. For an entire semester, *we* felt pregnant with congratulations. While I've been circumspect in conversations with family, friends, and coworkers, this spontaneous blurting-out—to a stranger, midday, in an ecological theater west of Tucson no less—feels careless. I scold myself for my bad discipline.

Andie's first pregnancy was so brief we didn't even get the chance to tell our pets. She had barely broken the news to me before she miscarried. What began as a tiny results window with two red lines, outstretched over a sink with all due gravitas, ended in the adjacent toilet bowl—a few weeks and feet apart.

"Could you?" the mother asks, clutching her other child closer to her hip. Elsie is wailing now.

I barely fit inside the mold. This is my one chance to crawl beneath proxy prairie, its byways cramped with clay composite. I want to believe it is an endless hole, one that continues into the museum's ducts, and then outside to the dry wash that plunges to the even drier Camino de Oeste Wash. In this space, designed for a child's shape, I feel like an oversized oaf: some gawky intruder from the raccoon clan. I signal my arrival to Elsie so as not to scare her.

"Hello?" I yell ahead.

I sit next to her in the tunnel. She leans against the burrow's wall, her face sour and arms folded.

"What's wrong?" I ask.

She explains how she thought it would go farther. She talks about another, more impressive kiddie burrow she had encountered elsewhere. She says she wishes her mother and sister had followed her in. Additionally, she is disappointed there aren't any ferrets inside. I imagine all of these complaints lodged in a scornful Yelp review. Considering the depth of the diorama, she's right: this play burrow is deceptively shallow, not at all "complex." Wanting to help her, I ready my paws for digging, scratching at the fiberglass. Between barks and yips, I tell her I'm part prairie dog. That I'll find us another way out of here. She quickly regains her enthusiasm for burrow life and reminds me she's a ferret. I wonder if she knows this means she's supposed to ambush me while I'm sleeping. Puncture my neck. Devour every last morsel of me.

As she mumbles to me about the dead ferrets, telepathically retrieving their private thoughts—something like "they have to pee" or "they like to sleep"—it occurs to me that their death *hasn't* occurred to her. While very young kids may theorize the interior lives of animals, by six, they begin to imagine their actual interiors. A six year old knows a dead animal when they see it because it lacks internal organs. It lacks animation. Gradually, researchers say, children grasp all facets of death: universality, nonfunctionality, irreversibility, inevitability, and causality. Elsie touches the glass, tracing the outline of the baby ferret corpses, not knowing.

Understanding is mostly gradual, and yet. I remember interacting with my mentor's kid, juggling her beanie cats in the air while she cackled at the comedy of their potential energy. The cats' arms, legs, tails splayed midair, shuddered at apex, and sank to my palms. A dozen adults lurked a few feet away, sipping cocktails and talking shop. "Cats are her thing now," my mentor whispered from afar. I remember that, just months before, it was penguins. I intuited the shift was due to a sickly cat they had nearly lost earlier that year. I juggled until my arms ached. Next, we put the cats into a jail—the hollow part of a circular iron table with dozens of vertical bars. The cats went in and out as if some feckless deputy had misplaced the key. I alternated between hoisting and lowering the table, which was a little too heavy for the girl. By accident (I swear), I lowered the table on one of the cat's tails. "That hurt Frank," she said, referring to her beanie cat. I apologized, assuring her I'd be more careful next time. But she said, "I wonder what other parts you could drop it on." She instructed me to lower the table on his lower torso, upper torso, then his neck. Each time, I resisted until I complied, a toddler's version of the Milgram experiment. Neither of us could have expected how gruesome it would look: this private guillotine ceremony, in the corner, away from the adults.

"You killed Frank," she said, looking at me like I was some kind of jerk.

"No, no, he's okay," I promised, unsure myself.

She crossed that imperceptible line from play into theater. "You killed him. He's dead. You killed him! Frank's dead!"

By the time I recognized her sudden aptitude for acting, it had accelerated into self-fulfilling prophecy. She was plainly upset, grieving. This was her spontaneous education in the causal and nonfunctional criteria of death. There is nothing gradual about witnessing a murder.

In her father's essay in *Cat Is Art Spelled Wrong* (2015), about internet cats and the self-same International Wildlife Museum, he quotes the naturalist John Ripley Forbes, who says, "A child's response to any living thing is emotional." I felt bad—I had made his daughter the victim of her own dare. It was equally visceral for me. Before that moment, I'd never been accused of murder— except maybe in a dream. She was led out of the door, my mentor restraining her. It was the climactic courtroom scene from a *Law and Order* episode. The adults took turns glancing at me like I should have stuck with my juggling act. Thankfully for me, she hadn't mastered irreversibility. My mentor texted a few days later: "Good news: after eating enough brains as a zombie cat Frank has been resurrected." I wrote back: "I'm so glad to hear it. I did some internet searching for replacement gray beanie cats, but then thought better of sending her a reminder in case she had moved on."

Elsie puts her lips against the glass—to whisper or kiss, it's unclear. Just 0.9 inches from the pelage, her breath fogs the pane. I imagine Elsie is telling the kits, "I know you're not really alive." Or maybe she's just starting to suspect it. After each huff, the glass clears, revealing the ferret over and over again, each instance a new chance to process the reality.

———— ⁂ ————

"Larry!" My wife had called from bathroom to bedroom. Not the usual get-your-ass-out-of-bed intonation I had become so adept at disregarding—first as a child and now, as a man-child—but something more panicked, emergent. We leaned on each other, peering into the toilet bowl at its puzzling contents. It was an uncanny valley like I'd never visited before.

Before I could say anything, she flushed it away. She must have felt me growing sentimental, feared I would try to save it like I do the cat's fur, bird's feathers, my own fingernails. We hobbled downstairs, traveling parallel with the walls concealing the pipes that carried it away.

In the kitchen, we made raspberry smoothies, not acknowledging the way we recognized the embryo-nearly-fetus in a single thawing raspberry. She had flushed the being (or nonbeing) away without ceremony, and now our lost one returned to us as if waylaid on the voyage from upstairs toilet to sidewalk plumbing, making an awkward mushy pit stop on our cutting board. I had the urgent notion to distract my wife from the sight of it.

In *Hyperobjects* (2013), ecophilosopher Timothy Morton writes, "For some time we may have thought that the U-bend in the toilet was a convenient curvature of ontological space that took whatever we flush down it into a totally different dimension called *Away*. . . . Now we know better." *Away* is a child's myth. Earth is too confoundingly viscous to do away with anything. Everything sticks to everything else. Viscosity is the reason we are all still mastering object permanence. It is the reason why adults still go to see the sleight of hand of Penn and Teller in Vegas, and allegedly enjoy it.

———— ⁂ ————

By now, Elsie has gotten bored with me and crawls away, not bothering to say goodbye. No matter how old I get, I always feel sad when I'm abandoned in an extradimensional space like this—whether it's a fort tent or crawl space, playground tunnel tube or highway underpass, bedroom closet or museum burrow for children. It is the unsharing of a secret. To go from "away" to *away* from each other. Elsie's mother coos gratitude into the abyss. "No problem," I say. I sit and stay. Lean against the curved wall. Tie my laces. Try out the chamber's tight echoes. I am calmly claustrophobic. For years to come, when I spotlight for ferrets, this is how I will imagine them in the moments before they pop up: bored and dejected.

I text Andie before I crawl out. "How are you feeling?"

"Pregnant," she replies immediately. She knows I have no idea what that feels like. It's a great nonanswer, a quiet plea for empathy.

I think a lot about how I mishandled the season following her miscarriage. I did a lot of vacant listening those next days. Spoke very little. I was cognizant of not being the person she needed me to be. Bereavement doula Elizabeth Bechard writes, "a pregnancy loss is a death we experience in our own bodies: there is no death we experience more intimately than one that literally passes through us." For a while, I made it so that she had to mourn the loss of both of us. I recognized my wife in an animal process. She became what Purpura calls "a mother pacing and grieving." Me? A different kind of animal—one I'm not proud to have been.

I often described wanting to go *Away* too—first to her, and then to others, professional and not. My melancholy, always coupled with recklessness, probably wasn't even about the miscarriage. "Hello, lover who is dangerous," my wife greets me in a poem. *Hello*, I want to say when I reread it, as if I could be that man's second chance. She goes on: "[He] drinks Scotch until he lights a sparkler in the dark bedroom where I am asleep." I am mortified that she publicly remembers that white-hot fountain of aluminum and magnesium, how it flowed like wire filament without the protection of a bulb. I want to make her forget my bad behavior, but once it's been codified as an image in a poem, it's like I've been inducted into some kind of imbecile hall of fame. Now, when I come late to bed, she'll sometimes shriek awake. I raise both of my hands in the dark to show her I'm harmless, emptyhanded: no sparkler, sometimes even no Scotch.

In another poem, she writes about the time I put one leg over the balcony. There are ravens in the poem too, reeling in the air over our backyard. I imagine my wife imagining my other leg

crossing the rail too. The ravens portend me as fresh-fallen car-
rion. I want to write back: *Hello, lover who has long suffered me.
I promise I'll—. Hey, don't laugh.*

Like the grisly potential of the toilet and balcony as *Away*, the
prairie is an ontological space too. It is an open range version of
Whac-A-Mole in which my vision is the mallet, my eyes barely
whisking the nape before its plunge. It's utterly unlike the diorama. In the fragility of a museum, the animals always seem
"*about* to disappear, the communion *about* to break," as Haraway
puts it, but then "the gaze holds, and the wary animal heals those
who will look." If there's therapy to be had in this burrow, it's
through the concrete reminder of universality, causality, nonfunctionality, irreversibility, inevitability.

———

To the proverbial Martian, a wildlife museum might better be
understood to be a mausoleum, and the diorama a kind of tomb.
Taxidermies are on display like the incorrupt bodies of saints,
secreting the "odor of sanctity"—or whatever scent the taxidermist's water-soluble organic salts and oils give off. We come
to these dead animals to learn, but wouldn't it be just as natural, equipped with our biophilic intuitions, to come to them to
mourn? Ignoring their lifelikeness now, I instead try to register
their deathlikeness. It's weird, the way these baby ferrets were
placed alongside a strange mother in this tomb.

It calls to mind the dubious ethics of *Bodies: The Exhibition*,
where flexible corpses of mysterious provenance were dissected
and plastinated and put on commercial display in museums, interacting with one another in perpetuity. While the local public
schools went on field trips to *Bodies*, the bishop in my diocese
forbade it. Our religion teacher even prohibited us from going
on weekends. "What about the incorruptibles?" I asked. We had
just finished our lesson about canonization, with brief morbid
mention of those canonized, beatified, and venerable saints on
display throughout the convents, churches, and catacombs of
Rome. Why was Saint Cecilia's corpse more fit for gazing at than

that of an alleged Chinese prisoner? Memento mori, but only the saintly? Of course I went. The most memorable station featured miscarried embyros and fetuses right up to the third trimester. It was the only time I gave myself license to gawk. In the decade since, similar exhibits have featured skinless nonhuman animals, what one museum in Edmonton called an "anatomical safari." Skinned elephants, giraffes, camels, and ostriches. Many reviews of the exhibit refer to the specimens as being "inside out," except there is no out. It's all taxi, no dermis. It is the closest one can get to the surface of an animal: muscle, organ, and vein.

My visit to the International Wildlife Museum ends at McElroy Hall, which I had planned on skipping. One route in the hall encourages me to crouch and waddle beneath the twiggy legs of a giraffe. I uncrouch to find there are hundreds of busts mounted to the wall. It looks like all these ungulates are being choked out by the wood paneling. My mind gravitates toward the interior walls that belie an ontological space from which these animals' force-filled torsos are trying to burst forth. Tucson native Lydia Millet writes of the hall in the *New York Times*: "It's this old-school trophy chamber—a victor's hall of imperial conquest, plunder, and braggadocio—that seems to lay bare the museum's core." It's time to remind myself that this castle of sarcastic conservation is funded by Safari Club International, a group Millet characterizes as "world-traveling endangered-species shooters [who] are a far cry from the hunters who spend weekends in the American outback near their suburban or rural homes." It's all about as gobsmacking as when one visits the Smithsonian's exhibit on climate change or its gallery on the atmosphere only to discover the donors responsible for these spaces are climate change denier David H. Koch and oil/gas supermajor Shell, respectively. One blog commenter surmises that the killers have simply paid storage fees that masquerade as endowments to avoid the posthumous humiliation of their wives hauling their prizes to the dump.

If you're wondering how these two rooms, one devoted to honest-to-goodness conservation and the other to bourgeois barbarism, can coexist in the same pretend desert castle, look no further than the museum's central thesis: wildlife management—the preferred euphemism for stalking, trapping, and killing animals—is the best conservation corrective. The only problem is that the International Wildlife Museum would have you believe that hunting and conservation are always compatible. In this light, the captions begin to read like poorly spelled apologia. If you want to challenge this thesis, you'd have to trace your footsteps back to the cash register, because there are no personnel within the museum. When it comes to the promise of discovery and education in the brochures, the captions do the heavy lifting. As Haraway puts it, "in the upside-down world of Teddy Bear Patriarchy it is in the craft of killing that life is constructed, not in the accident of personal, material birth." I begin to suspect the absentee keepers of this castle of conservation are hunting presently. "Beneath these forests of antlers, beneath the hundreds of pairs of gleaming glass eyes," Millet writes, "a dark fairy tale remains to be decoded if we wish to know what unseen hand has stilled these living beasts and made them ghosts." The joke is on me. As I leave the museum, I find myself turning around in the parking lot, paranoid, as if there are crosshairs stamped on my spine—an army of bows, rifles, harpoons poised to fell me on my way to the car.

In the car, the sun is searing. It's enough to make one want to return to his burrow.

The last known specimen of a species is also known as an endling. Like Martha the passenger pigeon, Benjamin the Tasmanian tiger, Celia the ibex, and Whatshisname the black-footed ferret, an endling represents an evolutionary terminus. While Morton roundly rejects the idea of *Away*, I continue to turn over Dawn Lundy Martin's riddle: "Are holes things with ends to them, or do they go on forever?" I've decided that even if the clay is firm enough, your arms spindly enough, the animal docile (see: dead) enough, a hole can still end nine-tenths of an inch too soon. Most burrows discontinue just short of earshot. Endlings, though, seem to travel a line known as a ray—beginning at a set point, but then going off in a certain direction, forever. It is a never-ending descent that simultaneously signals the end of descent.

Weeks later, Andie has bought a new bag of potting soil and there's a hatchback full of hearty plants that will survive even my black thumb. Geranium, African daisy, dianthus, sage, and a paper bag of red-hot pokers from our friend Ann. She's even upgraded the plastic and clay-colored pots to ceramic and stoneware. I think this might mean she has finally come to terms with turning this place into a home. The pots represent the end of years of searching for the next place to rent or buy and I love them instantly.

I turn to a task I've been putting off for nearly a decade. I sense it's now or never—now being the rarefied weekend when spring cleaning meets nursery nesting. Our house was built to be bright. It is the tallest in the neighborhood, rising above the tree line, the bedroom and balcony oriented dramatically east, serving the traditions of its first occupants, who were members of the Hopi Sun Clan. Walk the hall westward to discover the darkroom once used by a Hopi photographer whose work appears in local galleries. Our en suite bathroom plumbing connects to the darkroom. As a nonphotographer, I've adapted the rinse bath into pet tortoise habitat.

Windsor paces beneath a levitating faucet and UV sun lamp. Instead of storing chemicals and developer, the shelves above are filled with stuff I have been lazily calling "Windsor's Shrine." It gives the mélange an air of intentionality. In reality, I know it has nothing to do with Windsor. It's just shit I should probably throw away. And because I've strategically added the possessive—Windsor's Shrine—it seems it was all his idea. As if he selected its contents. That it'd be his disappointment, and not mine, were it to be dismantled. This is how I disguised the sentimental detritus of my bachelorhood. A lousy pack rat, I found or stole or bought these items cheaply over the years, but they never fit into the visible life of the house.

Sun-dried cholla wood. An eagle pole topper. A vodoun fertility doll, a cowboy Christmas ornament. Hunks of mica, granite, pumice, obsidian, sandstone. A Himalayan salt rock lamp. A sea turtle lamp. A domino. A temporary roadrunner tattoo. Two-by-two-inch square of artificial grass. A Zuni wedding vase. Turkey feathers, raven feathers, parrot feathers. Wind-up unicorn. And baby doll parts.

The bag of doll parts is an enigmatic gift from my mentor, something he awards all his mentees for a thesis well defended. We suspect it means something like, "You've written the parts to your book. Now you just have to put it all together."

The first problem arises when I take the parts out of the bag and realize there's no torso. Later, I notice the arms are identical: two left thumbs. And one leg bends more than the other. I stare at a rubber arm's finger's nailbed. Several mornings ago, Andie mentioned how our real baby's nails have each grown to the ends of the fingers. In other words, it's week thirty-two. We discuss app developers' fascination with piecemeal fetal development, the way it diminishes the womb to a storehouse of baby parts.

I wonder if my mentor buys the bags in bulk or waits until the end of each academic year to place his eBay order. I wonder if his daughter has ever wandered into that room where, to arrive at the lifelike, some assembly is required. I keep thinking I'll put the doll together when the actual baby arrives. Lay them side by side in the crib. It will be baby's first toy—not a newborn taxidermy but a grotesque re-creation.

I study the tortoise, who chomps at diced yellow pepper, and I wonder if he appreciates the shrine after all, but I know I'm justifying the mess I've accumulated. If Andie can do her part to make this place feel more like a home, then so should I. I throw out all the organics: the cactus parts, rocks, fur, feathers, and fingernail clippings I started collecting back in 1999 in the hopes of being cast in an episode of Nickelodeon's *Figure It Out* (a show that's been canceled for nearly two decades). I walk the lamps to the donation heap in the garage. Toss the plastic things, trying not to wince. All that's left then is the fertility doll and the doll parts. They make psychic sense together, I think.

I take the baby parts to the backyard. "The shrine is gone," I say proudly. I tell her I just can't get rid of these. She somehow understands.

Halfway through my cutting the grass, a dozen diagonal stripes punctuated by hard gulps of beer, the mower's chute cover bumps against some unused pots and a transparent vase. Andie has purchased more pots than plants. I accept the pots' hollow invitation, packing them full of soil before planting the baby doll parts. I add some decorative moss, a handful of pebbles. I show them to Andie, and she instantly realizes what I've done. "Is this your way of starting a new shrine?"

I admit it probably is.

"Then what's the point?" she asks.

The pots end up in my office on campus, a compromise. When students ask about them for days and weeks and semesters to come, I mumble something about stem cell research. It's a joke whose punchline has become too convoluted to remember. Though really—and I don't tell anyone this—when I look at them, I find myself meditating about the miscarriage.

———— ◊ ————

Andie shows me another of her poems, this one printed in a journal. "I Am Going to See a Mass of Cells" is her portrait of the miscarriage: "Whenever they leave my body / nothing." Her standing over me as I read it aloud is as close as we've ever gotten to having a true conversation about it. She writes of "a pair of small ears out there." I wonder if these ears are mine or the baby's. At nine weeks, indentations appear on the side of the head, a month before they can do any hearing. She helps me see the one and only resemblance to my would-be child: our ears, small and distant, are barely a part of our bodies. "I take you disappointment . . . for two months / maybe three."

Years pass between that poem and this essay. When I ask her to take a peek, she says, "It just makes me sick sad that I have to process it again because you're processing it for the first time." Sick sad. As if both at once. Andie is in tears. I wonder if I'm even biologically equipped to process something for which I won't receive "social credit." I glance back at the essay, this selfish thing / this part of me, and realize I should just stop.

MOURNING A FERRET

—•—

Día de los Muertos 2011

Chichi, from Chīsai (meaning "small" in Japanese), is dragging across the floor, not acting like any version of himself we've ever known. Also called Cheech Marin and Tsichi Fly, Chi Wee or Chi Weasel, Parcheezy and Young Weezy.

We need a different wavelength to see your insides. How common it is for spleens to enlarge and rupture.

Chi is the wee one with the white knees, the Waardenburg weasel. He's cold now, nose and gums pale. I hammock the others, his foster brothers. *Los tres amigos* are minus one. Our apartment B chi is off, life force unflowing.

We swaddle Cheech in the blanket and go: U-turn, brake, right turn, maybe wrong turn, curb crawling until we've found the emergency pet center, open twenty-four hours. The vet's form asks for his name—and any other name he may go by. This is how we pass the time in the waiting room, adding sobriquets to the backside of the paper.

"Don't forget Cheeto Magito," she says.

I write that one down.

"Or Pezhead," as when he looks at the world upside down.

Chichi, runty and deaf. We sometimes wrestle too hard. You weasel plaything: your ears are ornamental. They say he can feel vibrations. How I recline him on the bridge of the guitar, pluck strings until he tries crawling into the hole to get at the heart of sound. His whiskers dust the rosette inlay.

Chichi, we also call Chimney or Chi-ma-ny, Chi Money, and Chisus: little savior. Chichi, not perfect, not innocent. Nebshit and wirechew. Recount the many versions of his name, each born of a different brand of love.

Chichi is in the clinic. Restless, we should have brought his toys: coral loofa, the belled Indian elephants, and Gambel's quail bolo tie. Bright tinkling objects. Strange talismans he paws into oblivion. On a proverbial island with his three favorite things, all of them would be on strings.

She rewraps the cold blanket-bundle of two pounds, one ounce. In the field, she begins with density maps and radio telemetry, empirical tools to ferret out the ferrets. But now, this Chichi is right here, everywhere to be found. His consciousness is flickering.

These domestic variants (*Mustela putorius furo*) are soft and sleepy. Descented, nonaggressive: ready to be purchased by we eager glass-tappers one distant day in Akron, Ohio. We sing his name to "Rocket Man," "Dream Weaver," "Tiny Dancer," "Notorious," and that one song by the Ting Tings.

It will cost to stabilize him. We're talking plasma donations again, our desperation ATM. Later, I'll look for things to blame. Magellan GPS as murderer. Duk Soup as murderer. Me? (We sometimes wrestle too hard.) The surgery is "exploratory," and we haven't got the money. I am grunting at the itemized estimate, hundreds we don't have. Most insulted by eighty-seven dollars for surgical prep.

"What for?" I ask the vet.

Something about shaving fur from the crotch and abdomen.

It was hard then, not having any money.

I wanted to be the one to tell you, so I leaned in and whispered "death" in your ear.

We started mourning right away.

Chisai, meaning small. Big life. We loved. Chichi, you're secretly chimera, a ferret for sure but with something limbic about you we've detected. Maybe, you were my first son.

They called him Chichi. They called him Chi. That was his name. That was his name!

A FERRET BY ANY OTHER NAME

—.—

Rumor has it there is a remote population of black-footed ferrets east of Flagstaff on the Navajo Nation. Every time I've mentioned it to an Arizona Game and Fish official, though, I'm met with skepticism. "Have someone call me," Jennifer Cordova says dismissively. She probably thinks by now I'm the one who's started the rumors. I can understand her incredulity. I mean, how could the costly and uncertain reintroduction effort she's heading in Seligman have the same results as an autonomous population in this unlikely setting beyond Winslow, bereft of science, monitoring, money?

If there are ferrets on the rez, must they be immaculately conceived? "The beginning of the new creation," or so it says in Jeremiah 31:22. But enough evangelizing of the Navajo. If not immaculately conceived, then improbably distributed. There are too many discontinuities in the ferret's habitat for them to have somehow scuttled toward the Four Corners region from semiadjacent reintroduction sites—west from Espee Ranch in Arizona; south and east from Coyote Basin in Utah; south and west from Wolf Creek in Colorado; and east from Vermejo Ranch in New Mexico. If not this, then the most far-fetched explanation of all: an extant population with no genetic linkage to the relict population from Meeteetse circa 1987. Indeed, they would be considered the continent's only extant BFFS.

It's safer to assume these rumors are just ecomythology, the stuff of snipes and jackalopes, chupacabras and yetis. I'm reminded of Henry Quintero's poem "Quetzal Mustela," a Nashcale Mexican Apache adaptation of Mickey Mouse, in which the anthropomorphic Disney mascot is rendered instead as the hysterical plumed weasel.

Because I vow to go wherever the ferret goes, I decide to see if I can see for myself. I leave early with Will, a nondriving poet and amateur geomorphologist. There's a tortoise on his hat, and a ferret on mine.

"It helps keeps the species precisely on my mind," I say with a knowing wink.

———— ◇ ————

Earlier that month, I watched as a friend's kid designed a desert diorama; she rummaged through a kit filled with barrel and columnar cacti, saguaro and prickly pear, tall grasses and short grasses, and lots and lots of glue. She sorted through the allotment of scrub brush and pinched a clot of foliage fiber in her fingers. It kind of looked like—

"Is that tumbleweed?" I asked.

She nodded without looking up.

She prepared the glue and my gut churned. I wanted to slap the little plant out of her little hands. Until then, her desert landscape was free of invasive species. I wanted to ask: *Do you know how hard it is to remove Russian thistle once you've introduced it into an ecosystem?* Instead, I watched her affix the forb to the landscape just as Russian immigrants did in the nineteenth century, a generous globule of glue keeping it in place. At least there's that.

Unlike an actual tumbleweed that, well, *tumbles*, hers will stay put. It's so genius that for a moment, I wonder if ecologists have ever tried it: gluing the weed in place before it ever casts itself and its spores across the desert world.

Whereas in Westerns, tumbleweed connotes the passage of time in a desolate frontier town, a moment of visual reflection before an outlaw shootout or a bandit's comeuppance, in the living, breathing American West, tumbleweed *is* the bandit: stealing the water stored preciously in the land.

The kit's label reads: "Warning: Sharp objects. Choking hazard—small parts."

If real Russian thistle came with a warning label, it would probably say something about declining property values, falling water tables, and paralyzing dune creep. In fact, residents of the Navajo Nation have begun the Sisyphean task of daily bulldozing sand off of its roads, rerouting the dunes with a modest metal blade—to keep it away from the doors, windows, even chimneys of their homes. For one farmer north of Winslow, Arthur Yazzie, the biggest hazard is the postponement of his children's education. Each morning, he starts the glossy yellow dozer to clear the way for the glossy yellow school bus.

With her diorama complete, the girl asked me, "How do you like it?"

"It's cute," I said, glaring at the tumbleweed.

She rotated the scene, silently congratulating herself, not knowing I meant it as a criticism.

———— ❦ ————

While Will is in the restroom ogling the neon paintings, I am paying the entrance fee to Homolovi State Park and chatting with park ranger Ken Evans II. "There are black-footed ferrets here," he says. "There are black-footed ferrets here," he says again. I am trying to get him to say it as many times as possible.

"Says who?" I ask.

The name is on the tip of his tongue. He goes looking for someone's contact information in a back office as Will comes out of the bathroom.

"Ferrets," I say, raising my eyebrows.

"Here?" Will asks.

"Yep."

This time Will raises *his* eyebrows. "Well, that was easy. Let's go home."

We're only 65 miles into our planned 846-mile trip.

I remind him about the time our colleague insisted there were

BFFS having sex in a tree in her backyard. "She wanted to show me the video she took of it."

"And?"

"What?" I ask.

"Did it get your rocks off?"

"I never asked to see it."

"Why not?" Will asks.

"Because ferrets don't have sex in trees," I said, thinking that should be obvious to Will.

"So why would you turn down such rare footage?"

Will is like this.

Unable to find the name or number of his ferret contact, Ken Evans II explains the boundaries of the park—how there's this one wedge where state, tribal, and local lands converge.

"That's where they saw it," he says. The third-person pronoun makes things dubious. *They* saw the ferrets, and not Ken himself. "They went spotlighting after one of their star parties," Ken says.

As one of the Anasazi star cities, Homol'ovi is part of the Orion Zone and a center of Hopi cosmology. About once a month, Hopi elders and the Basque farmers who own the adjacent ranch will meet at the state park and chart the constellations. The Basque ranchers know a thing or two about stars as well: at least two of them have side careers as Hollywood stuntpeople, most famously in *Star Trek*.

Will and I tromp a path past potsherds and salt licks, pivoting from one prairie dog burrow to the next until we arrive at the point where the three fences meet. We stare the length of each vector, notice some burrow networks are bisected by the fences.

On the walk back to the car, I mention the sonograms to Will. "I saw my son for the first time this week."

"A son, huh? How does that make you feel?" Will asks in a lackluster way.

I say something equally predictable. *Seeing is believing*, or something like that.

Will's affected apathy has been a source of amusement the first trimester.

We discuss the Sawmill Fire, which singed 46,000 acres of state and federal land earlier that year midway between Tucson and the border at Nogales. We agree that it's the quintessential Arizonan news story: an off-duty border patrol agent starts an $8.2 million wildfire by shooting a rifle at a Tannerite Gender Reveal Boom Box, which erupts in a blue or pink explosion, as appropriate. From the product notes: "The Boom Box . . . contains cornstarch, which may light on fire due to friction." According to *Fortune*, the reveal site is notoriously flammable, sometimes igniting from a horse "clipping a steel shoe on a rock." In the video, the shot is fired and a light blue smoke bursts into a cloud (it's a boy!), and then orange trickles over the dry grass and chalky plumes expand over the mesquite (it's a fire!). There is a burst of black smoke veiling the human-high flames. Blue, orange, black . . . what gender is that? A man starts yelling, "Start packing up, start packing up!"

Will, who won't even ascribe a gender to his Chinese Crested Dog, Tiki, is grumbling about the hubris of the shooter. "Just like that, tens of thousands of acres of wildlife habitat are destroyed just so a handful of people can shoot a gun at a representation of not their kid's gender—that's a misnomer—but their biological sex." He goes on to address the possibility of a different assigned sex, or intersex. "I wonder what color dye the company uses in that case," he says.

I don't suspect Tannerite, mostly known for its nondescript rifle targets, will break out of the blue and pink paradigm anytime soon. The real irony, I point out, is that the 799 firefighters who fought the fire used a fire retardant containing heat-absorbing compounds that are dyed hot pink.

Will, who is always keen on reminding me how much it costs to raise a child, says, "The best part is, he's already into this kid for $220,000 in restitution before they're even born." That gender-neutral pronoun is Will's last dig, his coup de grâce.

We walk a few more steps, chuckling at the scene.

"How will you reveal *your* baby's biological sex?"

"I thought I just did," I said.

"Oh, right. Boy," he says, facetiously.

Our necks silently synchronize as we pass an abandoned uranium mine.

"Anyway, the sonogram was something else. I'll get you a copy for your wallet."

"Make it two. I'll need one for my desk as well," Will says.

I pretend to need the restroom on the way out of the park, hoping Ken Evans II has tracked down his BFF contact in the interim—*I was hoping you would stop by again,* I hoped he might say—but he is preoccupied with German tourists. We move on. Start the car, nudge up the AC.

———— ❦ ————

Whereas endangered species may not be trapped or killed or used by members of the general population, there is a religious exemption for Native American religious ceremonies. In *Navajo and the Animal People: Native American Traditional Ecological Knowledge and Ethnozoology* (2014), author Steve Pavlik quotes Navajo zoologist Debra A. Yazzie, who consults with traditional education specialist Earvin James. The following uses for the ferret corpus are presumed to be a feature of the Mountainway or Beautyway ceremonies: "The gallbladder of the ferret is dried and ground into fine powder that is administered in an unnamed ceremony. The nails of the ferret are also ground up and used in the same manner. James also confirms that ferret pelts are used to make ceremonial pouches and are cut into strips that are wrapped around the patient."

These pouches, also known as *jish,* may be composed of nearly a dozen ferret pelts and are handled by ceremonial singers. The ferret has also been known to play a part in the birthing ceremony: "A live ferret is captured and placed on a sheepskin. Corn pollen is sprinkled on the ferret while a prayer is chanted by the medicine man. The corn pollen is then gathered and placed in a pouch and used to bless a newborn baby at a later time."

In *Diné bizaad* (the People's language), black-footed ferret is known as *naa dloo lizhin,* or so says a single source used by the Navajo Nation Zoo. That source is not a text but a medicine person known as Anderson Hoskie, the only person on hand to recommend a translation. *"Naa dloo lizhin,"* he said at the zoo's ferret-welcoming ceremony, and that phrase was transcribed and printed for the placard and brochures—to be read by the Nation in perpetuity.

After the U.S. government sent successive generations of Navajo to boarding schools where their instructors spoke only in English—this is just one of the origins of intergenerational trauma that I witness in my university English classrooms to this day—*Diné bizaad* was stolen from right under the People's tongues. Because a whole generation of parents couldn't pass it on to their kids, a linguistic and cultural rift formed. In Navajo, language *is* culture. The first Navajo Nation poet laureate, Luci Tapahonso, writes for *Smithsonian*: "because speaking Navajo was forbidden, many children did not speak at all. Some disappeared or ran away; many never returned home." She writes about how those kids are now parents and grandparents, how they are still "beset by nightmares, paranoia, and a deep distrust of authority."

Gen X severed from their parents, millennials from grandparents, Z from great-grandparents, and onward.

A colleague tells me of how it spliced the culture into two, en masse. "Imagine a society where people must honor their elders but cannot always understand them. That," he says, "is our predicament."

The ramifications extend ominously into the natural world, where a single medicine man must conjure the language for a species, and by extension, its sociocultural place in this, the Glittering World. It seems fitting that ecosystem revitalization should be accompanied by language revitalization, which is underway throughout the southwestern United States.

New Mexican attorney Tina S. Boradiansky points to a Congressional House debate in 1962 in which speakers recognized that certain animals, particularly eagles, are "important in enabling many Indian tribes, particularly those in the Southwest, to continue ancient customs and ceremonies that are of deep religious or emotional significance to them." This is how lawmakers came to draft amendments to simultaneously protect wildlife *and* the integrity of Indigenous life.

Will and I end up at that free zoo in Window Rock where the Nation's only confirmed black-footed ferret scurries—not in the overgrazed grasslands but through her photogenic habitat, carefully arranged by a team of zoologists. The lead zoologist hasn't heard of any ferrets on the reservation, but he says there's been "talk about a formal reintroduction plan." I ask if the zoo works with the U.S. Fish and Wildlife Service to oversee the ceremonial exemptions. "Nothing like that," he says. "We're permitted for eagle feather distribution, though. That's about it."

I wonder if this *naa dloo lizhin* or whatever she is will live long enough to see the day her species returns to Dinétah. She flops and corkscrews through her bedding, the most well-adjusted mustelid I've ever seen in a zoo setting. Too long a captive, she's been retired from breeding at the Phoenix Zoo and will likely remain an "educational tool" for the rest of her life. I imagine her dusted with pollen, her whiskers charged with a sneeze. I look at her pelage, nails, and with X-ray vision, her gallbladder, imagining all of it sliced and ground, deposited into saltshakers.

"Hello," I whisper, unsure if the glass between us is soundproof. "Thank you for being here."

<hr />

When tumbleweed detaches from its vascular core, it becomes a diaspore—as in *diaspora*—and begins its signature wobble across the steppe. The tissue, all of it dead, fractures and scatters, carrying with it propagules that spawn more and more of the mobile menaces.

Tumbleweed is only one contributor to the desertification east of Flagstaff. Others have pointed to the dramatic impacts of overgrazing and climate change. Regardless of the cause, the effect is indisputable: the soil has lost its structure. When the surface of silt and clay becomes impenetrable to seeds, the land, according to conservationist Thomas J. Elpel, dries up and blows away.

To capture a black-footed ferret, I must stab the open end of the trap into the earth. Often, though, the holes are already clogged with snags of mature thistle. Reinforced by spiderwebs, the bits of tumbleweed nestle for weeks waiting for anything—a gust, a hoof, a beak—to free their seeds into the ground. All across the landscape, the inconspicuous green sprouts blend with the sagebrush, sucking water through their body's straw before bounding toward their next long sip.

When Arizona Game and Fish interns confirmed they were preparing to collaborate with officials from the badlands of the Painted Desert in the hopes of reintroducing the BFF there, my jaw must have dropped a little. With Tolani Lake just forty miles away as the crow flies, a parched and dystopic emblem of climate change in the American Southwest, I wondered what their plan would be when the habitat degrades further, when the last drops hover in a vapor over the earth.

A prairie dog's burrowing is dependent on a certain type of soil. There's a reason desert kids don't take their beachy sandcastle molds into their own backyards. Dry sand is soft sand, and soft sand complies with gravity, not make-believe. I remember my hair stylist telling me that he used to make mud pies on the rez, filling a tin baking sheet with a layer of dirt and covering it with a cup of water. He'd leave it in the sun to bake. Within a few minutes, the sand would dry like a brittle piecrust. He'd repeat the process to make cement, repairing mud cracks in the front yard by emptying his Tonka truck into the channel with wet sand. If anyone walked near it, he'd warn them to watch out for the drying cement. Without water, though, the sand loses its structural integrity. Its grains slip as if in an hourglass. If the burrow complex in the field adjacent to my house was to spontaneously lose all its moisture, convert immediately into sand, every living creature would be instantly buried alive, entombed by drought.

I go with Will to see Tolani Lake. We mention it to a cashier who mentions it to his coworker. Both look at us like we're tricking them. We're a little lost, and essentially asking for directions to a place that's more void than destination. They're kind to temper our expectations.

"You know there's no lake there?" one says.

We nod, assuring them we're not planning on snorkeling today.

To make things more bewildering, I add, "Hey, you've never seen a black-footed ferret on the rez, have you?"

They stare at me like I'm some kind of callous bounty hunter, a Wile E. Coyote sort who should be producing a photo of the critter from my hammerspace.

There are no maps at the gas station, so after some basic directions, we find ourselves backtracking, driving parallel with train tracks toward Leupp before veering toward the Tolani Lake Chapter House. Gradually, the road becomes painted in sand. Dune shelves rise on either side like buttes, and the road is carefully whittled for our passage.

At sunset, I park the car on a precarious berm, and we climb the slip face. From this vantage, we can see the barely damp crater known as Tolani Lake that was once so full that "streams flooded the road"—this according to Flagstaff reporter Laurel Morales.

"Damn." One of us says it, and the other agrees with silence.

It's a lake that needs a good long drink. I imagine the poet Sherwin Bitsui filling it up with his famous poem, reading into the crater through a megaphone, *tó* and *tó* and *tó*. *Tó* as many times as it takes. In his book, the word drips down the page in spare concrete poetics. When he reads it aloud, Bitsui's throat becomes a faucet, an aquafer—the droplets of *tó* strengthening then weakening. Until he turns off. He says that when white people hear it, they suspect it's a prayer, not a poem. When Navajo hear it, they run to get him water.

The sun begins to slump, and we pivot toward the parabolic dune behind us.

We stumble around a bit, following the echelon formation of the eolian sands. The leeward side of the mounds resemble dugouts. After some walking, we find a wide cache of colored glass in one dugout—along with tubes and clamps, coffee filters and crumpled plastic, scraps of rubber and plastic nubbins. At first, we think it's random and beautiful, perhaps an outside studio for an outsider artist. But we both wise up at once. It's a telltale meth lab in the bunkered secrecy of a dune field.

Historians have said that addiction in the Diné community is symptomatic of the transgenerational trauma of the Long Walk, the murderous relocation of Indigenous people to Kit Carson's "savage-taming" prison camp, Fort Sumner. Some only survived by plucking oats from horse feces. We kick the glass around, watch it scintillate in the sun's last waves. As we trudge toward the car, we exchange anecdotes of our own families' drug habits back in Delaware and Pennsylvania. Will has a niece with drug-induced birth defects. She's been on a ventilator through her first year of life. I have a cousin whose vein collapsed after excessive heroin use. I tell Will about how he'll have to get it amputated, and it's not clear if prison healthcare in Alabama will cover the costs of the prosthesis he wants.

Now there's a car parked behind mine. Before we can even work ourselves up and imagine the trouble we might be in, the driver puts down his window.

"Tamales?" he asks.

Henry's selling his wife's famous tamales out of a passenger-seat cooler. We buy him out, unfold the foil, unwrap the husk, only to discover they're studded with sinewy pork and mutton.

"Didn't he say they were corn tamales?" Will asks. Will, who barely tried jellyfish at a Chinese restaurant earlier that year, is a more principled vegetarian than I am.

I shrug, tossing the bag in the console. We decide we'll take them to Orlando as a thank you for letting us stay at his hogan that night.

There are two lawn chairs shimmied into the sand on a bluff overlooking Tolani Lake. I pull over like there's no other option. We take deep dragging steps through the sand like we're struggling toward the shores of a beach vacation. Once seated, we notice the empty beer bottles at our ankles and wish them full.

"Did you ask Henry about the ferrets?" Will asks.

Like the cashiers at the gas station, Henry looked nonplussed, like I was pulling his leg. "Never seen one out here," he says.

Come to think of it, how could he? If he sells tamales by day, returning to the chef/his wife before dark, and watches TV by night—it's the semifinals of *Dancing with the Stars*, he said, like we should hurry to the nearest set—he'd be asleep by the time the first ferret pops up its winsome head, and awake again as the last goes hiding. Ferrets and humans rely on inverse zeitgebers for their sleep cycles. If anyone knows about the existence of BFF here, it is probably the few who come out at night—to make Desoxyn or to search for a cell signal or to get an early start on a long-distance grocery run.

When I ask after ferrets, I have to make my intentions clear. I'm not looking to gain uncommon access to generations of traditional knowledge.

I'm reminded of a question a young girl raised at the Emerging Diné Writers' Institute at Navajo Technical University. "How do we know if something is too sacred to share?"

Elder Philmer Bluehouse responded to her by making a distinction between common knowledge, ceremonial knowledge, and esoteric knowledge. "Our *bilagáana* friends want to know what makes the Indian tick," he said. I was the only *bilagáana* (white person) in the full room, and despite the fact that I was sitting on the floor, in the absolute periphery, he still managed to find my eyes. "Our esoteric knowledge comes with a built-in protection mechanism. Our healers will protect that database. I will protect that database." Then he chanted in *Diné bizaad*, pointing to the universe beyond the sky and the ground, the universe and the ground, universe and ground.

Afterward, as Bluehouse caught his breath, I told him I had to leave the institute early, that I wouldn't be able to make it to his guided tour of the Navajo Nation Zoo the next day, but could I ask him a question anyway. In a matter of seconds, our handshake became handholding. He is handsome, sincere.

"Go ahead," he said.

I practiced it again in my head, making sure I wasn't angling for esoteric or ceremonial knowledge. *It's a narrative question*, I assured myself.

"Let's say an animal disappears."

He raised his eyebrows.

"A black-footed ferret becomes endangered, goes extinct," I clarified. "What happens to the story then?"

"Ah," Bluehouse nodded, clasping my hand some more. "Then we say the story is undergoing change." He used a Navajo word that means "change in the story." "And so, when we tell that animal's story, we have to acknowledge our own mortality. We have to admit we might not be around when that story becomes stable again. That it's not a guarantee we'll get to know the next part."

"No matter what, though," he continued, "the ferret's code will still be out there."

In asking after the BFF, I only want some common knowledge. I swear. If it's here, then where? If it's not, then, well, Jennifer told me so.

The Diné lived alongside *Mustela nigripes* for hundreds of thousands of years. Compare these hundreds of millennia of side-by-sideness to the swift population decline each experienced after the first and fatal contact with Europeans who expanded west as part of settler colonialism.

Less than a century after the BFF's discovery by settlers, *non*–Native Americans managed to convert its native range to cropland (1880s–1920s), poison its prey base (1918–1972), and occasionally shoot them for sport (1940s–present), all this before sylvatic plague spread itself over the prairies. For loss of native range, see the diaspora-inducing Long Walk to Bosque Redondo. For poisoning, see the EPA's atlas of abandoned uranium mines. For blood sport, see the rash of all-out massacres throughout the Indigenous Holocaust: the razing, raping, scalping, mutilating, and slaughter (sometimes euphemized as "reduction"). It's no accident that the colonial force that reduced an endemic species to less than 0.1 percent of its former stock simultaneously decimated the Indigenous population of that same landscape, according to *American Philosophy: From Wounded Knee to the Present* (2015), to 5 percent.

———— ❖ ————

Near Second Mesa, we pass a church whose marquee reads: HURTING? A few cars have turned off the main road, climbing the long dirt drive to the church. I try not to interpret the drivers' trajectory as ipso facto call-and-response.

Because Will is partially deaf, I turn the music up louder than usual. Theremin oscillates as we pass from one nation to the next, Hopi to Navajo. It's dusking by the time we reach Seba Dalkai. The sandstone's red dims to a full-moon blue. As we approach Orlando's, I search for a grocery store on my phone. I figure I should bring something more than the cold tamales to nibble on.

Back in Flagstaff, if Will invites me to his house, I'll swing by Whole Foods, where I buy fresh macarons with chocolate and pistachio meringue. If I'm going to Nicole's, I buy a bottle of red wine at the Safeway, maybe some guacamole. To Gavin's, I pluck up craft beers, some mix-and-match six-pack at Bashas'. Plus radishes. A Steelers game at Justin's means frozen pierogis with sour cream and chives at the Fry's off Route 66. I even went to Natural Grocers once with the antinuclear activist Uncle Don— to pick up some oil for the mushrooms we had just foraged. And once a week, I'll go to Sprouts for dandelion greens and a yellow pepper for my pet tortoise. There's a grocery chain in every direction, for every diet. And yet most Flagstaffians lament the fact that there is no Trader Joe's in town.

Meanwhile, on the Navajo Reservation (larger than ten U.S. states), a quarter of a million people are sustained by just eleven full-service grocery stores—all of them Bashas'. People make 276-mile round-trip grocery commutes—from Ganado, Arizona, to Farmington, New Mexico, for example—just to fill their pantries with fresh produce and other healthy foods. That's nearly five hours round trip. Others don't or can't bother. Which has led to a nutrition crisis. Which has led to a diabetes crisis. Which has led to an amputation crisis. Our friend Orlando, who has designed lessons at Diné College around the topic of soil sovereignty and food sovereignty—as a way to redress the practices that have enabled this veritable "food desert" to exist—still looks delighted when we show up with chips and salsa con queso from the Chinle gas station.

Come to think of it, there *is* a natural strain of soil adhesive. Like the glue in a desert diorama kit, "biocrusts glue the soil together." Maya L. Kapoor makes this case in a recent article in *High Country News*. The biocrusts "slowly [build the soil's] fertility by pulling nitrogen from the air and converting it to a form usable by plants, as well as storing atmospheric carbon." I remember the first time I was told to watch my step due to the presence of this precious nutrient-cycling soil. Hiking toward a panel of petroglyphs on a Navajo tract of southern Utah, where the San Juan's riverbanks choked with invasive tamarisks and Russian olive, our river runner implored us to look down before we look up.

Indeed, the ground was shaggy with lichens, mosses, and cyanobacteria. Upon closer inspection, the supernatural gray is more like a work of pointillism: pale flecks of mineral rest atop a layer of what seems to be blue coils of lint, emerald sprigs, and pulverized bay leaves. Each color, each texture plays its part in "holding the place in place," as soil ecologist Jayne Belnap puts it. "In the cold deserts of the Colorado Plateau region . . . these crusts are extraordinarily well developed, often representing over 70 percent of the living ground cover," she writes in an article for the U.S. Geological Survey.

I think of all the times I've sprinted absentmindedly across the nighttime fields of the plateau, inevitably crushing tufts of biocrust in order to chase down a ferret, a Frisbee, a friend. Of course, my boot print is limited when compared to the inestimable footprint of climate change. In an article in *Applied and Environmental Microbiology*, Blaire Steven and others write that "multiple climate change and land use factors have been shown to detrimentally impact biocrusts on a macroscopic (i.e., visual) scale." Because biocrusts "colonize plant interspaces," this kind of soil death has an impact on the entire environment, including wildlife habitat. Ironically, though, as Kapoor points out, while "a changing climate may be killing the mosses and lichens in biocrusts, [their] demise, in turn, may be actually [slowing] down climate change by making drylands reflect more sunlight back into space." This twist may help the U.S. Department of the Interior carry out "chaining" activities in Bears Ears and Grand Staircase–Escalante, a process that the Wildlife Society describes like this: "bulldozers drag enormous chains across the desert to uproot trees," incidentally hoeing swaths of critical biocrust along the way.

Soil regeneration is possible, though. Researchers bring the outside into their greenhouses, filling them with soil, seedlings, sprouts, plants, drips, mist, natural light. On a good day, soil ecologist Matthew Bowker has more plants than he had the day before. He is developing a way to "speed up biocrust growth significantly compared to the years, decades, and even centuries" it takes them to grow in nature. In a profile in the *Arizona Daily Sun*, Bowker claims biocrust is capable of "stitching soil together." Following rapid greenhouse cultivation, Bowker and his team transplant the filamentous biocrust to field sites throughout the Colorado Plateau, a process that could eventually mitigate erosion.

I am imagining the simulated Southwest, a landscape reconstructed by soil architects and wildlife engineers: the would-be extinct black-footed ferret nosediving into the would-be collapsed earth. An exquisite reclamation, these are the Daedalian measures required to achieve ecosystem stability in the Anthropocene.

———— ❦ ————

How many times I've asked the question today, and where:

ferret?

ferret?
ferret?

ferret?
ferret?

ferret?
ferret?

ferret?

I try the page as a "visual field" (bpNichol).
Try again without the high-rising terminal.
I try *"naa dloo lizhin."*
I try to nasalize, can't.
Try to elongate, can't.
Sounds like "andouille lesion."
I try, this time, with a note of desperation.
I try a different tone.
It's not my language to try.
I try then to draw its body (daytime).
Now only its eyes (for the night).
I try keeping the question to myself.
Also can't.

At Orlando's, we pluck poetry from his shelves and read aloud. Listen to punk from his speakers and sing aloud. Open a document to compose an exquisite corpse and type aloud. Draw ambigrams and turn them like wheels aloud.

We waste our late-night minds on conditions of despair. Orlando is mumbling about his divorce, and about the stroke he just had—how he misses his daughter and his good health. I tell him about my habit of getting drunk and sneaking off to the bedroom balcony, where I mount the railing, teeter, and peer into futurelessness. We both hear the voice of vertigo. It commands us to jump before calling our bluff.

I tell Orlando he's my favorite living poet, and I think it's true.

He says I'm exaggerating.

And I say, with conviction, "I don't think I am."

He tears up a little about that and then kicks a path through hundreds of books and DVDs until he's made it to the mattress on his bedroom floor. He falls asleep within the minute, a grin just above his labret piercing. Will and I turn out the lights and sleep toe-to-toe on the giant couch.

We are following Orlando's directions to the uranium tailings outside of Shiprock. "You have to see it," he told us over breakfast at a Denny's in Chinle. "If you have the time." We had spent most of the morning hoofing through the gliding sandstone formations of Canyon de Chelly, discussing settler-colonialism, bordertowns, American Imperialism, and the fate of Palestine—in no particular order. It was only natural that uranium, the ill-fated ore associated with decades of Navajo labor, would come up. On the way back, he saw two former students on the side of the road, the trucks of their skateboards fitted into their knuckles as they hitchhiked toward Tsaile. He mercifully transported them back to the college, a twenty-five-mile climb through the contours of the national monument. The skater next to me wore a Misfits shirt, so we talked about Danzig and some native crust-punk bands I'd never heard of. We all parted ways at the top of the hill.

"Come back soon," Orlando said outside of his lonely hogan. You could tell he meant it as he hugged us goodbye. We promised we would.

Before we reach Shiprock, Will leans into the dashboard.

"I think this is where—" he begins, his nose crinkled, sentence suspended. "Somewhere around here," he waves his hand magically skyward.

The methane plume that hovers over the Four Corners region is the size of Will's home state of Delaware. Despite the fact that it is visible from outer space, the naked eye can't perceive it.

"It's kind of *like* Delaware," Will says. "Barely anyone ever sees it."

"Did you ever see that episode of *Candid Camera*?" I ask. "There's a trooper parked at the state line. Maybe it's the Mason-Dixon with Maryland. He's set up a roadblock, and as the cars approach, he turns them away. He says, 'Sorry, ma'am. Delaware's closed for the day,' and the cars just U-turn back from where they came.'"

"They should try that in real life," Will says. "Like permanently."

Like Tolani Lake, the hot spot above us is yet another of Timothy Morton's hyperobjects. Pervasive but invisible like global warming, the methane cloud is categorically viscous, non-local, phased, and interobjective.

Even after we think we've passed it, we continue scanning for the methane in the rearview mirror. In an article published by the Environmental Defense Fund, "New Study Confirms (Again): New Mexico's Methane Hot Spot Largely Tied to Oil and Gas Pollution," NASA researchers attribute the methane accumulation to the state's unregulated energy infrastructure. The exasperated parenthetical in the title underscores the considerable energy that energy lobbyists' have invested in ensuring that everything is "debatable," a tactic that cultivates environmental ambiguity while extending the profitable grace period. The reality: carbon dioxide is to coal what methane is to natural gas. While methane accounts for only a tenth of greenhouse gases (compare with carbon dioxide at over eight-tenths), the Intergovernmental Panel on Climate Change has reported "methane warms the planet by 86 times as much as CO_2."

Our attention turns from greenhouse gases to heavy metals. There are billboards advertising no-copay-no-deductible uranium care for those poisoned by proximity. We turn right at a Subway and proceed along Ayani'Neez Boulevard until the road is dirt and the Department of Energy signage prohibits us from driving any farther. NO TRESPASSING, it says at the uranium tailings repository. The fence is several football fields in length. The tailings themselves are stored beneath a bed of gravel. The uranium repository is our third hyperobject: also invisible, but massively there. With over a thousand uranium mines leased on the Navajo Reservation during the height of America's nuclear fixation, decades-long lapses in uranium cleanup have led to shamefully high rates of cancer among the Navajo people.

As we duck back into the car, a voice calls to us. "Hey, do you want join us?"

We had certainly seen the compound as we drove along Ayani'Neez—a motley yard with iron tools, a cedar stove, and a chicken coop. The man who invites us is *bilagáana* like us. We worry he has no business summoning us into the organic lodge constructed behind him. Navajo men pass in and out of the doorway—drenched and heaving, some crawling, others hyperventilating.

"I can ask Benjamin," he says. "If that would make you more comfortable."

He ducks into the Bluebird Sweat Lodge, which is presided over by a broad-chested man named Benjamin, who comes out to greet us. He is shirtless with dozens of skin tags on his chest, shoulders, back. He explains that he is the leader of the Native American Church in Cove, New Mexico, and that we are most welcome in the sweat lodge. Will and I change into basketball shorts, scare up a towel, and fill up our water jugs.

⁎

While I can't write of that punishing/purifying sweat lodge—"I invited you and your friend, but not your readers," Benjamin cautions—I will mention that there was one quid pro quo in the lodge that led to another and then another. It all began when I gave a man a bottle of water in exchange for a hand-rolled cigarette. Weeks later, the stakes were raised via email. I rented a private study room at my university's library and illegally recorded some century-old Navajo chants on my phone, effectively returning them—albeit in a lower-quality format—to the People. With no access to the digital library that maintains and licenses the files, and certainly not to the ivy school that claims to own them, Bluebird's lodgers were able to hear a firsthand account of a chant in *Diné bizaad* they'd been singing all their life. They're delighted to realize just how faithful their own modern chants are to this "original." One man wonders if his great-grandfather's voice is on the recording.

Small talk leads, per usual, to ferret talk. That's when I am swiftly put in touch with a BFF witness in the first-person.

Over an awkward phone call, a man named Duane admitted he'd seen a ferret with his own eyes.

"Whoa," I said. "Do you have any evidence?" I don't mean to sound skeptical. I'd take anything at this point, even a video of it perched in a tree.

But the real surprise is in his language. "I have seen the black-footed ferret on my father's farm," Duane said, only he didn't say "black-footed ferret." Nor did he say "*naa dloo lizhin.*" He used another *Diné bizaad* term for the BFF.

"What did you just say?" I asked.

Duane repeated the phrase.

I was so stunned I had to make sure we were still talking about the same species. "Black feet? Black eye markings? Black tip on its tail?" I asked.

"Yeah," he said. "Real low to the ground. Like an El Camino."

I laughed at the comparison. "How do you spell it?" I asked.

"I'm not really sure."

And I wasn't going to make him try. Sometimes an English teacher needs to know his place. I cracked my knuckles, began drafting an urgent email to Jennifer.

VENTRILOQUISM FOR THE EREMOCENE

—•—

This trimester, we call him Whatshisname. One friend thinks it is a commentary on my mild anomic aphasia. I've always been bad with names. But it's just that the baby is unborn, and my wife and I haven't agreed on a name yet. Whatshisname is equal parts placeholder and genuine question.

In the first trimester, I called him Superpredator. As in:

MODERN HUMANS HAVE BECOME SUPERPREDATORS.
SUPERPREDATOR HUMANS ARE HUNTING OTHER ANIMALS
    OUT OF EXISTENCE.
HUMAN SUPERPREDATOR MORE TERRIFYING THAN BEARS,
    WOLVES, AND DOGS.
THE HUMAN SUPERPREDATOR IS UNIQUE—AND
    UNSUSTAINABLE, STUDY SAYS.

Read enough about the subject, and it will trigger early onset misanthropy. You might soften your stance on China's erstwhile one-child policy. You might even thumb through a Bible and read up on Herod the Great's megalomaniacal infanticide or agree with Australian ethicists' case for why after-birth abortion should be permissible (from an ethical standpoint, not a legal one).

One article begins, "if you're looking for the world's top 'super-predator,' look no further than your own reflection."

I am standing in the mirror with an unbuttoned shirt, bleary and bloated. My left arm has been replaced by a ferret puppet. I practice animating its neck, its paws, its awkward hindquarters. My wife would prefer me to focus on the more essential items on the registry—car seats, onesies, diaper bags—but I want to perfect my ventriloquism before Whatshisname arrives. When I talk ferret to baby, I want to know my lines. I work my knuckles until the fuzzy jaw looks vaguely alive, articulate. I work myself up to the first speech act.[1]

There's a neuroscientist/ventriloquist named Michael Graziano who puts it like this: "Many people think [ventriloquism] is a visual-auditory illusion—your voice sounds as if it's coming from the puppet's lips. But the real illusion is social." He demonstrates our desensitization to visual-auditory illusions by pointing out the flimsy magic of microphones. We see the voice, time-locked in speech, but it's been thrown to a distant corner speaker. Nobody gets excited about that. By this same logic, it would be unimpressive to watch a puppet flap its lips in tandem with my own. Audiences barely pay attention to the quality of the vibrational speech acts. Instead, what excites us about ventriloquism is the "feeling that there is another mind in that body."

I am staring at the ferret's black-bean eyes in the mirror, trying to interpret the BFF faithfully—to hear, comprehend, and translate its notes through waves of middle-night silence. Even the artificial language Yerkish would do. Nonhuman primates were able to pick up its few hundred lexigrams to communicate with researchers at Georgia State University. There is no such signal analysis among endangered mustelids, though. I briefly fantasize about enrolling in a PhD program in linguistics just to become an adequate ventriloquist for my son. I dream up a dissertation that lets me talk with my son as BFF, indeed to become my son's BFF.

My cat opens the bathroom door with her forehead, and I almost tell her about my plans. She gawks at the ferret on my arm. Anthropomorphism is more than just pragmatism, though; maybe, in an era of mass extinction, it's a way of coping with our impending species loneliness. It's last-minute empathy, a way of saying, "We hardly knew ye." We cultivate the gift of tongues just

---

1 "I see you, Whatshisname. Do you see me? Can I be your BFF? Your black-footed ferret?"

in time to behold multitudinous swan songs. In *About Looking* (1980), John Berger calls anthropomorphism "the residue of the continuous use of animal metaphor. In the last two centuries, animals have gradually disappeared. Today we live without them. And in this new solitude, anthropomorphism makes us double uneasy." To ventriloquize the puppet, I must wave through its neck, as if goodbye to the real thing: a vivacious fluttering of fingers in its throat.[2]

There's a napkin in my wallet with a dozen blue autographs on it. I read these baby names at a local open mic in Flagstaff just to see how the crowd would coo or caw. I read them to worry the names aloud. "If you don't like the name," I said, "then bully it."

"River," I said.

"Cry me a river, pussy," someone taunted.

"Hugh" was another.

"Boo!" They hectored my unborn son. They were really getting into it.

"Hall," I said.

"What the fuck?" It was my favorite reply of the night. Whereas Andie had been politely uninterested in that name (which belonged to my grandfather's brother), this stranger's response was immediate, sharp.

As the next reader slammed poetry, I stared at the napkin, upset that the ad hoc focus group didn't help to whittle down but instead just ramped the worry up. I ordered another whisky sour and turned bioethicist Travis Rieder's paradoxical words over in my head for the hundredth time that month: "Maybe we should protect our kids by not having them." Legally, it's too late for that.

What would a ferret say? I imagine its message would be faint. No louder than what Punxsutawney Phil, that supercentenarian meteorologist, whispers in Groundhogese to the president of the Inner Circle: "Get out the shadow scroll" or "Get out the no-shadow scroll." What are endangered species if not whispers

---

2 "Hey, Whatshisname," the ferret says hoarsely. "Would you tell your dad to stop speaking for me? My vocal cords are starting to get inflamed."

of their former stock? Though once, while transporting a black-footed ferret back to the inoculation trailer, it chittered as loud as a motion-detecting Halloween ornament. It was witchy and squirrely. Savage and jocular. The sound snapped like a sprinkler at the end of its rotation as it recoiled for another oscillation. A ferret can be more than a whisper. It can be shrill menace.

I practice my best chitter in the mirror, wondering how to get the throaty sound out through just the corner of my mouth.[3] I wonder how Jeff Dunham, one of the highest-grossing comedians in the world, sneaks all that human speech out of his face and into the puppet. Maybe he's got an expansion prosthesis to stretch his oral commissures. I wonder if Dunham knows what the ferret would say. Probably something racist. In an interview, Dunham says: "That's the trick of ventriloquism: it puts the taboos in someone else's mouth. The humans in the room are innocent, including the one with a hand up the doll's shirt." He then refers to some kind of bullshit psychic valve that divides ventriloquist and puppet. I hope Jeff Dunham's career capsizes before my son takes notice of him.

Now that the semester is over, I've been driving to parks around Flagstaff, sizing up the fields where I'll coach soccer, argue with umpires, and finally learn to stab the Capri Sun pouch with the spear end of the straw. One such place about a half hour east of town is called Peaks View County Park. I go there on a blustery day, sit in my car, and feel nauseous as the wind rocks the car's carriage. There are empty ramadas constructed along the foul lines of the baseball field. Mount Elden is to the northwest. Women are riding horses in left field. Solar panels line right field. And in center, children climb playground equipment, yelping and laughing like the opening seconds to MGMT's "Kids." Only the synth never comes.

Developers are keen on extirpating keystone species from Doney Park, which was once home to a million prairie dogs. Take this Astroturf field for example. When a handful of kids

---

3 "Eck-ck-ck-ck-ck-ck-ck!"

rolled their ankles on the pocked field (prairie dog towns some-times have up to thirty entrance mounds), the county decided to do away with grass. According to local conservationist Kelly Burke, until then, the field was "a prairie dog heaven. You would drive past, and it looked like a miniature view of buffalo on the prairie. They were all so fat." But then the park was excavated with no effort to relocate the prairie dogs. They were buried in layers of gravel. Those that survived the gravel were slammed by horizontal hurricane fencing. It was all designed to keep the animals from poking their heads into our lives ever again. If any one of them happened to survive the assault, it was sealed in by a layer of Astroturf. Looking at the turf, I think I see a small section undulating, as if a paw is knocking the underside of the synthetic field, trying to escape the mass grave of its kith. But these underdogs stay under. When my future son hops up and down on this field after scoring a goal, I'm ready to temper his celebration: "Don't you see that this goal was made possible by the massacring of thousands of prairie dogs?" I am trying not to be so joyless.

Ferret on hand again, I am feigning the animal's hunger. The puppet pats its tummy before glimpsing ravenously into my arm-pit. The ferret whimpers. It shudders. It collapses.[4] Because fer-rets have a specialized diet, a prairie dog town is as good as a buffet. This ferret needs to eat, so I add a *Cynomys* puppet to the registry too. Don't tell Andie.

The ferret's velvetine nose is there to caress the child, to make contact in the softest and most telepathic way. Maybe the ferret says more when it says nothing at all. To make its jaw move, I wag my middle finger. From the outside it looks like a tongue is trying to sprout through the palate. When ferret talks to baby, I am covertly flipping myself off. When ferret talks to me, I am covertly flipping baby off. No matter what ferret is saying, *I* am saying, *fuck you.*

4 "Hey, Whatshisname, I'm famished. Can you see if they've got any of those prairie dog pops in the freezer?"

Psychologists have claimed stuffed animals are a panacea for toddlers struggling with separation anxiety. The stuffed animal has ontological potential in an otherwise still and lonely room. When my wife sees the ferret limp on the couch, she says, "It looks dead."[5] With just the right arm erecting its neck, though, it could look alive. Perhaps the best evidence of the puppet's resemblance to a real animal is that the cat chatters at it just like she does for living creatures who visit her window: finches and ravens and rabid squirrels. If I get too close, she boxes with it.

At a time of unprecedented zoological impoverishment, we should find a new way to pacify children. In the absence of parents, why substitute emotional encounters with animals whose existence on earth is as tenuous as it gets? E. O. Wilson has dubbed the human longing for commune with other species "biophilia." This urge will become increasingly implacable in the Anthropocene. In fact, Wilson would prefer to call the human-induced epoch Eremocene, not Anthropocene. As in "the age of loneliness." Maybe in the age of loneliness it is wiser to cultivate our separation anxiety, not eliminate it.

When I return to Peaks View County Park, I peek into the sagebrush periphery for prairie dog survivors. I think I hear one yipping, but it's a child lingering on the playground. Leaning into the wind, I am nearly toppled on the trail. In the distance, the horse riders swivel in their saddles. The horses themselves seem out of sorts, imbalanced, as they trot ovals in the fenced-in dirt. I hear more yipping. This time, I know the sound—like the arrhythmic squeaker of a domestic dog's toy—is definitively prairie dog.

Local professor emeritus of biology Con Slobodchikoff has spent three decades analyzing prairie dog signals, trying to translate them into a language system. A self-ascribed Dr. Dolittle, he believes that prairie dog vocabularies are so differentiated and complex that their sounds can be nothing short of language. Biologists and linguists are generally outraged by his claims.

5   "Hey Whatshisname, did I ever tell you about the time my entire species was declared extinct? Crazy, huh?"

Ferris Jabr in the *New York Times* puts it like this: "[Con's] would be an audacious claim to make about even the most overtly intelligent species—say, a chimpanzee or a dolphin—let alone some kind of dirt hamster with a brain that barely weighs more than a grape."

A prairie dog crosses the footpath, diving into its entrance mound, bipedal and squeaking at me. Her language is pure verbal surveillance. According to Con, this one's telling her neighbors there's a being of a certain size (six feet tall), shape (mesomorphic), color (my jacket's red), and velocity (zero). A second and third prairie dog cross my path. I feel my acute anthropocentrism through my inability to perceive difference among them. In a police lineup, the first prairie dog would be indistinguishable from the other two.

After my walk, I approach the lone school bus in the parking lot. The bus driver, John, wipes mayonnaise from his lip before tugging the lever. He's wearing a Superman hat, Iron Man shirt, and crucifix necklace.

"Is it always this windy out here?" I ask, sticking my foot in the door.

"Let me put it this way. If you don't have a tin roof in Doney," he says, "you don't have a roof period."

I sit in the first seat, shooting the shit with John, assuming my son's eventual school bus vantage. "It's funny," John says. "Once school's out, the kids come to the park and they're so weightless, the wind nearly bowls them over."

"I have to see that," I say.

Within minutes, children are unspooling kites, divvying up into teams on the field, rolling on the infield. John and I cackle at their struggle. Small dust storms accumulate on the horizon as if nature is preparing a comeback. Maybe the wind will pull the Astroturf away from under their tiny feet, unveiling this field's secret history of wildness, the unmarked cemetery that spoils under each and every one of us.

Using Con's schema, I work out a rough translation. What a prairie dog might say before being ambushed by a ferret: *There is something here. It is low to the ground. It is long and willowy, sa-ble colored with black feet. Its speed is lethal.* If the ferret speaks back, I imagine it's probably just your average predator brava-do.[6] But beneath the yellow boom, dipper, bucket, and cab of a fifteen-ton excavator, the prairie dog becomes stupefied.

Within a few weeks, I've got my handful of catchphrases. I feel like I'm programming a Pixar pull-string toy. Despite the script, I can't seem to overcome the anatomy of linguistics. I practice with a pencil between my lips, resisting the urge to enunciate the no-no labial consonants. "Eck-ck-ck-ck-ck-ck." This nonperson-ified ferret vocalization is easiest, so I do it often. With my jaw fixed in place so as to hide the tongue and the lips just slightly open, the middle tongue rebounds off soft palate. My Adam's ap-ple jounces a bit in my throat, but even Dunham hasn't found a workaround for that.

Some words are not suited for ventriloquy. "Black-footed fer-ret" is a mouthful. Or rather, it's a lipful. The name is laced with labials that require one or both lips to actively articulate, and I must find a new way to say it or employ substitutes. According to linguist Marc Ettlinger of UC Berkeley, ventriloquists "take advantage of top-down processing to make you hear the sounds they're not making." Instead of *m*, I try *n*. Instead of *b*, I try *d*. Instead of *f*, which would mean teeth to lip (spoiling the illu-sion that I'm nonverbal), I try *th*. I say it again and again, the ferret's jaw overcompensating for my stillness: "I'n Therris, the dlak-thooted-therret." A friend suggested I name the puppet Ferris the other night at the bar, and despite my resistance then, the ferret seems to accept it now, as if autonomously. Suddenly, I'm less skeptical about Dunham's claims about the "valve of consciousness."

In the third trimester now, we're down to just three names. The crib is constructed, and I rest the ferret's chin on the rails. His paws swing through the spindles. He sweetly sings out each name. So this is what they call nesting. I'm reminded of a Bill

6   "There's no use resisting. You will be my lunch."

Callahan song, how he converts his panic room into a nursery for his son. I flap the ferret's gums some more. For this moment, I think of the names only in terms of their potential for easy ventriloquism. None begin with the nuisance labials: *b, p, m, v, f,* and *w,* which validates the hard work of nixing the 50,997 others in the naming tome. "I'n Therris," he says, reminding me of *his* name for the twentieth time this hour. I throw my voice as far as I can. The sound resonates in my nasal cavity.

My wife keeps insisting that the puppet is for me, not our son. In Roland Barthes's essay, "Toys," he distinguishes between the child-homunculus who plays with prefigured toys scaled down from the adult world and the child-demiurge who invents his world, creating forms that walk, that roll. Barthes writes that the child "creates life, not property: objects now act by themselves, they are no longer an inert and complicated material in the palm of his hand." Every time I insert my hand, it feels more like a collaboration. It may be that by learning how to "speak ferret," I am preempting what will one day be the posthumous puppetry of the black-footed ferret. If I speak ferret well enough—if I can radically amplify the social illusion—then maybe Whatshisname's biophilia will radiate from crib to prairie. Rather than liquidate the species, he might be the one to save it. I tentatively add that rationale to the "pro" column for reasons to have a child.

PROVING UP IN THE NEW WEST

—•—

I'd seen him a dozen times that summer, striding through Flagstaff in buffed leather ankle boots, his silhouette framed by Moenkopi sandstone walls. Always in an expensive-looking Western shirt yoked front-to-back with pearlized snaps, Billy Cordasco is a surfer-looking cowboy who resembles every insouciant model that's ever been cast in a Viagra commercial. In short, he's how I pray I'll look when I'm north of fifty.

This time, rather than ogle, I work up the nerve to follow him through the door on San Francisco Street. Once I'm up the creaky stairs, I ask Juana (his administrative assistant) if Billy's around and if he has time to talk. She welcomes me in and points toward the corner of the oversized office where Billy's torqued in his chair.

"You have a minute?" I ask.

He waves me toward him.

When the Babbitt Brothers arrived in Flagstaff, Billy's great-grandfather among them, the city was, according to Chip Brown, "a chapped outpost in the ponderosa pines." The brothers managed the CO Bar Ranch from within the saddle, dressing like hired hands, often "mistaken for range bums by their own employees." Brown writes about how they "roughed it in tents, eating sowbelly and white beans washed down with coffee." The frontier version of American shared plates, I suppose.

Billy, on the other hand . . . I look at him, his face tanned from a recent honeymoon. His new bride, set as his beaming desktop background, peeks over his shoulder at me. I know he grew up on the ranchlands, and that he probably ran more cattle in his teens than I'll see in my entire suburban lifetime, but there's something hygienic about him that I don't recognize in a rancher. I blame the yeasty depictions of an Old West, which this man has presumably left behind.

"Nice shirt," is the first thing that comes out of my mouth. "Where'd you get it?"

Most days, I wear a crushable felt cowboy hat, plaid flannel, a pair of junky jeans; on rare occasions, an additional affectation: a toothpick, maybe a bandana—all this besides the fact that I'm undeniably a mid-Atlantic tenderfoot, a university professor with a penchant for masquerade. All hat and no cattle, they probably say behind my back. I've always been a poseur with barely a scuff on my deck. I was punk with no bite, sporting flaccid liberty spikes. Then a big-box anarchist. Next, a bindleless hobo. In college, a writer who forgot to write but always remembered his Scally cap.

What does it mean to look the part, Billy?

He tells me he got the shirt at his own store—Babbitt's Backcountry Outfitters, just downstairs. Over the years, the Babbitts have been merchants, car dealers, morticians, but most of all landowners. As president of the Babbitt Foundation, Billy is the largest landowner in Arizona. He's listed among the "fifty landowners who own most of America" (MSN Money)—number forty-five nationally, though the *Land Report*'s had him as low as number twenty-eight this decade.

A trailblazer in the ranching industry, he has been described as the Aldo Leopold of ranchers. Recently, Cordasco rallied shareholders to "set aside Arizona's largest conservation easement to protect ranch lands from development," a dramatic shift in the land-use ethics of the last century. In fact, the Babbitt Constitution signals this shift through its multiple epigraphs from Aldo Leopold's *A Sand County Almanac* (1949). In the book, Leopold, rebuking those who take wild things for granted, writes: "One must make shift with things as they are. These essays are my shifts."

Cordasco, on the other hand, makes shift by interpreting his job in a way that responds to community before company. "That land is a community is a basic concept of ecology," Leopold writes. Environmentalists admire Cordasco, and maybe some of his peers do too. There are a lot of ranchers, though, who are indifferent about Babbitt's easements, even annoyed.

"Why is that?" I ask. "What are you doing wrong in their eyes?"

"When a rancher hears I've put forty thousand acres into conservation, they might ask, 'Why are you doing that?' Folks get a sense that you're giving in, that you're not sticking to the line in the sand."

"No good deed goes unpunished," I say.

I look up to see if he reacts to the phrase, so often muttered to the media by his uncle, Bruce Babbitt. Over the years, Babbitt transitioned from "ranching aristocracy" to beloved Arizona governor to Clinton's U.S. secretary of the interior, making him—in many regards—the largest landowner (or at least land manager) in the country, with 503 million acres of public land in his custody, much of it in the West. His ancestors were enticed to the West by the startling promises of the Homestead Act: 160 acres to farm, all for the pittance of a filing fee.

HO FOR ARIZONA! BRETHREN, FRIENDS & FELLOW CITIZENS: IN PURSUIT OF HOMES IN THE SOUTHWESTERN LANDS OF AMERICA, CHEAPER THAN EVER WAS KNOWN BEFORE

LANDS FOR THE LANDLESS, HOMES FOR THE HOMELESS: MILLIONS OF ACRES ALMOST DONATED TO BRAVE PIONEERS OF THE WORLD BY THE GENEROUS GOVERNMENT OF AMERICA

COME FORWARD AND TAKE YOUR HOMESTEADS NEAR SOME RAILROAD. YOU NEED A FARM!

Arriving in Flagstaff just a quarter-century after Lincoln opened the West for settlement, the Babbitts opted to own significantly more land than did the 1.6 million haggard yeomen who went west before them. I imagine what they might say of their progeny, Bruce, whom *New York Times* staff writer Timothy Egan called the "scion of a legendary Western ranching family [who] lashed out at big cattle operations as rangeland villains." It's important to distinguish the intimate family operations of the past with the corporate affair presently known as Big Ag. As the face of the "New West," it did not seem "at all incongruous to [Babbitt] that a man whose family owns a ranch nearly as big as some Eastern states is leading this charge. If anything, he says, protesting his own privilege makes him more qualified."

Babbitt's tenure as secretary of the interior began in controversy due to his push to increase grazing fees for twenty-seven thousand leaseholders, effectively ending "what many [had] called a government-sponsored giveaway that [had] outlived its original purpose of encouraging settlement in the Western states" (*Los Angeles Times*).

In *Code of the West* (1934), a Western written by Flagstaff's own Zane Grey, the author records a conversation about homesteading between flapper frontierswoman Georgianna and her cowbeau, Cal.

"Homestead," Georgianna says. "The word's a new one on me, but it sounds nice."

And Cal goes on to mansplain it to her, adding some colloquial affect to the tenets of the act itself:

> In unsettled parts of the West the government encourages homesteaders. Now a homesteader picks out one hundred an' sixty acres of likely ground that he can clear an' cultivate. The better soil an' water, of course, the better his chances to develop a good ranch. He builds a log cabin an' a corral. The government requires him to do so much work on this place—so much improvement a year for three years. Then if he proves up, as they call it, he is granted a patent for the land an' owns it. That entitles him to certain range rights. He can run so many cattle on an' near his ranch . . . An' that's what I'm goin' to do.

The only problem, though, is that to "prove up," yeomen had to do little more than butter up their neighbors with a basket of sourdough biscuits from the local chuckwagon. With a couple signatures from the next-door neighbors, the yeoman could claim his deed once and for all. In fact, though, most of the 160 million acres doled out in the name of manifest destiny were not improved but severely diminished.

Encourage the population to go, get west of that hundredth meridian, and 3 percent might just give it a try, land in what posters declared the "Gardens of the West." Tell them to farm (but not how), and you might expect a black blizzard on the horizon, ready to overtake those gardens, that you might catch those "dust pneumony blues" Woody Guthrie sang about. *Settle*, they were told. *Yeah, settle in*. But they didn't know how eolian processes would make the dust settle too, how it would one day take "a steam shovel just to dig [their] darling out."

Code of the West was released in 1934, the same year the Taylor Grazing Act was passed in direct response to the debilitating Dust Bowl that choked American prairies. The act authorized the secretary of the interior to "stop injury to the public grazing lands by preventing overgrazing and soil deterioration, to provide for their orderly use, improvement and development, to stabilize the livestock industry dependent upon the public range, and for other purposes." The secretary even created a Grazing Bureau. Regulation became a necessary evil in the post–Dust Bowl agricultural sector.

By the time Babbitt became secretary of the interior (1993), the EPA had reported that, due to overgrazing, riparian habitats were "in the worst condition in history." By charging ranchers $4.28 per animal unit per month—up from the $1.86 pittance of the past—Babbitt figured he could protect over 272 million acres of land. Just like that, he was the maestro of the cowboy's lament. Listen to the slow drum and low fife of countless cowboys whose livelihoods became unsettled. Imagine the ranchers cursing, kicking at the dust of their own animal unit's creation. Staff writers at *Beef Magazine* smarted at the unanimous Supreme Court decision in favor of Babbitt. For his part, the secretary was proud to bring attention to the issue: "It's not just a quiet outrage in a dusty corner [anymore]" he said. When he was overlooked twice by Clinton for a Supreme Court nomination, Babbitt took it in stride, claiming it would allow him to forego the great indoors for the continued thrill of the great outdoors.

Billy Cordasco is scrolling through an album on his desktop, sometimes double-clicking at thumbnails that reveal photos of him on the range, looking a little more folksy in his waterproof jacket and work boots. He says he has something that could be "of interest" to me, something to do with "the ferrets." He says "the ferrets" as if they're elicit, black-market.

If I'm skeptical of Cordasco, then blame Mark Frost and David Lynch for their cynical take on weasel conservation in *Twin Peaks*. Come to think of it, Flagstaff *is* Twin Peaks—what with its all-American diners and antlered lodges, snow-capped peaks and ponderosa pine stands, dark skies and sky islands, lumberjacker pasts and high-rise futures—not to mention its penchant for cultural and territorial appropriation. In *Twin Peaks*, it's through the headdresses and statues, murals and totem poles, what ethnobotanist Geoff Bil calls the "visual prominence of Aboriginal symbolism" and iconography. In Flagstaff, it's the preponderance of kachina dolls and Kokopelli silhouettes, turquoise settings and petroglyph brochures, Bluebird flour trucker hats and Pendleton knockoffs, shitty takes on Navajo taco / Navajo tea and toddler teepees in the nurseries of five-bedroom model homes.

I am watching Billy Cordasco's eyes as he clicks through a gallery, waiting to see if there's a glimmer of Ben Horne in there. One of *Twin Peaks*'s most diabolical characters, Horne owns a lot of land and a department store, kind of like Billy. He wants to burn down the local sawmill and develop it into a bourgeois country club, kind of like Flagstaff. For anyone familiar with *Twin Peaks*, though, there's a strange ferret plotline that makes any comparison between Billy and Ben uncanny.

Cordasco's photographs are repetitive: a sun-splashed yucca plant here, a dimpled anthill there, the horizon swollen with so many suns, rising or setting. There are photos of him with employees and contractors—sometimes in a lineup, other times in that semicandid *Reservoir Dogs* approach. There are photos of hands pointing at the damaged parts of post sleeves and clamp fittings and brackets and screens. He seems to document the work as proof of services rendered: progress on new structures, repairs on the old, water hauling, dirt-tank cleaning, road clearing and road grading, the miscellaneous maintenance of high-desert ranching. I imagine this album zipped into a file for the company's next audit. Most of all, though, there are snapshots of fence repair. When you own this much land, fencing is a continuous project. I imagine these doubled-over fence workers sharing Michelangelo's sentiment about the incessant painting of the vault of the Sistine Chapel: "My haunches are grinding into my guts." There are photos of all the cowboys too, and a sampling of the livestock in their care: 7,500 Hereford cattle and 150 American quarter horses with the hashknife brand. Most of Billy's employees, though, work in the office—in accounting and leases and administration.

"Here," Billy says as his scroll finally comes to a halt. "Here it is."

He double-clicks, and I'm looking at a photo of him, crouched, tilting a cage at a sharp angle into loose earth, letting gravity do the work. This is a photo of Billy Cordasco releasing a black-footed ferret into Babbitt ground. But not just any BFF.

"This is the first ferret we let out," he says. "They let me have the honors."

He tells me how the opportunity ended up on his lap. He'd heard researchers were assessing the prairie dog towns in the region to see if they were healthy enough to support the release of BFFs. First, they noticed the prairie dogs on the Navajo-owned Big Boquillas Ranch seemed plague resistant, so they initiated the release there.

"Then there were rumors they wanted to do it on Babbitt's too," he said. "On our private land. We were excited. We had just put all those acres into conservation just south of the Grand Canyon. We hoped they would ask."

"And they did."

"They did," he says. "Game and Fish determined Espee Ranch and Cataract would be good locations for releasing the ferrets. It was swift. It got approved quickly. Since then, we've released quite a few on that country—between ninety and a hundred, I think."

In the ecological marketplace, species have become a currency. The U.S. Fish and Wildlife Service (USFWS) maintains conservation banks, a market enterprise that allows landowners to profit by "selling habitat or species credits" to developers "who need to compensate [for the] adverse environmental impacts" their projects could engender. USFWS further entices bottom-line landowners to come over to the green side with promises that they can "generate income, keep large parcels of land intact, and possibly reduce their taxes."

In *Twin Peaks*, Ben Horne presides over a board meeting for Horne Industries, opening with a platitude before a literal unveiling of his scheme.

"What's the greatest gift one human being can give to another?" Horne asks. The board is predictably nonplussed, so he provides his own emphatic answer: "The future!"

From the script: "He goes over to a DRAPED EASEL in the corner, and removes the cloth, revealing a large Audubon-style drawing of a WEASEL."

"I give you," Ben says like a showman, "the pine weasel—found only in our tricounty area. Targeted by the Environmental Defense League and the Wilderness Society. Nearly extinct."

If you're wondering what a pine weasel is, you're not alone. In the next episode, the emcee dandy Tremayne asks, "Oh. Lovely. What is it? A raccoon or something?" And Ben's daughter, Audrey, sets things straight: "It's a ferret."

Back in the board meeting, Ben's buffoonish brother, Jerry—yes, their names are Ben and Jerry—responds to the image of the pine weasel with insensitive lip smacking: "They're incredible roasted. A ginger and garlic marinade, a glass of sauvignon blanc—"

Ben cuts him off, gestures again to the image on the easel, which come to think of it, *does* resemble Audubon's famous 1851 painting of the BFF. "According to an environmental impact report I commissioned, what few pine weasels remain"—Ben says this while giving Jerry a look of condemnation for having nearly eaten them all—"will be all but wiped out by the Packard plans for Ghostwood Development."

By invoking Ghostwood, Ben's real motives are laid bare. Having lost the bid to develop real estate in the national park to a cutthroat businesswoman named Catherine Martell (née Packard), his loyalty to the pine weasel is now suspect.

Bobby, a high school jock who's conspicuously present for this board meeting, tries to sum it all up: "You wanna 'save the pine weasel'?"

Ben seizes on this softball question, embellishing with false notes of gravitas. "Not just the pine weasel. Life as we know it. I want Twin Peaks to remain unspoiled in an era of vast environmental carnage."

Another board member, a fresh-out-of-business-school type, lauds this as an opportunity for virtue signaling. "Not just a vehicle for making money, but for expressing values too," he says, noting how rare that is in the business world.

But it's Jerry, who knows his devious brother best, who translates the whole scheme for us. Sure, the conservation is the means, but what are the ends? Jerry takes a crack at it: "So we block Catherine's development until the wheel turns and we get another shot. Brilliant Ben, brilliant."

Ben doesn't disagree with his brother's assessment. He vows to make the pine weasel a household name.

"And then what," his daughter, Audrey, wants to know.

Ben considers her question for a moment. "I'm considering a run for Senate."

It's like Frost and Lynch took a page out of the Babbitt biographies, right down to Bruce Babbitt's tenure in politics. I look at the way Billy points at the photograph with pride. You kind of suspect he even likes the look of the ferret. As for Ben, though, when the pine weasel appears in the next episode of *Twin Peaks* at a benefit dinner—a "pine weasel," sure, but it's played by a domestic ferret from Hollywood and flanked by easel photographs of the BFF—he is way off on the sidelines, still scheming.

I ask Cordasco, as pointedly as I can, about the financial implications of Safe Harbor Agreements and conservation banking, and he stops his digital rummaging to make careful eye contact: "Everything is qualitative for us."

I stay silent, hoping he'll expand on this abstraction.

"Look," Billy says, leaning into my skepticism. "Almost everybody aspires to be a landowner even if it's just a family home on a fifth of an acre. And when that happens, they become protective of their land in various ways. No matter if it's the homeowner association or the county or the Fed, people want to protect themselves against needless regulation. The issues you see in your own neighborhood are the same ones we're up against on our land. It's just applied on a larger scale. We all have different ideas about what it means to own land or real estate. I'm not in the habit of getting upset when a landowner interprets things differently from me. For Babbitts, though, we follow one principle: it's important that with every decision we make, we're always making that decision with an awareness of something larger than ourselves."

As I leave Cordasco's office, I make eye contact with his desktop background. I congratulate him again on his nuptials. He blushes and advises me to check out her art sometime.

"Where can I find it?" I ask, assuming he'll direct me to a pretentious gallery in Sedona.

Instead, he says, "You know the bridge over there by the pond?"

"That's hers?" I ask, referring to the broken-tile mosaic that spans the Rio de Flag.

He nods.

I walk to the bridge directly, crouch at the cement interior of the parapet, where broken-tile mosaics are arranged in panels depicting local wildlife. The tiles are filled with sanded grout and sealed over. My favorite beautification project in the city, Karen Knorowski's *Rainbow de Rio Mosaic Project*, stretches across the bridge like a complete storybook. I can't wait to bring my son here someday and read its images aloud.

I look up at the moon, and I'm reminded of the Margaret Wise Brown book I'll be reading in just a few months' time. Goodnight, herons and hawks. Goodnight, frogs and fish. Goodnight, tarantulas and butterflies. And goodnight to you, watershed mosquito species whose name I don't yet know. Goodnight orange and yellow flowers, all familiar in your design. Goodnight, ducks rafting in the reeds. Goodnight, turtle teetering on that rock. Goodnight too, crawfish waving with claws akimbo. Goodnight, dasher dragonfly zipping toward the clouds. Goodnight, Abert's squirrel, I whisper through your tasseled ears. Goodnight, whirling blackbirds. How lovely are your flashing red wings! Good morning, furtive owl. Good morning, gawky raccoons who hunch under middle-night stars. Good morning, kachina, assembled by Karen's former students at Hopi High. Can you hear my "good morning," jackrabbit, with your erect ears?

And good morning, most of all, to the black-footed ferrets. One bounds westward while the other barely makes it into the frame, as if popping out of a burrow that lies just beneath the bridge.

For a lot of Flagstaffians, this will be the closest they ever get to seeing a BFF. I polish the tiles that constitute the ferret's head—twenty in all, a circle for the eye, pentagon for the nose, the rest all snecked carefully into place.

With his board all on board, Ben Horne takes the campaign to "save the pine weasel" (and stop Ghostwood Development) to the public of Twin Peaks. He recruits Tim Pinkle, an expert on the species, to give a talk on the pine weasel. Just before taking to the stage, though, the emcee takes exception with Pinkle's visual aid, a hideous taxidermy of the pine weasel he's got in a headlock.

"It's just so people can see what a pine weasel looks like," Pinkle says.

"I understand the concept perfectly, Mr. Twinkle . . . But what I'm trying to make clear to you is that using a stuffed animal to represent an endangered species at an ecological protest constitutes the supreme incongruity."

Instead, Karen's mosaic is an ideal style by which to show the people what the black-footed ferret looks like. Broken-tile mosaic is also known as *pique-assiette* (French for "plate thief") because poor mosaic artists once had to scrounge, even steal, their materials. It's a fitting style by which to render the "ferret," a word derived from the Latin *furittus* for "little thief." In this century, though, ferrets are way more likely to be the victims of theft.

As the last tracts of viable BFF habitat are demolished for cropland, it's clear that many farmers prioritize profit over prairie. And yet, as Tyler Lark and others show, farmers' yields in these converted grasslands are marginal at best and come at a high cost to wildlife.

I really want to believe the cowboy when he says, "everything is qualitative for us," and that easements will truly make things easier for the ferret. I want to believe that what the Old West plundered, the New West will redeem—that a century of blunder could all end tomorrow, at Espee Ranch.

UP YONDER

—.—

George is stocking liquor in a hurry, crouching at the heels of the bartender, who is being seriously heckled by the woman to my right. The heckler's name is Earlene, and she wants to play the jukebox but doesn't have any money, so she resorts to bullying the bartender, wearing her down until she gives up a few quarters.

"Flash us those itty-bitty titties," Earlene says to her. "Go on. It's OK to be little bitty." I don't know at the time she is paraphrasing "Little Bitty," a country song that's about small-town pride and not cup size.

George, whom I immediately recognize from a conservation event a couple months back, rises from his crouch. A short man with a soaked bandana, he locks eyes with Earlene and, without a word, manages to put an end to her cruelty. It's a silent but effective *Quit it.*

"It's not like we'd have even seen them." Earlene swivels her neck to me and whispers, "Because they're so bitty."

I shrug.

The bartender tells me she'll be right with me, just as soon as George finishes with the Jim Beam.

"Take your time," I say.

"Oh, she'll take her time," Earlene says. "She doesn't need the encouragement."

Another patron, Roger, gestures for Earlene. "C'mere!"

He offers her a few bucks for the jukebox if she'll drive his truck to the Family Dollar and get him some smokes. The store is only a few lots away.

"I'd rather hand over my keys than my life," he says, quoting some stale PSA slogan. A few chuckle. He gropes Earlene's thigh, and she squeals.

"Buy me a drink, too," she says.

"OK. But none of that hoochie-coochie shit." He glances at the jukebox.

With that, a deal is struck. She picks her songs and leaves.

"That was dumb," George says. "She won't even get to hear the songs she was carping about that whole time." He is on the patron side of the bar now, on the stool next to me, slurping a beer, nodding his head to her first pick, a John Prine–Iris DeMent duet.

I remind him that we met before.

"I know," he says. "You're the ferret guy," he says.

I nod at that, proudly.

George reminds me he owns the feed store in Seligman, that he is also a stocker and a trapper and has a few other odd jobs in the town. As if to congratulate himself on being the only over-employed worker in Seligman, he takes a big gulp of beer. Then, he inadvertently sings along to the next line about sniffing undies. You can tell he regrets that by the way he wrinkles his nose.

I say Seligman seems like "good livin'." I cringe at my hokey voice, which tends to surface when I'm getting chatty in rural Arizona. "I can imagine myself living here," I lie to him.

George groans in sympathy. "I moved here when—well, I woke up one day in Prescott, looked out my front window, and saw a backhoe," George says. "That's when I knew it. They were developing the wide-open field in front of me. That field was the only thing I liked about my old place. So, I moved to Seligman. It's cheap, and there's nothing but wide open."

I tell George about the article in the *Onion* that says the Phoenix suburbs are expected to sprawl over the entirety of the continent by 2030. At first, he doesn't get it. I find the article and read it aloud to him. "They even say Phoenix will cross the Pacific and encompass most of Asia by 2040."

Recognizing it as satire now, he starts giggling.

"And it's going to add 1,200 to 1,400 hours to the daily commute."

He laughs some more, even contributes an exaggeration of his own. "We'll all be citizens of the United States of Phoenix."

Alan Jackson's "Chattahoochee" is on the jukebox now, and Roger, who unknowingly financed the song, is irate. He tells the bartender he's going to do a hard reset on the jukebox. Actually, he says, "I'll unplug the fucker." But she talks him out of it.

The Fox 10 Phoenix News, which rarely makes mention of Yavapai County, let alone Seligman, hangs above our heads. Trump—not yet president, not even president-elect—stands side-by-side with Joe Arpaio, "America's Toughest Sheriff." There's an air of general admiration for both men as the footage shows Arpaio's Tent City, an outdoor extension of the overpopulated Maricopa County Jail, which Arpaio himself referred to as "a concentration camp," and where prisoners' shoes melt in 145-degree heat.

"Even Phoenix's jails are sprawling." Another voice to my left joins the conversation.

The Valley of the Sun is the ultimate sprawl: its unchecked population growth has swollen to 4.5 million people, which would qualify the city of Phoenix alone as the thirty-second most populous state in the nation. A single exurb like Mesa now has more people than the city of Saint Louis, where the Gateway Arch, a symbol of territorial expansion, is now just an omen signaling "Mission Accomplished, Now What?" Even if Phoenix doesn't grow to the Onion's hyperbolic proportions, it's at least on pace to extend to the United States–Mexico border. As Growth Nation reports, Phoenix has experienced an annual population growth of 4 percent for the past forty years, much of it southward toward the Phoenix–Casa Grande–Tucson corridor.

"What will you do if the backhoe comes and gets you in Seligman too?" I ask George.

"Then I'll find my next slice of nowhere."

"Maybe you should move to Nothing, Arizona," I say.

He snorts. I can tell he knows the place.

I think about the paradox of "the road to nowhere," about this place called Nothing off of Arizona Highway 93. The village, once inhabited by four people, is now completely abandoned. Next to the sole garage, there's a sign that reads "Nowhere, Arizona." But the sign sits on terra, faithfully adheres to the coordinate plane: N 34°28'47", W 113°20'7". The road to Nothing approaches nowhere like an asymptote, continuously destining. "When you live a long way out, you make your own fun," Annie Proulx writes in her story "Fifty-Five Miles to the Gas Pump." But what happens when the city starts to go a long way out too, purging the pastoral imaginary?

By the time George slides off his seat, I realize I'm in pursuit of that old fantasy again: a "naive but noble rube," some charismatic yokel who knows how to turn a phrase. I look to my left at a stockman in a Stetson. To my right, there's a brakeman in a camo trucker hat. The others are retired or unemployed day drinkers who are already, or perhaps always, slurring. I hate to think I'm the cliché here—a day-drinking writer poised to take their sound bites to the bank.

"One more?" I ask him. "My treat."

He squints one eye at me, trying to discern whether I'm coming on to him.

"Naw," he says, leaping off his barstool. "I'm off to another job."

"Suit yourself," I say.

"I'll take one," Roger says by way of introduction.

"Me too, one for me," his friend chimes in, his speech a little crapulent.

I raise three fingers, and the bartender pivots to the tap.

"So, ferrets?" Roger says. "What are they like?"

"Like piranha with feet," I say.

"They're little fuckers, huh?"

I glance up at the sportscaster as he rattles off Phoenix Suns' preseason injuries. That's when I think to tell my company about the English tradition of ferret legging. I explain the rules of the bar game—how men cinch their trousers' ankles, dump two bitey ferrets in, and tighten their belts.

"That sounds more like one of those *Jackass* stunts. What's the point?"

"It's about endurance," I say. "How long can the ferrets last down there?" I note how this is also the driving sentiment behind black-footed ferret conservation.

"Well, how long *do* they last?"

"It really depends. It can go for five seconds like a bull ride or five hours like a coast-to-coast flight."

Earlene, who's back from the Family Dollar, gets an idea. "We should have a ferret legging tournament here at the Black Cat."

"Hey, you think Jen would let us borrow a few from Game and Fish?" Roger asks. "Give her a call, ferret guy. Give her a little *por favor.*"

"I'll see what I can do," I say. "But you better hope the ferret's already fed. Like I said, they're piranhas."

"Don't worry," Earlene says. "Nothing much down Roger's pants for them to nibble on anyway."

MY SON WAS BORN TO ROB ME
OF THE GLORY OF SAVING THE BLACK-
FOOTED FERRET FROM PLAGUE

—.—

When the nursery is ready enough, I shimmy a tent into the back of my car, plus a notebook, some reading, and a change of clothes. I swerve off the Williams exit toward the kitschy Grand Canyon corridor on AZ-64. My wife is on the hands-free for as long as reception will allow for it. We debate which would be a worse fate for me: missing the birth of our firstborn or contracting the plague. It is not a theoretical question—nor, as my wife points out, are these options mutually exclusive.

"It doesn't matter. They could both happen to you tonight," she says through the Braxton-Hicks contractions, which the books describe as a kind of crampy false labor.

They're just about the last words I hear before the call drops. I drive past Grand Canyon Junction, past Joe's Route 66 Hot Dogs, and past the gates to the Big "D" Ranch, which feels like the ill-advised name of a Western-themed fraternity house. Just before Red Lake Valley, I see the sign for Espee Road. In just one month's time, an article in the *Williams News* will open: "After fleas tested positive for plague last month near the Red Lake area north of Williams . . ." I turn toward Babbitt's Espee Ranch and play Smog's *A River Ain't Too Much to Love* like I always do.

The second track, "Say Valley Maker," matches my mood this morning: mortal, poetic, juvenile. Bill Callahan sings of a heart that's covered in either dew-dew-dew or doo-doo-doo.

Much the same, the Espee range is dew-dropped and tangy with manure. As the road weaves on for ten miles and then ten miles more, losing its pavement then its gravel until it's just a hard strip of dust, I begin to wonder if I've missed a turn. I approach a wind farm with dozens of carbon-fiber turbines collecting to-day's little breeze. With my head tilted upward, I nearly fail to see the drove of donkeys obstructing the road. I stop, charmed by what other's might perceive to be their insolence, and enjoy the way they greet my car. Only one seems to notice me within the car. It stands at the passenger window, staring through the glass. His eyes bore into me until he has made me understand: *I would sooner hitch a ride in a car than have a cart hitched to me.* A few seconds later, and it moves to the front of the car, lowering its head to the hood, warm from the long drive. It shakes its muzzle against the smooth metal and swishes its tail and then completes its semicircle as it arrives at the driver door. It feels like I should be paying a toll: corn husks or similar roughage. Its nostrils flatten against my window. There are clusters of donkeys before me and beside me. They accumulate in my rearview mirror as well.

Parked on a ribbon of rust in the sage landscape, I'm convinced my car is the most static thing in this scenery. The donkeys continue to circle me. I've turned catatonic, not daring to move in the midst of this magic. Babbitt Ranches may be famous for its summer colt sales, quarter horses bred for penning cattle, but I think I would sooner leave with one of these handsome burros. By the time they all condense into a rearview snapshot, the windmills whirling overhead, I realize it's a ready-made adaptation of Miguel de Cervantes's *Don Quixote* (1620).

Since the four hundredth anniversary of Cervantes's death, I've been flipping through the picaresque. I'm reminded now of how Quixote names his horse, modifying the noun *rocín* (work-horse) with *-ante* (formerly), therefore elevating the retired nag to a noble steed—just as he himself declares the man in the mirror a knight-errant when he is actually a "madman" (his own words). In one of the most unhinged scenes of the book, Quixote gives "the spur to his steed Rocinante, heedless of the cries his squire Sancho sent after him, warning him that most certainly they were windmills and not giants he was going to attack." The sails of the windmill shiver his "lance to pieces," and Quixote, rather than admit his mistake, claims they were transformed by his mystical adversary, Friston, to "rob [him] of the glory of vanquishing them."

Some slow miles later, my car passes between artificial embankments, and the windmills disappear from the rearview completely. As promised by an email dashed off by an Arizona Game and Fish official, I cross a cattle guard at 27.8 miles. Before getting out of the car to open the first gate, I stuff the cuffs of my pants into my wool socks. Like the long-sleeve shirt, cotton-latex gloves, and bug spray, it's a form of insurance against the fleas, a primary vector of plague. I have been reading about plague all week as if I'm a casual scholar and not some neurotic game-and-fish volunteer.

The basics: A pathogen is carried by a vector to the vertebrate host, which is then stricken with the disease. For example, the bacterium *Yersinia pestis* is carried by a flea to a prairie dog, which comes down with the bubonic plague.

As for humans, I made the mistake of sharing *this* description from the Minnesota Department of Health with my wife: "people get bubonic plague from infected animals. The bacteria are spread by bites from infected fleas, bites or scratches from infected animals, or direct contact with infected animal carcasses."

"And what is it that you're going to be doing at Espee Ranch?" Andie asked me, leadingly.

"Volunteering."

She rolled her eyes, so I tried again.

"Saving ferrets."

The more truthful version goes like this: "I'm trapping known vertebrate hosts, knocking them out with anesthesia, taking blood samples, and combing vectors off their backs to send to the CDC, who will check for evidence of the pathogen, which is responsible for one of the deadliest diseases in human history." I don't mention the tragic case of Eric York, the wildlife biologist who died of pneumonic plague an hour from Espee Ranch after handling an infected mountain lion carcass.

Andie knows I'm not some tedious thrill seeker like her ex was, that I'm just a sucker for the black-footed ferret, the endangered species whose existence in northern Arizona is entirely dependent on the health of the prairie dog population. Senior biologist of the World Wildlife Fund Kristy Bly has called the prairie dog the McNugget of the prairie. In fact, she and colleagues in Montana oversee an operation in which: "Pilots fly [drones] across the prairie, dropping blueberry-sized pellets about every 30 feet. They are flavored to taste like peanut butter . . . The kicker is that they're laced with a live vaccine that protects [prairie dogs] from the plague." They have even shot vaccine-coated M&M's onto the prairie from their airborne apparatus, which has been likened to a "glorified gumball machine." "Save the food and you save the ferret," the article reckons. It's a logical wager. This is why I don't hesitate to lend a hand despite warnings from administrators, through national megaphones like *USA Today* and ABC, to stay away. "Officials are urging residents to reduce their exposure to the disease," one outlet says over a satellite map of *my* residential area.

That, and the black-footed ferret has always been more auspice than omen for me. Over the years, the volunteering has always aligned with important moments in my personal history—as if it was my own spiritual existence and not the ferret's biological one that was at stake. Even on my best days, despite the biophilic bookshelves and conservation conversations, I'm probably still an anthropocentrist. Worst of all: I fear that volunteering has allowed me to become some self-styled "good guy," something to suspend the reality that I'm otherwise a shithead.

Andie knows better than I do that this trip is more about the baby than it is the ferret. That's why she didn't ask the perilous question again. *Why insinuate yourself into a remote ecosystem when your own personal ecosystem is about to be so radically altered?* We made sure one of her closest friends was available in case she went into labor, and now here I am, rolling up to the primitive camp: a small village of tired trucks parked in a dirt roundabout, stacks of rusting cages under a canopy, a kitchen with locked coolers and a gas stove, and a semicircle of REI tents raised in the limited shade of the piñon-juniper woodland.

I spritz my torso with too much bug spray. By the time I cover my forehead, ear, neck, shirt, sleeves, wrists, palms, fingers, and thumbs, I've run out of the elixir completely. My vision sweeps the dusty floor, looking for Hollywood harbingers of apocalypse as I saunter through the site. Where is the distressed diary that concludes in feverish gibberish, the fan-belt-operated steam-punk generator, the cadre of cockroaches feasting on invisible desert crumbs? But everything appears to be on the up-and-up. It's just a rustic campsite, momentarily abandoned. Because the equipment is spare and the clutter minimal, I estimate there's only a half-dozen on the conservation team this weekend. I squat into a lawn chair, wondering where they have gone. *Maybe they've already succumbed*, I worry. Plague is one of the viral apocalypses after all, swift and sweeping in its lethality. But then I spot an aluminum pot. I stick my finger into the water, still hot from a recent boil, and realize I must have just missed them. Breakfast too.

The solitude is a good chance to try out my new headphones. I can't help but dance to the desert noir of Calexico. To the unini-tiated, Joe Tangari of *Pitchfork* puts it like this: "bluesy Mariachi, desert-rock, and jazz." I walk around with that home-alone vibe. If it weren't for the fleas, I'd probably be stripping off my duds and doing my best rendition of Tom Cruise in a rural *Risky Business*. I am dancing—kind of prancing—to a song named after my fa-vorite taqueria in Tucson, trying to recreate the essence of the rhumba, misremembering the steps I had carefully learned at the flirtatiously named desert dance studio Shall We Dance?

I had bought the Groupon back when Andie and I were dating, surely trying to impress her with some combination of money and vulnerability. When she was a no-show for consecutive weeks, I decided to go to the studio anyway. I danced for hours with our instructor, Bianca, an award-winning Argentinian tango *bailarín*. She endured my talentlessness with a slight and merciful smile. At the conclusion of our last session, she gave a masculine bow (she often took the lead) and wished me luck. She was clearly speaking to my dating, and not my dancing, prospects. My pride dares me to call her now to tell her that my no-show dance partner is now my wife. That we're having a baby!

When I can't tell the difference between rhumba and waltz anymore—and there are major differences, at least I know that—I realize my body's mostly forgotten its instructions. I look angrily at my feet, cautiously at my hips, crossly at my shoulders, and determine it must be a cognitive problem. I freestyle instead toward an open patch next to a juniper tree that looks suitable for sleeping.

I toss my tent on the floor and notice a giant white vertebra by my tapping toe. The rest of the skeleton is strewn about the area. It's not until I reach the cloven hooves that I discern it belonged to either an elk or a cow. No wonder no one else chose this otherwise cool haven. I kick the rest of the skeleton out of the way and stake the poles into loose clay.

"Oh good, you found us!" Jennifer says when the conservation team has returned to the camp.

I greet her with a thumbs-up, emerging from my tent, toothbrush poking out of my mouth.

"I just got a voicemail from one of the other volunteers. They made a wrong turn and just went home."

"You have reception out here?" I ask. I wonder if Andie still has Jennifer's number from our last spotlighting trip, if she'll think to use it in case of membrane rupture (water breakage).

"Kind of," she says, squinting at her phone. "Well, no." She explains they were just on an ice run back to Red Valley. Behind her, interns pour the ice bags into the cooler while others crouch at the wheel well of a truck.

"We'll get going in a little bit," Jennifer says. "When it cools down."

It's been a hot summer, and as we wait to set the traps, I read the rest of the plague literature I printed the night before. After the primer, I encounter a number of articles citing the role climate change will likely play in spreading vector-borne diseases.

Scientists like Yoshinori Nakazawa believe the vectors (again, fleas) are "indeed shifting in accord with patterns of climatic shift." Another group of researchers led by Russell Enscore gives *this* indicator for Arizona: "the number of cases actually observed . . . can be estimated by monitoring key climatic variables . . . [like] maximum daily summer temperature values." Because in North America plague only exists in the western states, zoonotic diseases are usually affected by the Pacific Decadal Oscillation (PDO) as well. The PDO is an atmospheric pattern in which the Pacific basin warms or cools over the span of decades. With its cooling trend over, the Pacific is now in a warming phase. The warming results in increased precipitation, which in combination with warmer regional temperatures, is "believed to enhance small-mammal food resources and flea survival," write James Mills, Kenneth Gage, and Ali Khan. Tamara Ari concludes, "warmer and wetter climate [leads] to increased plague activity."

A plane flies overhead as I shuffle through the papers. Most of the science is projective, its prose laden with modal verbs like *might* and *may*. But there's one report that manages to scare the shit out of me in an immediate way. For the skeptic, look no further than statistical wizard Nils Christian Stenseth and his team, who in 2006 demonstrated that regional climate conditions favored plague during the onset of the Medieval Black Death and the Third Pandemic of the plague in the mid-nineteenth century. I stare at the mathematical model used, trying to trace the relation between the variables, superscripts, logarithms, and covariates. It is annoyingly empirical, typically impenetrable.

That's when my "plague panic" transfers to another, more domestic, predicament: Who will help our son with his future calculus? If I start beefing up now, then in sixteen years, I may be able to get him through trigonometry and the derivatives of a function. Yet another hurdle we hadn't anticipated, I'm reminded of the ambiguously paced Jonathan Safran Foer story "Here We Aren't, So Quickly," in which a father narrates his son's childhood with devastating velocity: "He suddenly drew, suddenly spoke, suddenly wrote, suddenly reasoned. One night I couldn't help him with his math. He got married." Having sufficiently prepared for my son's arrival, I feel I am already bracing for his departure. I fear he will be a double asymptote, never quite landing on this sliver of a life, this trembling axis we augured for him. One anxiety begets another until I am on an extralong stroll to take an extralong piss, hoping my phone will be blessed with signal. The anxiety is so bad for a moment I even start to see it from Andie's perspective: *What the fuck* am *I doing all the way out here anyway?*

Volunteering, I remind myself. *Saving the black-footed ferret.* Good then. Good for me. I pat myself on my needy back.

Because one of the trucks was clogged with brush the day before and an engine spark started a little fire in the undercarriage, we're down to three trucks to attend to four sites. It's sunset, and I want to know how the intern at the wheel knows where she's going. She's only been on this nondescript farm road once before, and she makes masterful hairpin turns without consulting map or GPS.

"This next turn," she says, "I know because there's a burrowing owl just chilling."

Sure enough, when the truck turns again, wide this time like a jibing sailboat, I'm rubbernecking at an owl who stands on its twiggy legs at a steep entrance mound. While burrowing owls and black-footed ferrets are both squatters in the prairie dogs' colony, at least the owl is courteous enough not to devour its landlord. Due to the suspicion of plague, there is an uneasy fear among state conservationists that a ferret's next meal will be its last. The intercolony transmission of plague could be instantly fatal for any living specimens associated with the black-footed ferret project in northern Arizona, which in 2017, peaked at a minimum population of just nineteen.

The site is marked by a lollipop reflector. The traps are arranged all across the field, and the sun glints off their west-facing aluminum walls. We slalom the rows, giving each spring-loaded trapdoor a swift high five so that they catch on the treadle latch. We add a couple cotton balls for nesting and cast a spoonful of oats, millet, and kibble just beyond the treadle, enough to lure small Rodentia. After the Sherman traps, we switch to the larger Tomahawks with steel-wire frames. These are for the prairie dogs. We double the bait on *their* treadles and converge on the truck again. Each of us gulps some of the water stored in the truck bed before dropping to our haunches. We sit, silent, privately trying to process the sun's slippage through the broad horizon, the way the clouds bear the weight of all that color until they can't anymore.

Back at the campsite, the interns prep our meal. Jennifer peeks into the saucepan and notes they have big shoes to fill. Apparently, the last intern cooked up a prairie dog with lots of spices. "Wasn't that bad either," she says.

The interns look at each other, silently wriggle their noses.

Dinner happens so quickly—the chopping, chowing, cleaning—that it feels like the spaghetti is coiled inside my gut as one large noodle, balled up like yarn. Since we'll wake at 4:00 a.m., we hurry to the tents and try for sleep.

I unroll my socks and crack my toe knuckles, flick the lantern off and slip into my scalloped sleeping bag. When something keeps jabbing me through the tent flooring and bag's padding, I know immediately what it must be. I reverse the process: slip out of the bag, flick the lantern on, put on my socks, and pull the headlamp band against my skull. Reaching beneath the tarp I've spread under the tent, I graze another piece of skeleton. I was convinced I had toed them all aside earlier, but this piece of ilium must have been camouflaged by a clump of grass. I remove it, rotate it in my hand. The mineral intimacy gives me the creeps. I had essentially just dry-humped what was left of this animal's pelvic skeleton. I imagine the elk staggering toward this, its final resting place, and I suddenly feel gruesome for resting here too. *What had it died of?* I wonder. *Parasites? Nitrates? Respiratory problems?* I wonder how long until bacteria started breaking down tissue, until the scavengers started circling the recumbent body, until the buffet began, then ended. How much time had passed until I danced on the grave with my incompetent rhumba and REI dome tent?

Convinced the tent is contaminated by death, I creep away under a filmy moon glow, taking a spotlight with me. In the unlikely case of a black-footed ferret's green eyeshine. I haven't been sleeping for the past week thanks to my wife's tossing on the mattress. Her back pain, along with the Braxton-Hicks contractions, have rendered her sleepless as well. She even pointed out that I'd probably sleep better in my tent tonight than I have on our memory foam mattress. By night, I've been stepping into the living room to read books with small font, my trick for inducing fatigue.

When I finished *Don Quixote*, I couldn't help but rummage back to the protagonist's first sally. His idealism descends precipitously over the course of his journeys. Early on, he leaves his estate, "urged on . . . by the thought of [what] the world was losing by his delay, [the] wrongs he intended to right, grievances to redress, injustices to repair, abuses to remove, and duties to discharge." He mounts Rocinante and sets off to fulfill his grand purpose. Compare this bumptious Quixote with the groveling Quixano (his given name), who repents from his deathbed at novel's end. The swashbuckler grows faint. And his bravado is replaced by humility, apology, and a formal renunciation of his fantastical mission to revive chivalry.

I walk for twenty minutes—no more than a mile—swinging my spotlight over prairie dog entrance mounds, desperately hoping my phone will vibrate.

NO BABY YET
or
THE BABY'S HERE. COME QUICK!
or
YOU ASSHOLE

Anything will do. Instead, I catch the unmistakable sound of a herd of javelina, their hoggish snouts sifting the ground. I lower my spotlight, let go of the trigger. It's uncommon range for them, though a map from the Conservation Biology Institute shows a "very sparse" population a few miles to the southwest of this ranch. It's even more unlikely that they would be foraging at night, though during the hottest months (and *these* are them), they may eat as a team after dark, snuffing up all the tubers, rhizomes, and prickly pear in sight. Unsure if my rabies vaccines are up to date, I walk perpendicular from the sound of them under star-riveted sky, trekking farther from camp, rolling my ankle over the occasional bricklike cow patty.

I sit and watch the video of the donkeys from yesterday. I pause the video, take a screenshot of the one whose muzzle nuzzled the hood of my car. *There! That's my Rocinante!*

By the time I've returned to the camp, the others have woken to their alarms. Not even dawn, and it's time to check the traps. After a mug of instant coffee, I'm in the truck with the interns again. This time, we relish the silence. The burrowing owl is burrowed. A weak flash of blue urges in from the east.

We stalk the rows, calling out when we've got one. A few of the smaller traps have clapped shut without an animal. It's obvious, though, when a prairie dog has been captured. It stares through the cage—either with vengeance or dismay—and we hoist it carefully to the truck. We escort the live cargo to a midway point, where Jennifer and Heather set up the canopy. Equidistant from all four sites, another truck has arrived and is already processing the first grasshopper mouse.

Her eyes are two jumbo caviar, black and glassy, popping at her captor's nerve. A man has dumped the mouse into a transparent wholesale pretzel jar and is now clasping a mesh tea ball infuser around a cotton ball that's been doused in general anesthetic. Once the ball has rolled to the base of the container, the lid is screwed on and we wait. Immediately, the rodent staggers. Onlookers compare him to a punch-drunk boxer, a last-call boozer, a cartoonish dental patient. I try to laugh, but nothing comes out. Eventually, the mouse drops. They rattle the container and nothing changes. In the man's gloved hands, the limp mouse looks bitesize, a little bigger than a marshmallow Peep. We pay close attention as its toenail is snipped, and blood is collected in a vial.

"If we don't get blood from the nail, we can yank a whisker too," Heather says.

As she brushes its back with a toothbrush, hoping to loose some fleas into a small basin on the folding table, the mouse re-animates. The man, who has been using one hand to scruff the mouse in the event it regains consciousness, alerts the crew. Someone tilts the pretzel jar his way, and just like that, the mouse is anesthetized once again. A few minutes after the processing, she is back in the Sherman trap, ready to be returned to the exact spot she ate her last meal.

Once the samples are labeled, it's our team's turn to process a kangaroo rat. We repeat the procedure, each person taking on the role they're most comfortable with. Next up: another kangaroo rat. And another. When one of the interns spills the next grass-hopper mouse out of the container, though, it sails past his palm and ricochets off the tabletop. It's unconscious, concussed. Again, the crew resorts to caricature, treating the incident like a groin hit on *America's Funniest Home Videos*. Its fur is combed for fleas (two) and blood is drawn. Then it's returned to its cage and, turns out, casket. After that, everyone's a little more careful.

The procedure is a little different for the prairie dog, most of it relating to scale. A larger container, more isoflurane, a lon-ger wait time until paralysis. The biggest difference, though, is the scruffing technique and this warning: "Now, don't let these guys nip you. Their teeth are a whole other story." A prairie dog's cheek teeth grow continuously. It's only through constant gnaw-ing (that is, filing) that they don't drag their teeth on the ground with them everywhere they go.

As the first prairie dogs are processed—energetic juveniles who scramble against the walls of the container, trying to bur-row their way out—I can't help but recall the Department of Health's explanation: "People get bubonic plague from . . . bites or scratches from infected animals." I squint at them. *Are you infected? Are* you? Once they faint, these dogs are dumped and scruffed, snipped and combed, and returned to the Tomahawks from which they came.

When it's my turn to scruff the prairie dog, it's a very large adult who weighs in at a jumbo two and a half pounds; in other words, he's maxed out. The specialists give him the same amount of anesthesia as the others, which concerns me, but they have their procedures to follow. After a drawn-out wobble around the circumference of the container, the dog finally drops. I grip him like my life depends on it, like it's the "hold-my-hand" cliff moment in the penultimate scene of an action movie. He's heavier than he looks, and I manage him like a heavy barbell. When he thrashes not twenty seconds later, I tell the person on containment duty he's going back in.

We all stare at the prairie dog in the jar. No one dares to make fun of this one. If someone will be scratched or bitten today, here's the likely perpetrator. The anesthesia process is repeated, and perhaps we all look the other way when Heather gives the cotton ball an extra splash. This time, when the animal slumps against the wall, gravity pinning him in place, we're all convinced of his slumber.

Turns out medical-grade nitrile disposable gloves—famous for their flexibility, dexterity, and "dependable barrier protection"—were not designed to defend against the canines of a two-and-a-half-pound, agitated prairie dog. When he tosses back to life, he slips from my right hand. It's the left hand, swinging to support the prairie dog's torso, that sustains the bite that punctures the glove. The dog returns to the container, a flimsy holding cell, while I fling off the glove. The skin appears to be contused, not abraded. I'm the recipient of rapid concern and antiseptic, but I look beyond my finger as Jennifer and Heather quickly paint the prairie dog's blood on Nobuto sample strips. I remember the gist of Jennifer's ambiguous email a couple weeks back: "There is a possibility that there is plague at one of our trapping sites."

I trudge to the cage, lock eyes with the prairie dog, name him Brutus or Judas. As in *Et tu, Brute?* I'm scandalized by his kiss of black death.

The animals are unceremoniously returned to the easting and northing from where we plucked them up. After that, I leave in a hurry. My tent is stuffed, not folded, into the canvas bag; after going through the motions of being a team member—inventorying cages, lifting canteens, exchanging emails with the new interns—I am waving goodbye, my injured hand the last they see of me.

I close the gate on the Babbitt allotment, knowing I am leaving this tract, this project, behind for a short while. It took only a couple weeks of living in Flagstaff to realize Babbitt Ranches is very public about their land ethic. While they are truly model citizens of the national ranching community (ask anyone), one might describe their calligraphied constitution in the face of so much deterioration as quixotic. From Article V, Section 3: "Health is the capacity of the land for self-renewal. Conservation is our effort to understand and preserve this capacity." Or try Article V, Section 5, on for size: "A thing is right when it tends to preserve the integrity, stability and beauty of the biotic community. It is wrong when it tends otherwise." As a millennial, I should read it as righteous, but instead, I scan for sanctimony.

I think back to my conversation with Billy Cordasco and wonder what it is the foundation stands to lose. All a rancher has to give up is the combination to their padlock and they can receive government subsidies and public plaudits. Why *not* pull at the levers of green capitalism as long as it's fashionable to do so? I feel my cynicism flaring up again. No. Billy is one of the good guys. They may actually exist!

Meanwhile, my mere presence on their holdings this weekend could be a source of regret for the rest of my life. The way I see it: If twenty years from now my son wants to know why I missed his birth, I'll simply tell him: *This other thing, this ferret thing, that was important also.* Later, Will jokes that maybe my son will return the favor by ditching my funeral.

I pass the windmills and watch their blades chop the sky. By now, I'm checking my phone every 0.3 miles or something like that, waiting for the first trace of a signal. Knowing this will probably be my last time in the field for a while, I put that Smog album on again. The bite is imprinted on my flesh. It's still possible that

I've missed the birth of my son *and* that I've contracted plague. *I was meant to be a volunteer, not a martyr,* I think. It's possible too that the black-footed ferrets are the next in line, that this is their last summer ever in Arizona. "In last year's nests there are no birds this year," Don Quixote says on his laconic deathbed. Through this late sentiment, I sense a tacit acknowledgment: Despite my best efforts, I remain ineffectual.

My pocket buzzes. The brakes squawk. A dust cloud of my own making drifts over me. I listen to Andie's voicemail and gallop homeward.

EXTRAPOLATING THE GENUS

—·—

One can be too much in love with something. For example: the other day, I tossed you in the air (despite Mom requesting that I not), hoping to elicit a smile big enough to reveal the deciduous teeth emerging from your gums. Even though I was bound to catch you (I always will), I forgot the ceiling fan was on and nearly decapitated you. Love can be dangerous like that. I am not sorry but could have been. Ever since, I've been holding you in the basket of my arms, staring at your neck, imagining it severed. I decide the fan blades are too blunt to amputate even a foam finger. Still, I trace the creases over your trachea, wondering. Sometimes you smile for no reason at all. The teething has only just begun, and it's likely you'll be gummy for another year. I give you my pinky to gnaw on, and for the moment, you're mollified.

I add "decapitation" to the long list of concepts I don't yet know how to explain to you. Our "sex talk" will be easy due to an overabundance of resources on the matter. But where's the pamphlet on *How to Talk to Your Kid About* . . . any of the subjects du jour: migration, biopolitics, border ecology? I'll probably begin with the image of kids climbing walls or kids in nice cages. And how to introduce the idea of "extinction" when you've only just learned objects continue to exist beyond your immediate perception of them?

Another thing I love—and you probably know this by now since you hear me speaking its name all hours of the day: the black-footed ferret. It was the first animal (stuffed) to share a crib with you. *Ferret* was the reason I almost missed your birth. *Ferret* is the thing I try to pick out by itself, only to "find it hitched to everything else in the Universe," to quote John Muir. The "universe," Milo. I'm not even sure how to explain the "neighborhood" to you yet—let alone the "Colorado Plateau," "Arizona," "America," the "biome."

The real reason I'm writing: please don't get me one of those ancestry DNA kits for Father's Day. Not this year, not ever. Our extended family has denied any mystery worth the yarning. They've tattooed national flags on their torsos, struck up correspondences with long-lost relatives, and even bought purebred dogs that hail from the county of their origin. There are factions who would have you believe we're so Irish we shouldn't leave the house without a shillelagh. But I refuse to believe that ancestry is some self-fulfilling prophecy you can purchase with a credit card and a little spit. It isn't meant to retroactively inform your consumer behaviors, explain your freckles despite your olive complexion, or stoke tourism to some muddled motherland. I have this sneaking suspicion that the genealogy boom (the local news tells me the kits are the top-trending gift this Father's Day) is a temporary evil that has something to do with the rise of white nationalism and the suppression of cultural globalization. By discovering where we *do* come from, we are able to clarify we do *not* come from those other "shithole" places.

Let's always be honest with each other, finally admit: we come from earth, we come from worms.

I've always been a miserabilist. For that, I apologize now and forever. I know you're my descendent (in fact, you were named after the punk front man of *the* Descendents), and that's enough, genetically speaking, for me. Let's skip the tongue swabs and just spend Father's Day hiking the open spaces in this forest called Flagstaff. I'll dust off the old backpack palanquin, adjust the hip belt for me and the foot stirrups for you, and make half-empty promises as we trot along the Arizona Trail—saying to myself, "I promise to coach your hockey team one day" and "I'm going to run for the Open Spaces Commission next time there's a vacancy." If a man whispers in the forest with only his baby to hear it, all sound and no sense, who will hold him to it?

I am no father to a ferret, Milo, but it's important to think I could be. After all, there are thousands of men who abandon their biological children daily; how can we expect them to care for the next generation of wildness when they can't be bothered with their own domestic brood? For example, the other day, we were killing a couple hours in San Jose. I called six cemeteries in the area, hoping to find a "Nick Leonard." He was "definitely not" in the directory for cemeteries number one, number three, and number five; unlikely to have been buried in the Jewish cemetery (number two); and I just had a hunch, without ever meeting the guy, that number four's neighborhood was not his style. We went to the sixth cemetery, your mother and I stalking alternate rows, scanning the mausoleums for his name. I carried you for a while, whispering: "We are trying to find your father's father's father's father." You laughed—maybe at the sonic repetition or the way we kept converging on Mom. Or perhaps you know better than me: this is farce / he's not to be found.

For most of his life, that was true. When Nick left the family during the Great Depression—goodbye wife, goodbye son, goodbye daughter—he found work in New York, Indiana, and Illinois before choosing a new name, family, and coast. In the 1980s, Nick's second wife called to tell us how impressive his burial was. "It's a one-person mausoleum," she said. "Don't you want to come see it?"

At the time, my dad (your Pap), said, "Not really." But now. Now that I was doing the legwork, he called in a favor. "Piss on his grave for me, will you?" I won't be able to teach you about "desecration" or "grudges" or "intergenerational trauma" until after I teach you how to pee at a specific target. These things take time.

Most of the names in that Catholic cemetery were Italian, which seemed to mean we were in the right place. The more I had to pee, the closer I thought I might have been getting to the grave. Ironically, Mom took you from my arms when you wet your diaper, leaving me to continue the charade, now with more velocity. It was the first time I ever craved one of those small drones with the aerial cam. (The drone is the second most popular gift this year; don't get me one of those either!) How quickly I could have whipped through the cemetery, verifying Nick's interment—or not. I think not, after all.

Your father's father's father's father. Who cares, right? But keep tacking on possessives; say it enough times, and you'll exceed the DNA kit's capacity to convey an ancestry that makes modern sense. One product promises: "Held within our DNA code is the history of humanity." In reality, our genome reveals much more: the history of all life on earth.

Come to think of it, Milo. What I *would* like for Father's Day: a frame for my "Certificate of Adoption" for the black-footed ferret, a gift I reluctantly accepted from a student. I guess you could say this makes you a brother. More symbol than sibling, this "adopted" ferret from the World Wildlife Fund will keep to its burrow rather than your bunk.

When I teach you about death, Milo—and the prospect of extinction—how can I explain that sometimes beings are resurrected, restored? You will know how black-footed ferrets are my concession to faith. Every time I see a ferret, brilliant in a cone of white light—and every time it sees me too—I sprint jaggedly across the tufted steppe, feel hardwired in those strides and my beating heart an intense biophilia. The urge, as E. O. Wilson puts it, "to affiliate with other forms of life."

I felt that urge a few weeks ago after putting you to bed. I called up some friends and we drove to Seligman, arriving at the hour the Bible says Jesus died, Good Friday. But it wasn't until Easter morning that we saw it. I barely remembered to park the car, had hardly slipped on my shoes, before taking off in a rapturous sprint. The ferret dove into the burrow's funnel opening, rocks clattering after it. We gathered around like disciples—completely winded, our lungs wheezing like bellows.

"Come out, little Jesus ferret," a friend called. "Get thee out of your tomb."

And the ferret immediately complied. We had our little tête-à-tête at N 35°27'54.1", W 113°01'25.3", a perfect assembly just before our return trip at sunrise.

I slipped into bed at 7:00 a.m., just as you were stirring. Your eyes were blinking brightly on the baby monitor. Whereas I spent the evening trying to outshine the darkness by oscillating the heavy spotlight, I needed only to adjust the contrast on the monitor to see you at near-infrared. It's almost like wearing contacts with tapetum lucidum, the way the monitor allows me to see you like a ferret would. *There!* I thought. *I spot another.* But rather than sprint down the hallway toward you like I would on the prairie, I simply watched you do your thing. You were trapped in the Velcro grip of your swaddle—cooing and squirming like you might come free.

The thing about binging a live webcam is that it is unscripted. There are no natural breaks in the action. Sometimes there is no action. I think of the zoo's BFF webcams I watched years ago, how many hours I spent taking in that enchanting feed, never knowing when to peel myself away for fear the best was yet to come. But now, I've got something superior. On this machine, I can press a little button and send my disembodied voice directly into your room.

"Good morning," I said to you.

Your mom, not knowing I'd depressed the microphone button, assumed I was saying it only to her.

"You're back," she said, shuddering as she stretched her limbs. Her jaw unhinged for a satisfying yawn. "Did you find our ferret?" she asked, referring to the kit we'd found years ago.

I don't have the heart to tell her that one's almost certainly dead.

"Maybe so," I said.

Later, I toss you in the air. Toss you again. Don't worry: the fan is off this time. The blades are resting. I say to you: "Father's father's father's father." It's our inside joke. You begin to repeat it, bottom lip flinging off your top teeth. It sounds something like "fa-fa-fa-fa."

If you say it enough times, *father* and *father* and *father* and *father*, it begins to sound like *farther* and *farther*, like you're tracing a distant line. "Fa-fa-fa-fa," you say. "Fa-fa-fa-fa-fa-fa-fa-fa."

"Fa-fa-FA-FA." There is something urgent in your babbling, or it is the semblance of an urge. Call it biophilia. It's like you're stuttering the chorus of Talking Heads' "Psycho Killer." I think about how you are becoming a talking head yourself. Spittle slicks your chin. You kick until your toes curl into plantar reflex.

"What is it that it is?"

"Fa-fa-fa-fa," you keep sing-saying.

So I join in, our first duet, "fa-fa-fa-fa" and son.

We crawl now, across the kitchen floor. We're locked in this mantra ad nauseum, aiming to reach so many fathers back that our heritage may be natural, not national. We babble past bipedal hominids (fa-fa-fa-fa) toward the dawning of the Cenozoic, approach the ancestor of all placental mammals, humans and ferrets alike.

"We were shrews," I tell him. "Shrews!"

"Fa-fa-fa-fa," he responds.

We know the aim of our mantra, and it's all the way back. To fathers farther than Afrotherian. Past the conspicuous shift to when mammals morphed from reptiles, those terrierlike cynodonts. We wriggle and babble, wormlike to the window, sallying forth in a rectilinear ray like the world's oldest bilaterian, *Ikaria wariootia*. Let's get the hang of it, Milo. Let's try to enjoy. If not our own existence, then existence itself.

PETRI TO PRAIRIE

—·—

An ankle-high fog of liquid nitrogen drifts over the floor of the Frozen Zoo, coasting round the keglike cryotanks that host the world's largest collection of living cell cultures. The fog immediately lowers the room's temperature, a reprieve from the sultry June day in Southern California. This room—about the size of the beer cave at my local gas station—is probably the most biodiverse room in the world. (Well, this one and a duplicate collection assembled in some discreet facility in a different Southern California fire zone.)

Marlys Houck, the zoo's curator, climbs a stepstool and peers through protective goggles into one of the tanks, which steams like a frozen hot tub. She waits for the carousel within it to spin to the correct quadrant.

When I parked at the San Diego Zoo Safari Park in Escondido this morning and asked an attendant for directions to the Frozen Zoo, she clearly thought I was joking. Did I mean the polar bear's tundra habitat? I found my own way, walking the fence line to the facility next door. The Beckman Center for Conservation Research includes the twenty thousand square feet of laboratory space where the international nonprofit San Diego Zoo Wildlife Alliance makes good on its conservation mission. The Frozen Zoo is its crown jewel. "Come see," Houck says to me as the frosty carousel stops.

I tip my toes to see into the tank, and she rummages through the racks in what appear to be ski gloves. The racks resemble model skyscrapers, with each floor removable like a drawer and full of vials. Inside the vials are one million to three million gooey living cells. And inside each cell are tens of thousands of genes, some of which have endured decades in suspended animation, just one thaw away from reentering the gene pool of an extant endangered species. It's no wonder, as Houck says, that "the safety of this collection literally keeps her awake some nights."

When she finds what she's looking for, Houck wields foot-long forceps with her cryogenic gloves and transfers the rack to a stainless-steel table. Houck runs her eyes over a hundred vials until she IDs it: *Ceratotherium simum cottoni*, male. Northern white rhino.

Houck admires her decades-old script on the vial. "It's funny seeing my handwriting—to think, what was going on in my life when I wrote the label for this one."

Someone mentions that 1988 was the summer she first learned to spay mice as a zoo intern. Another person remembers it as one of the Frozen Zoo's last years with its late founder, Kurt Benirschke. I demure, don't mention I wasn't alive yet. Like time capsules, once the vials are submerged, they don't reemerge until authorized. When they are called up, it's because one of the wildlife alliance's partners has a specific genetic project in mind, one that promotes species recovery or extinction risk management.

Take this vial of northern white rhino, for instance. When a veterinarian snipped a lentil-sized notch from the rhino's ear decades ago—mixing it with enzymes, antifungals, antibiotics, and nutrients before incubating it in a flask, lettings its cells cleave and multiply for a month before cryopreserving it indefinitely—there were two dozen or so northern white rhinos left in the world. But now, when a technician prepares those same cells for thawing, the species is critically endangered, more than likely extinct in the wild. The two known living specimens, Najin and Fatu, are at a conservancy in Kenya. As both are female, the species is at least functionally extinct, with no male to sire another generation. That vial beneath my nose is as close as one can get to a living male northern white rhino. The researcher-recipients of these living cells might use them for applications in embryology, in vitro fertilization, stem cell technology, even—one day—cloning.

To produce a new northern white rhino, scientists would need to complete genome sequencing, create rhino sperm and oocytes from stem cells, and develop new assisted reproductive technologies.

"We'll be long gone by the time that happens," Houck says, referring to her colleagues. I can't tell if it's a euphemism for their retirement or death.

The process—from thaw to clone—was much quicker for the black-footed ferret, which in December 2020 became the first endangered species native to North America to be genetically duplicated. Its membership within an endangered ecosystem (prairie grasslands) and its specialized diet of endangered prey (prairie dogs) makes its survival that much more precarious.

It all began with an email from Seth Willey, U.S. Fish and Wildlife Service (USFWS) recovery coordinator in the Mountain-Prairie region, entitled "Out of the Box." He asked his addressee, the biotechnology company of resurrection biologists Revive and Restore, if the technology was "ripe" enough to genetically enhance the BFF. Ryan Phelan, Revive and Restore's cofounder, and Ben Novak, its lead scientist, spent the better part of a decade as biotech ambassadors, convincing USFWS officials, led by BFF Recovery coordinator Pete Gober, that genetic restoration was in the best interest of the ferrets. When Phelan and Novak were told to "slow down" at working group meetings, they realized it was because of the way the agency guards each and every ferret, especially following a devastating plague in 2008 that vectored through South Dakota's Conata Basin, once home to the only self-sustaining population of BFFs. Phelan explained, "We told them we'll take the criticism, we'll raise the money." And they did.

Once it was discovered that the Frozen Zoo curated a special cell line that belonged to a nonreproductive ferret known as Willa, it was clear that Escondido would become the auspicious starting line for the genetic restoration. The current BFF population, which numbers about six hundred—half of them wild, half in captivity—all originate from a measly seven founders from

Meeteetse, Wyoming, a stark fact that severely limits genetic diversity. Willa's decades-old genes, however, can't be found in any living ferret, meaning she signifies the potential of an eighth founder.

When the last extant wild population was infected with canine distemper in 1987, conservationists trapped the willowy weasels for safekeeping, jumpstarting one of the most comprehensive pedigree charts in the biological world. A studbook keeper at the Smithsonian acts as matchmaker for all captive ferrets, making breeding recommendations based on data. Genetically speaking, opposites attract. But there's only so much one can do for a species with seven founders. Over time, most of the BFFs have become the genetic equivalent of siblings, or cousins at best. Remarkably, in 1988, Fish and Wildlife had the wherewithal to collect cells from nonreproductive ferrets in Meeteetse in the event technology would later enable them to reenter the population. Or to cop the Frozen Zoo's well-worn maxim, quoting historian Daniel Boorstin: "You must collect things for reasons you don't yet understand."

Arlene Kumamoto, a prolific technician during whose tenure the Frozen Zoo's holdings rapidly expanded, received the cells. After growing those cell lines, she deposited a few vials in the freezer, where they've been boiling in a cauldron of liquid nitrogen for thirty-four years now—or, my whole life, give or take a few months.

Conservationists have cast *Mustela nigripes* as an ambassador species—a charismatic *mini*fauna, if you will—whose bonny features have been leveraged to convince the public that the prairie ecosystem is worth saving. Show someone a video of unremarkable tufts of swaying grass, and they're bound to shrug, but sprinkle in a few pop-going weasels, and suddenly, people give a hoot about the landscape. In this way, the ferret is an unwitting agent of the prairie, protector of grasses whose fifteen-foot root systems reliably sequester carbon. At a time when drought and wildfire threaten other precious carbon sinks, such as forests, researchers wager that grasslands, with their fixed carbon, will be the most resilient and adaptive ecosystem of the future. They're even the ironic protector of their own prey, the prairie dog, a keystone species that acts as a vital ecosystem engineer. Researchers at the U.S. Geological Survey have demonstrated how prairie dog foraging, nibbling, and digging provides essential services, like mixing the topsoil with subsoil, effectively fertilizing the prairie, keeping it moist.

A black-footed ferret obsessive, I'm unreasonably miffed nobody in the know thought to tell me about this cloning business. I contact Oliver Ryder, director of conservation genetics at San Diego Zoo Wildlife Alliance, to get the scoop.

"You have to remember, when we got those ferret cells in '88, there was no Dolly the sheep, and the Human Genome Project wasn't done yet," Ryder says. In fact, it hadn't even begun. "We might have wished it was possible to clone them, but it wouldn't have been responsible to say it aloud."

In other words, Benirschke's concept of a biobank, the first of its kind, was aspirational. It seems that, at the Frozen Zoo, futurity necessarily drives present action. Conservationists must think two steps ahead to preempt any future incursions on biodiversity that are already in motion. And there are many in motion.

Paul R. Ehrlich, president of the Center for Conservation Biology at Stanford University, coauthored a paper in *Science Advances* that established, using very conservative assumptions, that the sixth mass extinction has officially arrived. This means we are likely at the dawning of a lonely era in which 75 percent of species will perish from earth.

In September 2020, the vial containing Willa's cells saw daylight, its contents representing an untapped source of genetic diversity for the severely bottlenecked black-footed ferret population. A marvel of conservation-as-curation, this slurry of cells began as Willa and ended a few months later as the fang-baring Elizabeth Ann, the would-be eighth founder in *Mustela nigripes*'s gene pool.

Even agnostics who behold the cryopreserved snotlike cells of an endangered species—held up to fluorescence or clipped to the microscope's stage—have to reckon with the soul. How much of the immaterial spirit can stow itself away in this smudge of particles? In a paper exploring the metaphysical and moral implications of cryopreservation, Jason T. Eberl asks, "Does cryopreservation thus involve 'suspending' the soul?" When Houck thaws the cells—of the ferret, or the white rhino in the vial I saw—are they at all ensouled? I look around the vats of frozen tanks.

"When you think about it," Ryder said, "to have 1,000 species in something the size of a trash can, that's like a neutron star of biodiversity." The zoo holds 1,224 species and subspecies, represented across 10,500 individuals. "Here is an orca whale next to a meerkat next to a hippopotamus next to a California condor next to a Galápagos tortoise next to a kangaroo rat next to an elephant next to a black-footed ferret. I could go on and on. That just startles me."

It startles other biologists as well—and not always in a good way. Ehrlich, the Stanford biologist, likened it to "anticipating a flood and planning to bail with a thimble." He would prefer to see the immense resources of a $561 million not-for-profit like the San Diego Zoo Wildlife Alliance go toward redressing the root causes of the conservation crisis, such as population growth and climate change. In the *Washington Post* in 2015, he wrote, "Screwing around with science to save a white rhino might be fun, and I would like to see it preserved and am all for biodiversity, but it's so far down the list of things we should be doing first." One has to admit, though, the cryotanks in the Frozen Zoo make for a pretty big thimble.

But for every voice of caution, Ryder must contend with its eager counterpoint: those who wish the Frozen Zoo would go even further in its genetic rescue.

When he discusses genetic restoration with Revive and Restore, Ryder tries to temper their interest in de-extinction. Whether it's the passenger pigeon, the po'ouli (an extinct Hawaiian bird), or the woolly mammoth, a handful of biotech firms are intent on destigmatizing de-extinction.

If the Frozen Zoo was created to collect things for reasons

not yet understood—well, then, "not yet" has suddenly morphed into the here and now. Biologist George Church is proceeding with plans to de-extinct the woolly mammoth from the Siberian tundra; paleontologist Jack Horner continues to genetically edit the chickenosaurus; and for an actual example of de-extinction, see the Pyrenean ibex, whose endling, Celia, was cloned for all of ten minutes before the newborn succumbed to a lung defect, effectively resulting in a second extinction. If all of this seems tinged with ethical anxiety, then you might sympathize with actor Jeff Goldblum, who played Ian Malcolm in *Jurassic Park*.

In response to online chatter about the chickenosaurus, he reprised his cautionary line from the film, this time via tweet: "Your scientists were so preoccupied with whether or not they could, they didn't stop to think if they should."

One can't help but imagine Ryder doing his best to tune out all those competing voices as he considers what's best for the species represented in the zoo's holdings. Ultimately, he decided that the chickenosaurus and woolly mammoth and others were outside the scope of the zoo's charge, but he suggested two extant species that could benefit from some genetic rescue: Przewalski's horse (a Mongolian equid, also known as the "last wild horse") and that perennial survivor, the black-footed ferret.

Back in the lab, Houck thaws the rhino cells in a bead bath while chatting with a technician who stirs the eyeball of a white crown shrike. If the tech were to trade her white lab coat in for a witchy black cloak, the sight would send chills.

The lab is as antiseptic as one would expect: phenolic work stations, autoclave, and fume hoods. And there is a prized sketch of a rhino. At the microscope, another tech karyotypes the cells of an Indo-Pacific bottlenose dolphin that recently stranded itself nearby on the coast. Over her shoulder, I watch the crystal-violet-stained ovoids round up, cleave, divide. On deck is a fossa, a relative of the mongoose, endemic to Madagascar. I ask if species are still recognizable under the scope once they've been pureed into culture, into cells.

"I used to say 'no,'" Houck says. "But the ferret really has an odd morphology." It's one of the few species whose cells she could recognize under the microscope, she explains, "because it's more rounded. They don't have those long . . ." she trails off while looking at the dolphin's spindly cells.

"I'd recognize your cells anywhere," the eye-stirrer teases from the other side of the room.

Houck checks the clock and glances my way. I ask, "If the northern white rhino is functionally extinct, aren't any interventions to revive them categorically an attempt at de-extinction?"

"Well, no." She pauses. "Not precisely." She provides the International Union for the Conservation of Nature's definition of de-extinction, more or less. In 2016, the IUCN released a report called *Guiding Principles on Creating Proxies of Extinct Species for Conservation Benefit* (2016), which defined de-extinction as "any attempt to create some proxy of an extinct species or subspecies . . . through any technique, including methods such as selective back breeding, somatic cell nuclear transfer (cloning), and genome engineering."

But Ben Novak of Revive and Restore would have liked a more nuanced definition. As a concept, "de-extinction" has enjoyed two stints in the popular imagination: first, through the Crichton-inspired Spielberg franchise, Jurassic World, and more recently, when National Geographic Society and Revive and Restore partnered to livestream a TEDxDeExtinction event. Amid a media frenzy of specious reporting, the IUCN set out to define the phenomenon. Novak finds the definition too restrictive, based on a binary—extant versus extinct—that, for him, isn't intellectually honest.

As he pointed out in his thirty-three-page redefinition in *Genes*—which reads like a manifesto for de-extinction—there are gradations of extinction, which are variously termed locally extinct, extinct in the wild, functionally extinct, evolutionarily torpid, and globally extinct. "Such classifications of extinction are more helpful for conservation practice and intervention than a binary concept of extinction and survival," Novak writes. Somewhere between extant and extinct is the black-footed ferret, which Novak name-checks in the article. Ferrets are said to be "locally extinct," as they have been extirpated from many sites across North America. All reintroduced black-footed ferrets, known as "replacement populations," are translocated from captive populations. To reverse a local extinction, specialists use techniques ranging from husbandry to IVF to—now, starting with Elizabeth Ann—cloning. For Novak, these are all just part of the grab bag of conservation.

I ask Houck about the ferret genes. "What did you do after their cells thawed?"

"We regrew them, saved the newer ones, and then shipped the others out."

"Shipped them how?"

"FedEx overnight." She smiles.

It's hard to believe that earth's most precious genetic materials are shipped alongside America's pet supplies, yoga mats, board games, hair-care products, and toothbrush heads. I imagine the ferret culture tempering in frozen cryovials on solid carbon dioxide, being loaded onto delivery trucks, forklifted onto cargo containers, shuttled to airplanes, and stacked in boxcars before chuffing off to the regional sorting facility and, finally, to the local sorting facility in Rochester, New York, a few miles from the shrewd embryologist who awaits their arrival.

Over the past couple of decades, Dennis Milutinovich has worked in the agricultural, reproductive, and pet industries, where he developed expertise in husbandry, in vitro fertilization, and cloning, respectively. Currently an embryologist at ViaGen Pets and Equine ("America's Pet Cloning Experts"), he occasionally lucks into the "fun stuff," as when he's on the receiving end of rare ferret, horse, or snow leopard cells. While his work with pets is the science of the uncanny, one detects in his work with endangered species the art of the sublime.

It all happens in an eight-by-forty-foot shipping container punctured with a few doors and windows. Milutinovich's name for it—the steel coffin—is a misnomer, considering it's designed for life-giving activities like embryogenesis and fertilization. Parked outside of a Rochester strip mall, the shipping container is crammed with high-tech equipment, including incubators and a cloning scope.

"In order to do the conservation projects, we need to make money. That's the dog-and-cat stuff," he says.

Let's say your furry friend has one paw in the grave, and you'll wager anything—in this scenario, $50,000 for a dog and $35,000 for a cat—to "extend the special bond with your beloved pet," as the website says. Just snip the tip of its ear or get a biopsy of its abdomen, and Milutinovich will take it from there. If your pet is already dead, act quickly: transport its corpse to the shipping container and they'll cryopreserve the cells for you, prepping your pet for resurrection.

The majority are pets whose inconsolable owners can't imagine a world without them—or rather, without their dog's genes. This anguish calls to mind a woman Errol Morris interviewed in his 1978 cinema verité documentary *Gates of Heaven*, who upon burying her dog at a pet cemetery said: "There's your dog; your dog's dead. But where's the thing that made it move? It had to be something, didn't it?" Imagine if this woman had the option to purchase not just a burial plot but a resurrection. As best I can tell, that's the essential constitution of a ViaGen client.

"Is it all just an elaborate form of projection?" I ask during a videoconference with Milutinovich. "The pet owners are superimposing memories of Pet Number One over the genetically identical form of Pet Number Two?"

"I'm sure most of it is projection," Milutinovich admits. "As much as you can tell them, 'You're not getting your exact animal,' in their minds, that's what they want. There are very high expectations. There's a lifetime of love they're dumping on the animal."

"They want to pick up where they left off," I say.

"Yeah," Milutinovich assents.

Milutinovich has cloned hundreds of dogs and a hundred or so cats in the past five years, which, based on advertised prices, comes to around $20 million. Why so pricey? ViaGen's website boasts its cloning services are "the 'Cadillac' of animal care and technology development." It is just one of many companies in the global pet-cloning industry.

And here's where my ignorance shows. I assumed Dolly the sheep (born 1996) was the one and only of its kind—that, like the moon landing, we'd been there, done that, and generally lacked the will or permission to do it again.

"Didn't Clinton kibosh cloning in the nineties?"

"Human cloning," Milutinovich clarified, alluding to the Dickey-Wicker Amendment, which prohibited federal funding of research involving human embryos, including cloning. "At this point, it's routine to clone mice for certain types of research. Pigs and horses are cloned, but the government doesn't keep track of those. And there's a self-imposed moratorium for cattle companies who agreed not to put clones in the food source."

But given China and Japan's recent forays into pet cloning, with operations similar to ViaGen's, there are by now tens of thousands of clones among us.

"Our clients sign a pretty airtight waiver," Milutinovich says. "We tell them we can't guarantee it's going to look exactly the same. More than likely, it will not have the same personality."

A stately house cat launches itself onto a fabric tower behind Milutinovich. "Is that a clone behind you?" I ask.

"Cheeto?" He turns around to study his cat. "No, but she was a queen in our surrogate colony. We have to restrict the number of embryo transfers, so after her last one, I adopted her."

When compared to conservation projects, pet stuff seems relatively low stakes. It's easy to see why the chance to clone a black-footed ferret for the sake of genetic recovery would appeal to Milutinovich.

"There's a lot of cool stuff I want to do, like the woolly mammoth," he said.

For the black-footed ferret, Revive and Restore handled all the paperwork ("the hard part") while ViaGen started establishing a protocol.

"So the black-footed ferret was a side hustle? Was it similar to working with a pet?"

Milutinovich had never done ferret cloning before this. In fact, before him, only one other lab had ever cloned a *Mustela furo*, or a domestic ferret—the kind you can find curled up in a hammock at your local pet store, purchasable for around $150. That lab published a few papers on the protocol for cloning domestics, which became the blueprint for Milutinovich's own protocol.

"It was quite an undertaking," he says. "It's very difficult to work with ferret oocytes on the scope, because they're so soft."

So difficult, in fact, it took him a year and a half to produce a litter of domestic ferret clones. As soon as he was successful, Marlys Houck received a call, greenlighting the extraction of Willa's vial. She flipped on the frozen carousel, tonged and thawed the cells, 250,000 of which were put into a flask, grown out, and frozen down for new vials—backups—in a process that could be repeated ad infinitum, though a little quality is lost each time. Once FedEx fulfilled the order, someone at ViaGen signed on the dotted line, and Milutinovich repeated the cloning protocol, this time using *Mustela nigripes* genes. The embryos imperceptibly divided, enlarged, and differentiated until ready for transfer. When the time came, a licensed vet made a midline incision and pulled the ovaries out of the surrogate so Milutinovich could inject the embryos.

"That part is easier than a spay surgery," he says.

"How was the surrogate chosen?"

"Well, she was an established mom, a proven mom, with a couple litters of domestic ferrets. She was a good mom of the right age and birth history who we knew would whelp out OK, and she's good to her kits and everything. Oh, and she was in heat."

I am gobsmacked that the surrogate was a domestic, a completely different species of weasel. In other words, the dime-a-dozen pet store variety carried this multimillion-dollar wild ferret fetus. Milutinovich reminded me that it's common to employ different species with similar morphologies in surrogacy, especially if, as is the case with black-footed ferrets, it's difficult to obtain and risky to work with the actual species.

Three weeks after implantation, the vet performed an ultrasound on the pregnant jill, finding vesicles resembling living tissue. At twenty-five days, they listened for the clone's flickering heartbeat, which set the surrogate into motion. She was relocated to the National Black-Footed Ferret Conservation Center (BFFCC) in Carr, Colorado, to receive expert care from Fish and Wildlife Service staff. The trip began with a six-hour leg—Rochester to a hotel parking lot in Toledo, Ohio—where she swiftly changed hands, from one keeper to another, like a furry baton in a relay race.

From Toledo, Robyn Bortner and a technician from the BFFCC chauffeured the surrogate the rest of the way. Because of the coronavirus pandemic, Bortner, the center's captive-breeding manager, opted for ground transport to minimize risk of human-to-animal exposure. As someone who's repeatedly driven pet ferrets cross-country, I know ground transport involves anal glands emitting oily skunklike musk, pee with notes of battery acid, and a short digestive track voiding endless crud. By the time the surrogate arrived at the interstate facility in Carr, ten miles south of the Wyoming border, I imagine the whole caravan sighing in relief.

There are 168 low, wide metal mesh enclosures at the center, most occupied by a single ferret. Arranged in tight aisles, a captive breeding colony is carceral, but ferrets—who are solitary anyway—are mostly indifferent to their neighbors' messy mastication, ecstatic clucking, the rapid battering of the lattice during a fierce scratch reflex. Enter the surrogate.

Nudged into a vacant coop, a domestic among a hundred-plus captive wilds, she whiffed the air with her coffee-bean nose as she warmed to her new space. Not yet inured to the ambient ferret business surrounding her, she reluctantly turned in, scuttling down the corrugated tube to the nest box, which is partitioned into den and latrine. She needed the rest as the clone's fetal tissue tautened into a skeletal structure. Is there maternal dissonance in carrying another species? Does it resolve as the surrogate snoozes, knowing that what was within her now surrounds her completely?

By gestational day forty-two, a jill is usually ready to be whelped out. If the mom has a "healthy squeaky litter in there," Bortner says, there's no need for visual confirmation. She'll put up a literal red flag on the enclosure and let her be for four days. On very rare occasions, a mother will cannibalize her young; from a taxpayer's perspective, "baby ferret" is just about the most lavish meal one can eat.

"Usually, when breeding a wild animal in a captive setting, you need to accept some losses," Bortner says. "There's only so much you can do in the process. For our expensive clone, though, we had a lot higher stakes." It helps that a domestic surrogate is more tolerant of humans during labor, even permitting staff to handle her.

"We don't usually stay up all night waiting for the ferrets to whelp," Bortner says, "but for this one, we had a twenty-four-hour camera vigil."

A dozen staff rotated on two-hour shifts, ready to alert the overnight veterinarian. And it was a good thing, because the surrogate needed an emergency cesarean section. The clone kit was milked through an incision in the uterine horns. She was dried, warmed, and given oxygen therapy. At some point, she acquired the name Elizabeth Ann.

Elizabeth Ann was born outside of the black-footed ferret's springtime breeding season, so her birthdate (December 10) is an anomaly. Because the surrogate was recovering from a difficult labor and it's impossible for technicians to hand-raise a kit,

Elizabeth Ann was adopted by another domestic mother that the center arranged to have on hand. Born within hours of her foster litter of five, Elizabeth Ann nursed alongside them, nuzzled them, until she was about a week old.

So Elizabeth Ann is an endangered species clone who had an interspecies surrogate mother, wet nurse, and foster siblings?

"I don't think we ever put it quite like that, but yes. Essentially," Bortner says.

That makes them oddkin, a colloquial term defined in Donna Haraway's *Staying with the Trouble* (2016) as "other-than-conventional biogenetic relatives." A clone has no biological parents, per se. It's not the sexlessness that disqualifies this parentage but the fact that Elizabeth Ann is isolated by twelvish generations from her parents.

I ask my mother-in-law, a keen genealogist, how such a thing might be represented by the software she uses. But Willa and Elizabeth Ann share an uncoded kinship, a berserk in genetic spacetime: sisters once removed. Or rather, they are sisters once removed from a cryotank—thawed and shipped, duplicated and injected, transferred and born again—not exactly sharing the same tier on the family tree. "But I am a blasted tree," says Victor in Mary Shelley's *Frankenstein* (1818). "The bolt has entered my soul." Elizabeth Ann's existence is multidimensional, perhaps best represented as a twig floating spookily midair.

And, speaking again of the soul, in his article "Questioning Cloning with Genealogy," Emmanuel Ifeanyi Ani asked: "What is the status of a cloned being? Will it possess spirit or soul?" What becomes of a society sorted into clones and nonclones? Will natural beings regard artificial beings as superbeings or second-class beings? Such thought experiments might apply more readily to the dilemma of human cloning, but they still raise—on principle—the question of how Elizabeth Ann and the clones-to-come will negotiate kinship within their colonies.

Meaning that when I ask, "So, how's Elizabeth Ann doing today?" it's kind of a loaded question.

"She's doing really well," Bortner replies. "If you put her on the floor with every other ferret in my building, I'd have to look very closely to tell her apart." The morphometrics are within range of other black-footed ferrets, and she's of a typical size and weight.

"What about her behavior?" I ask.

"Ah, that's the big one," Bortner says. "I mean, she's on the curious end of the spectrum—one of the more curious individuals, for sure. But even when she was very, very small, her nature was outcompeting her nurture."

"How so?"

"Oh, when we came around, she would use a burrow as a refuge while her foster siblings popped up to say, 'Hey, what's up?'"

Elizabeth Ann is in the main building, the one with the backup generator and the best HVAC, where she's exposed to other ferrets, getting used to the routine of managed care.

Because of her offset birthdate, she was too young to cycle into estrus during her first spring, and so mating was delayed until spring 2022. To state the obvious, Elizabeth Ann was born to breed. Technically, all the jills here were. The species' studbook keeper is poring over genetic possibilities now, nearly ready to assign her to a surefire hob, a union that will create the most genetically differentiated BFF litter on the continent.

Technically, though, the best genes for hers are still in Southern California in an enigmatic vial that Revive and Restore can't wait to get its hands on. After spending over thirty years together, frozen side-by-side in a carousel in a cryotank, as genes in cells in vials, it seems that cellular Willa and her cellular beloved are destined to meet again. The clumsily named "Studbook 2" (SB2) is the ninth and last of the potential founders of the species. Together, the two might just be the ones to find a way through the bottleneck.

It's entirely possible that they met in life, zigzagging toward the same prey in Meeteetse, circa 1985. Maybe even in spring, when SB2 left his scent for her sensing, rubbing pelvis or dragging anus on prairie substrate. Did Willa's nose ever lead her into a burrow only to find a randy SB2? Did they sniff at parts or just part ways? Whatever the case, they both died kitless, and notches of their ears were pulverized and preserved inches apart in Escondido in the hopes they'd one day reanimate and consummate, making viable progeny to be released in Meeteetse or Seligman or whichever reintroduction site would have them.

It is, in my opinion, the greatest genetic love story never told.

If only it were as easy as pouring the vials into a cocktail shaker, mixing those genes up manually rather than technologically. Instead, SB2's cells must be cloned in an intricate process resembling the one last year, but with an added hurdle: his genes tested positive for canine distemper, the signature bacteria and virus that killed him and so many ferrets over the years. According to Revive and Restore, a pharmaceutical company has been enlisted to test methods for the removal of infection from SB2's culture.

Beyond her supervision of the husbandry team, Bortner also raises the kits, coordinates daily-care duties, including training them in preconditioning pens, at which point they might be ready for life in a zoo or, wilder yet, one of thirty reintroduction sites across North America.

"It's a lot of effort," I say, "keeping these things alive."

Bortner agrees.

"Is it worth it?"

She reminds me that the U.S. Fish and Wildlife Service is charged with conserving resources (endangered species) for the American public. "And it's not just the ferrets that benefit from this work," she says. "To save ferrets, you need ferret habitat. Ferret habitat means prairie dog colonies. It helps out the entire prairie ecosystem."

"So why not just focus on prairie dogs if they're the keystone species? Is it a PR issue like they say? Nobody will rally to save varmints?"

"You know, you could just say that the prairie would be fine without BFFs. And it might," Bortner says. "Other predators might take its place. But it can be dangerous to let one species slip through the crack like that. If ferrets can't survive on this prairie, then the ecosystem is missing a piece of its puzzle."

———— o ————

I'm late dropping Milo off at daycare again. I mouth apologies to his teacher and head out to the parking lot. Another father who's prone to chitchat is parked beside me. He clears stems of tumbleweed from the carriage of his pickup.

"Hey," he says. "Seligman."

It's not that he *calls* me Seligman as much as he recalls the time he was telling a story at a kid's birthday party about drawing a bow at a pronghorn, and I detected, based purely on the imagery in his story, that this antelope breathed its last breath alongside a particular water tank on a particular transect of a particular ranch outside of a particular rural Arizona town (Seligman) seventy-five miles west of Flagstaff.

"How's it going?" I ask.

"Doing okay," he says, his head stuffed under his runners. "Except for this shit." He snaps and flings more weed.

"Smart move," I say. "I've seen Russian thistle ignite under a chassis before."

"No kidding?"

I nod. "In Seligman." I say it almost flirtatiously.

"Seligman," he says again.

It's endearing: the fact that when he sees me, he thinks *Seligman*—even if, when he doesn't see me, Seligman makes him think of killing antelope. When *he's* not around, Seligman makes me think of trapping ferrets. Revivifying them. Our boys, who are in the same class, share a kinship that's seemingly inspired by the fact of their fathers' ambiguous bond. Most days, I drop Milo off at school and Hunter (his kid's name, seriously) is first to give him a hug or high five, ogle the graphic on his T-shirt. In this way, they become the odd kin of an ecosystem they've only ever experienced through pronghorn neck mounts (Hunter) and BFF puppets (Milo).

"What are you up to today?" the father asks.

"I'm actually heading to Seligman," I tell him. Which is news to me. Honest to God, I had no such plans before I heard myself say it aloud.

Just like that, I unlock my car, text Jennifer Cordova to see if she's up for lunch, and make way for the interstate. Another Willa native to the prairie, Willa Cather, once wrote: "Anybody can love the mountains, but it takes a soul to love the prairie." I always feel the weight of my soul when I reach the Arizona Divide, right where the mountain starts shrinking into sage steppe, and the soul heavies again when I swerve into town. I pass a feedlot and landfill where a breeze laps at the undone threads of a Trump flag, pass antique automotive ephemera scattered across gravel lots, pass German tourists shooting photos of an America that, like Schrödinger's cat, is simultaneously dead *and* alive.

At Westside Lilo's Café, I'm led to a table where I chug coffee and wait for Jennifer, an acquaintance who, for over a decade, has allowed me to shadow her conservation team in the Aubrey Valley. However, citing a fear of reverse zoonosis (human-to-ferret transmission of COVID-19) that could lead to an outbreak in the prairie dog colonies, Jennifer has placed a moratorium on volunteerism. This was mostly inspired by the fact that, last year, mink farmers in the Netherlands infected their stock and had to slaughter over ten thousand weasels. It's not a risk that wildlife managers are willing to take for a dwindling species like the BFF.

The party of four beside me squabbles about vaccine mandates, and it calls to mind the passive aggressive ADOT sign staged just before the Seligman exit, notifying an antivax populace that the rest of Arizona is taking care of business. As if on cue, Jennifer enters Lilo's.

"Sorry I'm late," she says.

"You aren't," I tell her.

She's immediately distracted by the bickering at the adjacent table.

"Vaccines," I say.

She rolls her eyes knowingly.

"I suspect you're all for vaccine mandates?" I probe. "I mean, the ferrets don't really have a say when you inoculate them against plague, right?"

"I guess not," she says.

"You're like the Fauci of the ferrets."

"Let's just keep that nickname between you and me," she says with mock worry.

We sip tea and talk low, have lots to catch up on. She tells me about the 2,500 acres worth of burrows they recently dusted with insecticide to suppress fleas (primary vector of plague). And she tells me about the drone operator who's using thermal imaging to surveil the ferrets at night. And she tells me, most excitedly, about Working Dogs for Conservation—about a scat-sniffing yellow Lab who's nearly twice as proficient as humans at ferreting out ferrets.

"Isn't it strange," I say, "to work in a field so analog and digital all at once? Scent dogs and spotlights by day, drones and clones by night?"

"It's whatever works," she says.

She reminds me that the Seligman site has always been on the bleeding edge of conservation: first to release pregnant females in spring, first to do on-site breeding, first with preconditioning pens, and first site with Gunnison's prairie dog on the menu.

"First to introduce cloned juveniles to its colonies?" I ask predictively.

"We'll see," she says, smiling.

Each year, wildlife managers request captive-bred ferrets for the sites in their region. Before the BFFCC can allocate ferrets, they must first consult with partner zoos, whose captive populations must be maintained, and with the studbook keeper, who plays genetic matchmaker for those breeding colonies. Of the 203 kits born in Carr this year, only a limited number will be suitable for the conditioning pens where they rehearse naturalistic behaviors. Those ready to assimilate into a wild ecosystem are divvied among the twenty-nine reintroduction sites. As clones and their kits enter the population, it won't be long until this genetic windfall comes to a prairie near you. Or me.

I pay the bill, and the owner makes small talk with Jennifer. "This rain situation sucks," he says.

She concurs.

"You still doing the ferrets?" he asks.

With almost two decades with the Arizona Game and Fish Department, Jennifer has tracked, trapped, jabbed, and tested more BFFs than are alive today.

"Still at it," she says.

I drive to a livestock gate by Double O Ranch just outside of town, not far from where I saw my first pop-going weasel. I count the entrance mounds, punctures of earth where ferrets eat, sleep, die, and give birth. I extrapolate my count to the horizon, where rose-colored cliffs bisect the range. For a ferret, there are thousands of ways to vanish. And as many ways to return.

I keep watch as long as I can.

I keep odd kin. Odd kin: keep me.

ACKNOWLEDGMENTS

Thank you, Andie, for your carriage. And everything since.

Milo, it was no contest after all.

Will Cordeiro, a real B-F-F.

Mom, Dad, Sharon, Mark, and Greta: for time stolen.

Jennifer Cordova, this book would not have been possible or necessary without you. Same goes to Heather Heimann and the Arizona Game and Fish Department's rotating cast of interns.

Thanks to the dozens who let me interview them, especially Billy Cordasco, Ken Evans II, Eduardo Ponce Guevera, Marlys Houck, Chriss Jass, Karen Knorowski, Kevin Krahn, Jim Mead, Dennis Milutinovich, Robyn Portner, Bradley Poynter, Oliver Ryder, and Jim White.

Thanks to Orlando White for a night in the Hogan at Diné College. Thanks to Manny Loley and Jake Skeets for the invitation to the Emerging Diné Writers' Institute, and the dorm digs at Navajo Technical University, where a draft of this book was finished. Thanks to Philmer Bluehouse.

Three cheers for three of Northern Arizona University's finest MFA alum: Weldon Ryckman, Jeanne Mack, and Mark Alvarez. Thanks to Nicole Walker and Steve Rosendale, who believed Aubrey Valley could be a classroom.

Thanks, Ander, always. And to Athena: long live Frank!

Thanks to Chris Cokinos and Craig Reinbold in whose Technological Sublime course I first had the inkling to write of ferrets. Thanks to the OG staff of Rendezvous, where so much of this was written.

Taylor Brorby, Maya L. Kapoor, Sean Prentiss, Clinton Crockett Peters, and Nick Neely, fondly. In debt to Bill Callahan, Timothy Morton, Donna Haraway, and E. O. Wilson, whose thinking left imprints on every page.

Thanks to the following journals and their editors, who let the BFF slink across their pages: *Creative Nonfiction, Orion, Passages North, Quarterly West, River Teeth, High Country News, Terrain, Willow Springs*, and *Territory*. Thanks, especially to Hattie Fletcher at *CNF*, for naming "If the Ferret Crosses the Road" Best Adaptation Essay for the themed issue. Thanks to Robert Atwan at Best American Essays for recognizing three of these essays in the notable section.

Thanks to the Waterston Desert Writing Prize and Ellen Meloy Fund for Desert Writers, both of whom selected this manuscript as a finalist. An excerpt from "My Son Was Born to Rob Me of the Glory of Saving the Black-Footed Ferret from Plague" was published in the anthology for the Ellen Meloy Fund for Desert Writers. "Dear Milo," was published in the anthology *Letters to America* (Terrain.org). Thanks to Sarah Gorham for her eyes on an early draft. Thanks to McKenna Stayner for visionary editing and Sam Yadron for facing the facts with me. Thanks to Juniper House. Thanks to Bill Wetzel and Charlotte Lowe for some desert refuge—and Bunter, javelina's best friend.

Brittany Bankovich, I'm sorry. Better late?

CRUX, THE GEORGIA SERIES IN LITERARY NONFICTION

Debra Monroe, *My Unsentimental Education*

Sonja Livingston, *Ladies Night at the Dreamland*

Jericho Parms, *Lost Wax: Essays*

Priscilla Long, *Fire and Stone: Where Do We Come From?
What Are We? Where Are We Going?*

Sarah Gorham, *Alpine Apprentice*

Tracy Daugherty, *Let Us Build Us a City*

Brian Doyle, *Hoop: A Basketball Life in Ninety-Five Essays*

Michael Martone, *Brooding: Arias, Choruses, Lullabies,
Follies, Dirges, and a Duet*

Andrew Menard, *Learning from Thoreau*

Dustin Parsons, *Exploded View: Essays on
Fatherhood, with Diagrams*

Clinton Crockett Peters, *Pandora's Garden: Kudzu,
Cockroaches, and Other Misfits of Ecology*

André Joseph Gallant, *A High Low Tide: The Revival
of a Southern Oyster*

Justin Gardiner, *Beneath the Shadow: Legacy and Longing
in the Antarctic*

Emily Arnason Casey, *Made Holy: Essays*

Sejal Shah, *This Is One Way to Dance: Essays*

Lee Gutkind, *My Last Eight Thousand Days:
An American Male in His Seventies*

Cecile Pineda, *Entry without Inspection:
A Writer's Life in El Norte*

Anjali Enjeti, *Southbound: Essays on Identity,
Inheritance, and Social Change*

Clinton Crockett Peters, *Mountain Madness: Found and Lost in the Peaks of America and Japan*

Steve Majors, *High Yella: A Modern Family Memoir*

Julia Ridley Smith, *The Sum of Trifles*

Siân Griffiths, *The Sum of Her Parts: Essays*

Ned Stuckey-French, *One by One, the Stars: Essays*

John Griswold, *The Age of Clear Profit: Collected Essays on Home and the Narrow Road*

Joseph Geha, *Kitchen Arabic: How My Family Came to America and the Recipes We Brought with Us*

Lawrence Lenhart, *Backvalley Ferrets: A Rewilding of the Colorado Plateau*